UNDERTAKING
IN THE FAST LANE

Timothy Penrose

Typeset, layout and design by Novel Design
www.karl-noveldesign.com

Illustrations by Karl Triebel

The only names changed in this book have
been clients for their personal privacy.

Dedication

*I unhesitatingly dedicate this book to my wife Ruth who has been
the most tremendously steadfast support over more than thirty
years and remains the most astute business person I have ever
been proud to be associated with. When I made mistakes, Ruth
never questioned where we were, she just got on with getting it put
right. I love her very much and always will. As you so wisely said
one day "We are very different, but we do together very well."*

Thank You Darling, I would never have got there without you.

W.M.

Index

Introduction

I have been aware for a very long time that I have been immensely privileged to lead the most interesting of lives. Partly though being in the right place at the right time, a lot of good fortune and meeting people who were encouraging at the right time, my funeral directing days are in the main looked back upon with great pleasure. I did work my nuts off.

I was thrust into funeral directing at a very young age, saw my first dead body at the tender age of seventeen and conducted my first funeral at the absurdly young age of eighteen. I was very fortunate to be working in the industry when it was undergoing a huge shake up and worked for the largest company in the country at the sharp end of their growth for seven years. I have now attempted to recall some of the memories I have from those times and some of the crazier ones from the late 80's.

I believe that all this experience shaped me for the next forty years and I am so grateful for such an opportunity.

Timothy Penrose

"Dreams and schemes and circus crowds.
I've looked at life that way"

Joni Mitchell

Chapter 1

The Beginning

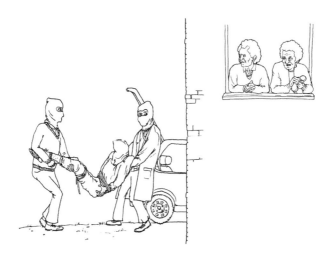

It is well past midnight, I am on my hands and knees fixated on cleaning the filthy encrusted grease from a commercial fryer in a McDonalds branch in Sutton Coldfield, West Midlands. My trousers are far, far too tight, I sport a baseball cap and a name badge with 'Tim' on. I have only been here four days and haven't yet been awarded any gold stars. I am absolutely exhausted and almost asleep. I know that I will have to cycle home three miles, mainly uphill, on a borrowed ladies bicycle complete with shopping basket. I am the oldest in the branch tonight, by a long way, but I'm only twenty-five. What was I doing here and what on earth was going on?

Less than a week ago I had a Rover fuel-injected company car, a share option, expense account, good pension and was earning an excellent

£18,000 per annum. I wore sharp suits, Grenson shoes, double
and gold cuff links. I met movers and shakers every day and was
very top of my profession, now that's all been lost. What had gone wro
and how had I arrived at this point? Well, it was all rather complicated...

How did I recover from this rather major set back? Well, with a display of
persistence, indefatigability, fortitude and hard graft. Where had all this
been formed? Well I went to Harvard business school you see, not as most
people would know it, but amidst a small company that was growing like
topsy and I worked at the helm with the Chief Executive who was quickly
turning his chosen profession upside down. Those years I spent with him
have been a huge part of my growing and nurturing. From the school of
hard knocks I claim graduation. But what about the beginning, where did
it all start?

Let me take you back... I was a high school drop out, a music obsessed,
radio lover who had somehow managed to get himself relieved of his
schooling duties through inattention and pranks. Dad wasn't amused,
he was a prefect who loved his education and was desperately hoping
his youngest son would educate himself to a higher level than he had
managed. My grandfather had died when my Dad was just twelve, he
had to grow up quickly and his Mum, on a widow's income, just couldn't
afford to send him to University. Dad's dreams had lain in tatters, until he
went to work for his Uncle Jack at Port Talbot, South Wales.

Uncle Jack was a character and a half, a prankster, good fun but also a
very good greengrocer. Dad took to it as if he had born to it, which he
probably had been. Upon arriving back in Cardiff he announced to his
Mum "I want to start up a greengrocery business!" He was only nineteen.

The one thing about my Dad is that he is a "doer". Always first to action
and never short of a plan. With Dad success was everything and I grew

il world where Dad was in control, he was extremely enormously hard working. I should have learnt at his ugh only seventeen, my business genes were already s I guess is common in such stories, at the time I didn't ted. Dad gave me a job as a Saturday boy earning five pounds a day. I served the customers, played the fool a lot of the time, but took refuge in the fact that even I hadn't been sacked as many times as my brother Steve who had got his cards for smoking in the toilet, reading Playboy in the office and blowing up the incinerator when trying to cook baked potatoes. He always had a fertile imagination and was keen to invent many ways of saving labour, I remember my major contribution to the business was installing the in-store AFJ (Alan Francis Joseph) Radio playing background music and jingles we'd made up with friends. I was ahead of my time clearly… unfortunately Dad put up with us for too short a time. Bah!

So Dad, my working-class hero, had an incredible work ethic, totally committed to his customers come rain, shine or snow – the latter was displayed in an unforgettable way in the Cardiff snows of 1982. Dad, the first to rise to a challenge ensured his shop always opened on time and his greengrocery orders were always delivered. Never mind that the Friday orders that week had to be delivered, on foot, through four feet of deep snow, he just did it.

Dad, my dear, wonderful dad didn't need a mission statement or customer charter, he had one in his heart and brain and when he retired twenty years on I saw old ladies openly weeping at the loss of a very good man. I thought he had retired at such a great age – he was only forty-six!

Much of what Dad had done at the time was ground breaking, though of course I had not realised it. He installed security mirrors and one-way glass so he could keep an eye on the occasional rogue characters that shopped regularly in his emporium. He had an intercom from the shop to his office, so that he was always in control, two way mirrors to catch the errant shoplifters and some rather wonderful runway rollers which he used to empty the van after the early morning market visit every day. There were enormous characters that came in; Dough Jones, Mrs Small, the only Jamaican woman on the council estate (my father would greet her with "Have you been on holiday? You've got a lovely tan!" She howled), Mrs Crock "the Maris Pipers have gone to mash Mrs Crock", Mrs Bowley the local rogue who held a collection for her husband's wreath – only problem was he hadn't died! There was a sense of fun and this was of course the lesson I would learn; that the culture came, always, always, always from the top. I didn't fully understand it all at the time but I never forgot that most important of lessons.

Dad was always busy on the weekend and we somehow managed to get invited on the hospital visits, visiting the "old people" from church and went far and wide in that most exciting of pursuits. However there were a few moments. Rhydlafa Hospital was occasionally on the agenda, we raced to go, we had to take Mr & Mrs Selwood to see their very aged Aunt, Miss Sandy, who must have been at least 120. The afternoon would always work out like this Dad would go and put Mr & Mrs Selwood into the visitors room whilst my brother and I went to get Miss Sandy. This was always the most exciting of days. The journey from hospital bed to the visitors room meant negotiating a two hundred metre corridor, dead straight and sitting at a rather tempting angle of about forty-five degrees. Well, it was too good an opportunity to miss wasn't it? And you just would, wouldn't you? We pushed to get Miss Sandy up to speed and then (making sure she was dead centre) let her go and raced after the wheel chair. My Dad caught us once and said with remarkable logic "I don't mind you racing her down but you mustn't let her go!" It was the highlight of our weekend.

Dad started mornings early, he was up and about every day by four in the morning. In those days, selling greengrocery was different, it was important to be there early to get the best produce and choice, oversleep by twenty minutes and you were already playing catch up in an immensely hard business. It was not until many years later that I realised just how unusual my Dad was, he was totally and utterly driven and this was why we always enjoyed good foreign holidays when they were not the norm and why in 1977, he had built a swimming pool in our back garden. Ralph and Pete our wonderful builders had become personal friends after an extension, a garage and a loft room.

Dad timed his exit perfectly, realising that he could get as much if he leased the premises in Llanishen, Cardiff than if he worked seventy hours a week turning a small profit.

The next few years were not quietest ones, over the following twenty years he started a Christian Charity, took 350,000 tonnes of aid to Romania in over a hundred trips covering more than a million miles, not one to sit back my Dad!

And of course like all driven men, he doesn't stop, woe betide me telling him I'm tired or that business is hard at the moment, he will bellow down the phone words that spur me on to better things. In short, the most wonderful hero you could ever have had. He is now eighty-four, and shows absolutely no sign of slowing down, tiring yes, worrying at times, but always inspirational.

Mum had led a very different life, but they were beautifully suited to work together. Her Dad had been called up to the army and sent away when Mum was only six weeks old. He was stationed in Malta and like so many of the soldiers, on both sides of the conflict, saw terrible things that they hoped after the massacres of the First World War, they would never have to see again.

Her Dad was then away with no visit home and not even a letter until Mum was five years old. She told me that she will never forget kissing a photo of her Dad goodnight on the bedside table every night and praying for him. In many ways, she was so fortunate; her Dad arrived home when she had just celebrated her fifth birthday. Her Mum had told her that her Dad would be home that day, so they went to Cardiff railway station and, there getting out of the carriage she saw this man who she recognised from the picture. He bent down and said softly "Hello, you must be Ann". He then put her on his shoulders and carried her home and when they got there, she stood on the kitchen table and sang to him "You Are My Sunshine".

My Grandad's war hadn't been particularly remarkable, but as with so many of the recently de-mobbed soldiers, after he came home, my Grandmother said he was a different man. He was morose, very, very quiet and very strict with my Mum. I remember a little, I enjoyed visiting them right up to the age of sixteen and they always made a fuss of me. I can still smell my Bampie's tobacco as he filled his pipe, and I remember with joy toasting crumpets in front of the fire at Gabalfa in Cardiff. I suppose you never think about their death, I wish so much I had seen more of them when they were alive. In a way I am making up for it now, rarely a day goes by without me phoning my Mum & Dad, they are now well past normal retirement age and Dad is still working flat out.

I remember little of my schooling. I had been a model pupil at twelve. "Timothy is always courteous, polite and well behaved." But at fourteen started to rather go off the rails. I always felt slightly different (which even as I type this sounds a little pretentious). I had inherited my Dad's love of music and maths, my Mother's ability to work incredibly hard at something if she enjoyed it, and the ability to organise came from both of them. I guess as we all look back on our early and formative years, particularly time with our family before the magic age of eighteen, we think that our family is "normal", well it's normal for you at that time as you have nothing else to compare it with. We appeared to be a very active family, not certainly in the sense of personal exercise but always in the area of "doing things". My Mum got massively involved in 1979 re-housing a large family of Vietnamese Refugees and we of course got roped in to collect the furniture with the vans and deliver it to the houses. I do remember snatches now, the highlight of which was probably my Mother (free from the shackles of my Father ordering her around every minute) communicating with the family in dramatic sign language as neither could speak a word of each others language. It did, as you can imagine have its moments, the Vietnamese father of the house, Voung a chicken farmer only in his early forties, agreed to assist my Mother reversing the van back with an OK, OK, OK…there was a huge clatter and we discovered "OK" was the only English word he knew, stop was not in his vocabulary!

So we muddled along with both our parents frequently getting involved in various mad cap schemes which either involved Grand Pianos being taken downstairs at midnight (no, I shall never know why either) or late night sojourns to collect somebody odd from somewhere even odder, it was all a little surreal. There was of course the immortal moment when upon cooking a huge meal for old people at the church someone had decided to advise my Father to place a piece of coal in with the potatoes to "keep them white" – you couldn't make it up. Mr Clem Bearpark wasn't informed and only discovered the coal when he started mashing them.

We seemed to ALWAYS be having people around for Sunday lunch, if not Uncle Bert (ex Somme veteran with a metal plate in his head), old

8

Auntie Gladys, a lady so immaculate in her attention to cleaning detail she even washed her light bulbs. So inevitably these are the things I remember. Uncle Bert playing snooker upstairs in the Garage Room every Wednesday but juddering quite dramatically with his Parkinson's disease.

We used to see Uncle Bert in Grangetown, a rough area of Cardiff, fairly regularly and I recall he was pinioned in his scullery, the other rooms were almost a shrine and all immaculate (maybe Auntie Gladys had sneaked in surreptitiously). I distinctly recall the black leather sofa and bouncing around on it as a youngster. Uncle Bert was always watching the horse racing – but pennies frequently don't drop at that age and it was only after he had been taken into hospital many years later that two days before he died he confessed to my Father that he had "quite a bit" of money stuffed up the chimney. Quite a bit was in fact £20,000 a not inconsiderate sum in those days and whilst there was a brief conversation about the wisdom of declaring it to the family (Uncle Bert's only surviving relative and therefore next of kin, was Reg who was a hopeless alcoholic) and my Father a strict teetotaller was aware it would all vanish rapidly. My Mother prevailed and indeed it was all passed down to Reg who in no plot twist whatsoever managed to get through it in six months, well he would, wouldn't he. However Uncle Bert's death also brought forward the discovery of the most brilliant of photos, Reg and his wife taken many years ago, with Reg's wife (no oil painting my Father said) in bra and knickers giving the camera a sexy, come hither look. My Mother announced she was "as ugly as sin", I certainly recall bottle glasses, wizened hair and not much else, it was quite frightening for a young lad.

The well driven Penrose fruit and vegetable van was often used for trips in the evening with the church youth club, days before Health and Safety. I believe thirty-two was the record number of youngsters we crammed in the back (no seats of course) for an evening out. I guess at that age you roll with the punches and whilst I picked up hints, my father was obviously wealthy because of two things, we had frequent foreign holidays, he had a new car every year and he smoked cigars, he will admit I am sure to being a quite absent parent over my early years. This was common in society then and I hold no blame to him. He was building a greengrocery business and working enormously long hours, but it was a bit divisive in some ways and there were frequent phone calls from my Mother panicking when she got the spaghetti jar stuck on her hand or managing to hoover the budgie's cage and also the budgie. To be fair Joey clearly enjoyed the ride at the time, it must have been like Alton Towers, although as there was no time to brace himself, he obviously passed away from all the excitement a couple of days later…

I certainly don't remember home life being dull. There was always something going on, whether it was collecting waifs and strays for the Church Christmas Day meal, or collecting and meeting just very odd people. There was I recall a gift of fishing equipment for my brother and I, from a man who had been in hospital and had his arms amputated. Mr Smitheringale, I thank you here Sir!

My father, an innovator to the core in retail, brought home the first ever aerosol cream that we were fascinated by. He tried to demonstrate it, the nozzle got jammed and then it exploded all over the elderly Mrs Hyatt's hat who had come around for a quiet Sunday lunch. Then there was the time we brought in the catering golden syrup from the garage (Dad was always keen to buy in bulk). We got it to the table and the visiting church minister opened it to find it was in fact Castrol GTX motor oil! So, lots happening, always.

I don't know who started all the practical jokes that seemed to be rife in our family, probably my Mother who famously had hijacked one of the staff's shopping one day at the greengrocer's shop. Specifically a packet of six white bread rolls. She decided it would be quite fun to open the bag up, make up a ham and cheese roll with butter and seal it back down again. The lady concerned was furious the following morning and had gone directly to the bakery to complain. I recall my Grandmother's wig being plucked out the air by a banana hook as she bent down and there was often a light air in the shop, to me it did not seem to be about making money, but having a laugh... how green I was.

As we got to sixteen/seventeen years of age we constructed far more elaborate pranks, probably the highlight of which was hijacking a Church Minister's Induction. This was the service where they get welcomed to the church. This was going to be a big affair with a bun fight afterwards so we knew Dad would be attending. I cannot remember who had the idea but it was decided that we would get hold of a copy of the order of service which always had a large picture of the minister on the front, and photocopy one of my Father. We then ran off eighty copies and were set for the day. To be fair whilst initially my Father had scurried around trying to gather up the copies in the church he wasn't that mad and was pretty much used to this sort of thing by now, looking back it still produces a smile.

I was probably up to lots of things I shouldn't have been at primary school. I certainly remember regularly shinning up the drainpipe in the school yard to get the errant football and being told to "Stand Under The Clock" as a punishment. One thing that is burned into my mind was the reports that used to come home, sadly rather frequently. I always did okay with the academic stuff, I was always top in maths, without even trying. Probably working with figures at the greengrocers helped, I used to win any competition in school for times tables, even beating the teacher. And drama was fun (I was a right old drama queen) but every single report at the top right was a line : Conduct: POOR.

The last ever report I had from primary school I had managed, I could not believe it, a "Good"! However Mr Ball had added an appendage "GOOD – Occasionally there are outbursts of stupidity" And the only thing I can add to that is... LOL!

I recall being desperate to get out to any sporting fixture at all. Football, Cricket, Rounders, I was at ease on the pitch and was probably (in my humble opinion of course) the best football player in the school. I was always prepared to try and light up the game, I didn't always achieve it, but it seemed to me that entertaining was as important a part of the game as winning. I loved any type of sport.

I was totally obsessed with football in primary and junior school and Friday football at school was the highlight of the week. However my messing around usually led to me being told "No Games Timothy Penrose" by my teacher Mr Ball. Mr James R Ball was a great bloke, pork pie hat, Welsh through and through and fearsome but fair always .....until I was persuaded by Adrian Jones to put a hamster in his hat. Actually he was still fair and I was thrilled to meet up with him many years later when Hodgsons had floated on the stock market and he had bought some shares! It was lovely to meet up and I suddenly realised he was not scary at all but looked like a great chubby teddy bear on short legs. I recall his great umpiring, with cries of "You're hanging your bat out to dry lad!" and "Help it on it's way" whenever a wide was bowled. Good times, but you never realise it at the time.

Despite my antics, I was very good at football. Being anarchic and a bit of a nuisance I wasn't ever allowed to captain of course, that accolade went to Iain Howells who captained everything as he was a very safe pair of hands. I was always in the school team and was a regular for Cardiff Schoolboys where I teamed up with Paul Bodin (soon to play for Swindon and Wales) as an attacking force to be reckoned with! Two goals against Western Valleys was my highlight and kept hold of the press cutting – it's probably in the loft!

We were sat waiting to get changed one Tuesday afternoon at Pontcanna with the Cardiff Boys squad when Mr Kite came in and wanted to talk to us. "Listen up boys, something special happened today, Bodey (Paul Bodin) scored ten goals for his school". I never forgot that, it demonstrated the gap between Paul and the rest of us! He was a quiet and lovely lad.

I really enjoyed practices at Pontcanna and those at Sophia Gardens led by the nutty, slightly eccentric Paul Kyte and the elder statesman Howard Spriggs. I remember Mr Kite asking for a cross from the wing to go "right on his peanut" (head) and I picked him out perfectly. Of course all I wanted to do was to be a professional footballer and at the age of thirteen duly wrote to Cardiff City and got a charming reply saying to contact them once I had left school! I was actually selected for Wales Schoolboys as well. We played at The Racecourse ground in Wrexham, but I was on the bench and didn't ever get on the field. Does that qualify for a cap? I like to think so.

When I got to the big school (Whitchurch Comprehensive) my obsession with football was partially translated into playing rugby. Being a Welsh school the rugby lads had all the best equipment and football was frowned upon as being the sport of the devil. I was a regular fullback for Whitchurch High up to fifteen years of age and enjoyed the goal-kicking duties. But I was injured on a tour to Ireland and then slowly fell out of love with the game. Partially I think because I was quite young and slow to develop physically, and the thought of regularly getting run over by larger lads week in and week out became less and less interesting!

I played cricket to a good standard and was selected for South Glamorgan and also for Wales. I don't remember much of it all, expect going down to Barry one Saturday, opening the innings with Lyndon Williams who had the most gorgeous technique. Lyndon scored a flawless century and I scraped, poked and fiddled my way to over fifty and we ended up undefeated after fifty overs. I scraped my way to fifty-nine and Lyndon had hit a tremendous 174. Again a huge gulf, but I enjoyed the cut and thrust of cricket and in particular the fielding where I could throw myself about with gay abandon. Always the showman. Lyndon went on to become an international badminton player and then international coach, you could certainly see the quality the guy had all those years ago.

One of the first things I remember when I got to Comprehensive School was being taken into the gymnasium by Steve Williams the sports teacher and told that we all had to compile a Rugby File, notes of how to pass the ball, how to hand off, a little history of the game. We had six weeks to do the work, they had to be handed in and marked and there was a prize for the best one. I wasn't interested at all really. And then one afternoon I realised that I knew Joanne Rowlands whose father was Keith Rowlands the Welsh Rugby Team Selector. If I could ask him for some material such as programmes or pictures, then I could make it interesting. Of course I went completely over the top, I always do with something I love to do. Sad to say it is a trait from my Mother and it is what I call a 50%er – depends on which way you look at it I guess? My file was ten times the size of anyone else's, had the most pictures, programmes and tickets and rosettes in and was crammed so full, it made a serious impression on Mr Williams. Not only did I win first prize, but I proved myself head and shoulders above the rest and (more importantly) I proved to myself that I could do whatever I wanted to do, if I set my mind to it. This would stand me in good stead for the next thirty years of my life.

Sport apart, I had lost interest in the formal side of education, for I had discovered that there were more important things to see and be involved with, girls for one! And pranks, oh loads of them and all the time! Most of them were unmemorable, silly and childish, but one will live forever in my mind and was the reason for me leaving full time education.

I, and a number of my friends, Banger (Philip Williams) and Andrew Walsh were the main plotters and we had fallen out with a lad a year above us in the Upper Sixth Form. Someone, okay me, thought it would be a really good idea to arrange a little outing for him... to accost him early one morning, bundle him into a car boot and tie him to a tree naked up in the Wennallt Forest. It was *not* a well thought out plan.

The fateful day dawned, so dressed in black SAS masks and white coats we pounced upon the unsuspecting lad and manhandled him into the back of Andrew's dad's car. Everything would have been fine had it not been for the two elderly spinsters who happened to be watching the scene from an upstairs window, and immediately telephoned the police...

I am very embarrassed writing this many years later, that we tied the hapless lad up and drove back to school as if nothing had happened. I never did find out how he got himself untied.

I went to registration, bit late granted, and almost immediately I was summoned to the headmaster's office. It was then that I saw the police cars and mobile incident van and recalled that we had actually heard some sirens when we were out in the car. Oh dear. It did not take the local plod long to work out what had happened and we were severely told that we could all be up in court for wasting police time. All for a little practical joke!

My Dad was not amused. Not riotously cross, but I guess hassled that I hadn't been as assiduous in my studying as I should have.

The time I first showed an interest in girls, I was fortunate enough to visit the Church Youth Club every Tuesday where meeting Caroline England and Carol Burkett became the highlight of my week. I must have thought I looked really cool in my drainpipe trousers and leg warmers. I was always a little bit different in what I wore without being wacky.

And as radio, music and girls became more and more important, school became totally irrelevant. I passed four O Levels, okay more 'scraped through' than passed, although I did manage an "A" in Scripture without doing any revising. I'm not sure whether I should be proud of that or not. Then I moved on to take two A Levels in English Literature and Scripture, both of which were totally incomprehensible to me. I started disrupting the class with practical jokes and my inattention led to me being asked to take the first year again, I had totally wasted it really!

My first real girlfriend (I think in those days a real kiss was the definition of that) was the gorgeously named Suzanne Barker. She was a real steal! Friends with Fiona Grant who seemed much older than her fourteen years (she had a quite magnificent and prominent pair of bosoms I recall) and also Karen Chichester. The three of them hung around together and goodness knows why or how Suzanne and I got together. It seemed to be going swimmingly well, until Neil Isaac announced he was having a party and would I like to come? "Oh yes" I replied "and Suzanne will as well if that's okay?". "Haven't you heard" he said "She's finished with you." Children can be very cruel can't they, but indeed she had.

So although between the jokes we managed to squeeze some studying in, I had always been a bit of a maverick, always happy to stand out from the crowd and be different. One day S4C, the Welsh TV channel came into school to use some of the sixth formers as extras in a Welsh play. I wrote a letter to the local paper saying how I couldn't understand that the headmaster had approved it, since when the play went out it had an adult theme and of course half the school had stayed up late to watch it. I hadn't imagined the fuss it would provoke! I was cross that everything at that time seemed to be about sex, it was everywhere, but the letters I got in response wound up the Headmaster and Head Boy and a rebuttal was also printed. But this only made things worse, since the rebuttal was seized upon by other readers who then wrote in questioning the judgement of the Headmaster for allowing them into school to film in the first place. It was an occasion when I truly felt I was on my own against the entire establishment and was ostracised by the entire school bar one or two very close friends. I liked being different and having a different view on matters – I enjoyed being the centre of attention and being the subject of debate – it was something that was going to stay with me for a very long time.

It was around this time I discovered music which became my first love, way beyond anything else that had captivated my young life. Certainly by now, school work was taking a back seat, part of the reason being that I couldn't see it's relevance to me. And I seemed to want so much more from my waking hours than my peers.

As part of the revolution of Independent Radio Licences, Cardiff had been awarded a licence to broadcast. In early 1980, not very long after the station had opened, I started going down to the Cardiff Broadcasting Company, helping out a guy called Dave Kitchen on some of the Christian programmes. My job was to look at news and events every week and present a three minute piece to go into the show. Sometimes it was live and on other occasions it was recorded. This then led to presenting the show when Dave was away and standing in for other chaps when they weren't there to present their shows and it was all done on a tape reel. So, by the age of seventeen I was hosting a weekly radio show at CBC, the Independent Radio Station for Cardiff. Remember this was the early eighties and by all accounts the music from this period has stayed with us, much of it had real lasting power and quality. Working in the station combining music and radio was about as good as it got! In the main I drove the taped shows, that is, I inserted the adverts and the music idents for such shows as Jeff Werst and his Country Hour (fairly scary), Binda Singh and his Asian music hour (extremely scary) and Welsh Folk Tunes with Frank Hennessey (you don't even want to go there). I was fortunate enough to work with one of my early mentors Will Waldron and remember being extremely impressed, as even at an early age I instantly recognised if someone was exceptional at their job, and he was! Will is now a senior barrister in Liverpool.

I had the great opportunity to work with people like John Hawkins (now LBC), Martin Shankleman (Radio 4), Pete Solomons, Diane Kemp (professor of radio production), Phil Miles and loads of very lovely telephonists, tea girls, typists and jingle makers. It was here I met the delightful Sue Lloyd. Sue and I worked together on Hospital Radio at Rookwood Hospital (I also met Maggie Singleton a lovely friend here) and we had a great time as the world of radio started to open up for us all. John Melville Thomas was a great buddy and together we hijacked the production studios some evenings to make spoof shows and radio programmes for fillers. They were heady and really enjoyable times, I had no idea that a job could be so interesting.

I was happy at CBC, I still have the garbled sports report from Newport on cassette at home in a very safe place:

> "Newport are playing Swansea at Rodney Parade and from there Tim Penrose reports: "Newport 10, Swansea 20, John, and it was this sort of mundane, run of the mill game that emphasised just why Swansea are fighting for the club

championship this season and Newport are attempting to pick up the pieces of theirs."

I was fortunate enough to be (spoiler alert and ongoing theme coming up) in the right place at the time and a lot of this was sheer luck. I remember in particular being despatched to Cardiff Arms Park on match day, being wired into the station and every twenty minutes giving an update. "Cardiff are at the Arms Park today with visitors Llanelli, from there live Tim Penrose with an update." I was seventeen for goodness sake! Brilliant, just such a brilliant opportunity. And I loved it, 100% it didn't seem like work it was just fun. Listening back to some of my tapes in the last few months (late 2021) I am quite impressed as to how professional and secure I sound. I had definitely found my niche in life, or so I thought.

I was always good with words and so desperately wanted a career in radio. I knew I was good, but I wasn't brilliant, I needed to work an awful lot in so many areas. In many ways I should have stuck at it, I was so young, but then you feel so old at the time. It's not easy being young and keen!

I tried to spend a lot of my time around Will and absorbing his knowledge. He was so helpful to me, he even took me home one lunchtime and cooked me eggs. And now he is an internationally famous barrister, well I never! Even in my addled youth I knew he was going to be a star at something. In addition he was a very lovely man and very kind to me.

I hung out at the station as frequently as I could. I made countless cups of coffee for just about anyone imaginable, I ran spools of spliced tapes down from the news room to the studio, I typed out the latest weather and road reports, I was there early in the morning (often when I should have been in school) and was happy to be there late at night for the closedown as well. I enjoyed the people, the environment, the atmosphere, and the setting. I had found my place, my niche, I was going to have a full time job in radio.

And then just as I was settling down to a good rhythm and feeling very comfortable in my own skin, the station controller changed. In radio, the station controller does everything, it is he who decides the tone of the station and just like a managing director it is he who provides the culture of the whole set up.

Jeff Winston had been tremendously successful at the independent radio station Devon Air. And now he had come to sort out CBC, to be fair we were extremely amateur, for example the girl that read the weather report in Welsh couldn't actually speak Welsh, she just read them in Welsh! Goodness knows how she knew where to put the intonations, well of course she didn't did she? The guy doing the late night programme would, every five minutes, say "Welcome to the late show with Me Gary Price" and was therefore known by all and sundry as "Me, Gary Price". We were renowned for the naff phone ins where listeners were trying to sell everything from a Labrador puppy to a chest of drawers, and our jingles sounded like you had made them up at home in the garage, although come to think of it...

Jeff immediately introduced a completely new and professional tone to the station. He revamped the jingles, re-organised the programme structure and even sat in between the two studios on an all-day marathon presentation making comments in the presenter's earpiece on how to improve their presenting. He was very much a control freak and almost immediately the whole flavour of CBC changed for the better. The station picked up listeners overnight and I suppose it was this new and radical approach of professionalism that made me think about moving on. I felt that I was too young to get anywhere. I really should have hung around, "Me Gary Price" did, and even he got a longer show!

Chapter 2

The Curtain Pulls Back

With the glorious benefit of hindsight, the whole thing seems too ridiculous to believe it even happened, but it did and I was about to embark upon a chapter in my life where nothing would ever be the same again. It would be like a core running through me. Dirk Bogarde once said that "Men had to go through a war to crack their balls" and in some way this was the same. I was part of an elite force, catapulted to stardom it would seem. When my peers would be escorting young ladies' bodies upstairs, I would be carting old (and deceased) ladies bodies downstairs. It was a rum job, but someone had to do it and why not a young boy, fresh and wet behind the years in all manner of subjects, a clean palette, a fresh virgin, a new piece of clay to be modelled – all of huge benefit in what was about to happen, my life would be changed for ever!

I'd had enough. School for me had become something to be loathed, I sat in front of the TV at home and cried. I was seventeen and rapidly discovering that I just didn't understand what they were going on about in the lessons. I had the capacity to remember nothing, although I enjoyed speaking (and latterly I would discover writing) I felt lost at sea and hopelessly out of place in any form of education.

"If he doesn't want to go to school then he won't." My mother's warm Welsh tones soothed me and stopped me crying for a moment. But what was I to do? Where would I look? The local paper that's where! What I couldn't tell my Mum was that I had a bet with my best friend Adrian Jones to find a job before he did. I knew he had one starting Monday and today was Thursday, so what was I going to do? I didn't like losing!

I was at a loss. What job would nobody apply for, I wondered? I shall never, ever understand why my brain thought funerals, I'd had no previous experience of death (that was all about to change, wasn't it?!) But something somewhere in that brain of mine must have turned a cog and pushed me into first gear, one that I was not to get out of for eight long years!

It all sounds so bizarre now, I don't know why but perhaps there was a bit of devilment about it, I hadn't excelled at school (they short-sightedly didn't give out prizes for biggest class clown) and this was my chance to prove to everyone what I could do. There was nothing like having a different job, one that raised eyebrows when it was mentioned... So I sat on the stairs, got out the Yellow Pages and looked up Funeral Directors. Being rather lazy by nature, I chose the nearest one, about a miles walk from our house, picked up the phone and asked if there were any vacancies.

This was the catalyst that led to me leaving, by agreement with the school, although I got the distinct impression that if I had not left I would have been pushed.

It was the jolt I needed and led to the most exciting seven years of my life – ones that shaped me for the future.

The answer was perhaps unsurprisingly no. Crestfallen, I replaced the receiver and went into plot mode. It's a mode I guess inherited from my Dad; it is the unwillingness to accept a situation that you are not happy about and you immediately start plotting how you are going to correct it, a great asset, at times. The next thirty years would see me go into that mode many times and mostly with huge success. Or perhaps I choose to not remember the failures…

I know, I thought, I'll go around and wash his car, nothing like a bit of straightforward, up front crawling. I got a bucket, hot water, soap and a sponge from the garage and walked around to the looming building which declared, in rather a grim font, "D. Caesar Jones" Funeral Services. It was all about to begin and I hadn't a clue! Of course, I'd only been there two minutes when an extremely ruddy faced individual came out to see what I was doing.

"Who are you?" he demanded. His red face seemed to soften a little as I explained my mission.

"I'm seventeen, have a full driving licence, left school and I'm keen. Surely you must have something for me?" He looked, and now I know that this was the look that started it all and opened up a world of secrets, enigmas, mysteries and skills. I was about to see the curtain pulled back.

"Have you ever seen a dead body?" he asked and I followed him into the chapel of rest. Now, like most of my peers I had never witnessed death before, but here in the coffin was my blooding and in a way it couldn't have been any easier. As Mac lifted a coffin lid and peeled off a face cloth (very much a Welsh thing I learnt later), I saw the face of an elderly woman who looked just like my Granny Jenkins. There was no horror, just mild intrigue and a little shock, I looked and murmured ummmmmmmm, there was no pre-set script for such occasions. He looked at me and said "Alright you can start on Monday."

"Could I start on Saturday Sir, please?" I whimpered. I knew Adrian had a job starting on Monday and I wanted the bet to be safe before the weekend!

"Okay, Saturday it is" he said. He gave me no idea of what to wear, or what time to turn up, this was the way it was in those days. It is difficult to recall, forty years later, just how crazy the whole situation was. Perhaps good timing, good fortune favouring the brave and the foolish? But I do know that I had won and I almost ran home rejoicing, I was going to work at an Undertakers! That would make people laugh wouldn't it?

Malcolm Groves, known as Mac, was quite a strange individual, although I was soon to understand that many of those I met over the next eight years had a similar impression on me. He had bought the business from Maude Jones' father (D Caesar Jones) and was now working long hours to make the small company, arranging 250 funerals a year, profitable. His wife Lynn was rarely seen in the funeral home and she lived next door with their daughter, who was to be my first fantasy, Debbie. Lynn appeared to have nothing but disdain for the business, leaving Mac to get on with it on his own, a situation that didn't seem to bother him. I was told early on that his temper was something else, I appeared to not be bothered about this, I was so green!

Maude was now officially retired, but helped out when they were very busy, or when Mac went on holiday. Maude, or Miss Jones as everyone called her, looked like a cross between Miss Haversham and Dame Edna Everage, she seemed incredibly old to me, but I guess she was probably only about sixty. She lived half a mile up the road with Tegwyn her housekeeper. She had never married, but was extremely forceful, strident and in charge, you didn't mess with Miss Jones that was a certainty. There was something about her I loved, she had a stage presence, an aura. If Mac was small town amateur repertory theatre, Miss Jones was Royal Shakespeare, she was a performer down to the last detail and I grasped very quickly that hers was a show that was always applauded. Mac was a functional business man who just happened to have bought a funeral business, the same way he might have bought a Londis franchise. He didn't have that X-factor and in that way he was particularly unusual, many of the people I would meet on my journey had it in spades, but Mac's didn't even stretch to a teaspoon.

Of course almost every job, large or small, that I was asked to do the following Monday seemed unusual or bizarre. Stack the coffins, count the name plates, tidy the gowns, wash the hearse, help with removals. Mac threw me into the deep end straight away, the best way I guess. I went out with Miss Jones on removals to the local hospital and met Barry Hanks. Three rings for Hanks, Miss Jones declared as she stood outside the mortuary thumbing the doorbell. One thing I had discovered was that the mortuary was not signposted.

Barry one of those almost but not quite mythical creatures, the Mortuary Assistant. Yes, he did keep his sandwiches in the mortuary fridge and had a rather creepy look about him, but my mother always said I had a vivid imagination! Once I'd known Barry for a few weeks, I decided he was okay, and not unusual at all... until one day, as the clock struck noon in the mortuary, Barry disappeared into his office, and returned wearing a stationmaster's cap and brandishing a whistle. He blew the whistle to announce the next train on a model railway he had built throughout the mortuary. The train was in fact *bringing his lunch.*

Miss Jones kept up my education with a constant babble of what was right, what was wrong, and how Mac was cocking it all up since he had bought dear Dada's business. She wasn't bitter, and it never came across in that way, she was just telling it like it was. She was free with information and I was an eager pupil under her tutelage, she liked me, I liked her and it was a good partnership. I drove her around while she sat queen-like in the front and gave instructions and observations, all pearls of wonderful wisdom, I wish I could remember them now, so many years later!

It was her really, more than Mac, who introduced me to the many traditions and methods of funeral directing. She was so interesting, she had purpose, she had style, her every movement was focused and purposeful. Thinking back now, she must have been absolutely mortified that someone so lacking in stage presence had bought Dada's business. But she made the best of it and with Teg her sidekick, strode about the churchyards of the Welsh Valleys dispensing her wisdom and sympathy in equal measure. She was in many ways a little like Hetty Wainthrop the detective. One afternoon, after quite a drive to the valleys to arrange a funeral, the door was opened and a middle aged lady threw herself on Miss Jones wailing "Oh Miss Jones, now you're here everything is all right!" It was the beginning of my introduction to a secret society that had its own rules and these lay outside the normal rules of society, this was something else instead.

I had convinced myself pretty early on that there was nothing to be afraid of in the funeral home and this was fine, when other people were there. However, at the start, when I was on my own and dressing bodies or

26

moving coffins around, my mind started to play tricks on me. It built up slowly, you imagined all sorts of ridiculous things and I am ashamed to say (well perhaps not really), that on more than one occasion in those first months I ran out of the funeral home spooked by nothing and hid around the corner for ten minutes. But in general I managed okay. Although there was no particular training, Mac showed me how things worked and I just got on with it. I was the only full time employee he had ever had, although I didn't realise this at the time. Training me was as new for him as it was for me, and he wasn't particularly patient! But we got by, and in a few weeks I was au fait with most things and very comfortable with my duties. I always enjoyed working with Miss Jones, she was quite something else and an entertainer down to her boots.

During funerals I was generally tasked with menial and physical jobs, I came to realise why, much later, as I seemed to be continually employing bearers who were the wrong side of sixty. One of the more unusual jobs took place in a client's home; it was a tradition in the Welsh Valleys and to a certain extent in the older parts of Cardiff, to have the body home for a while before the funeral. Much of this tradition stemmed from before the days of modern funeral homes with chapels of rest. Neighbours wanted to pay their respects, so many a D Caesar Jones coffin was manhandled by retired bearers, puffing and wheezing, into a little Welsh cottage.

Once inside, the lid was unfastened and the clothing re-arranged, as when a coffin is tipped on its end all sorts of muddles can occur. The lid would be stood in the corner of the lounge or drawing room and the body viewed, normally for a period of twenty-four hours before the funeral. My job came into play when we went into the house to seal the coffin down. Normally, there would be at least twenty minutes of people having a last drink of sherry or wine in the same room as the coffin. Now, when the coffin had its lid off this did not present a problem, but the moment the lid went on the coffin... disaster! The closed lid seemed to attract all sorts of empty sherry and wine glasses and (this was definitely the worst) empty beer bottles, mainly Double Diamond I seem to remember. So, my job as the youngster was to continually clear these glasses, trying at all times to maintain a sense of dignity about the place, surreptitiously polishing the beer rings off the wooden finish and trying to make it all look as if nothing had happened. What a palaver my mother would have said.

It was here that I was initiated into all the practices and methodology of funerals. And where I discovered that yes; they really are the individual's ashes you receive after the cremation. Each coffin is cremated exactly as it is received on the catafalque according to The Cremation Act and then a nameplate identifying the remains travels with the coffin and stays with each small oven (or cremator). The final pieces of bone that don't quite burn up are pulverised into the ashes and placed in the receptacle you are handed upon collecting Granny's ashes. It was here I realised that once a body has been left for too long (not unlike a raw chicken left out of the fridge) will start to attract flies, which lay their eggs and maggots will hatch. I learned that a body left for too long in the water will blow up like a balloon and quite possibly pop if you are not too careful, and that dead bodies can make noises. I discovered this to my great alarm one day when the excess air escaped from a deceased old lady, not with a burp or a fart, but a loud wheeze from deep inside, which came out as an ominous groan! All this time, I was accumulating secret knowledge that would be with me for the rest of my life. I was very privileged to be in such a special place and I was an eager student. Miss Jones and I, we could conquer the world (oh Mac, he was just an irritant along the way!)

There were moments of disaster of course, Mac asked me if I could drive an automatic. "Yes" I said. Of course, the answer was no, but I assumed it must be easier than using gears and I could drive my Dad's fruit and veg van. After all hadn't I driven it through deep snow the afternoon of passing my test at the age of seventeen? Dad was supremely confident in my ability, what a hero of mine, he still is actually! So, it turned out that driving a geared veg van was rather different to tackling an automatic Daimler limousine, which purred when underway, and underway was fine, however stopping was another matter. I made the classic mistake of jamming my foot on the brake as if it was a clutch and the flowers I was carrying (thankfully no coffin on this test run!) flung themselves forward and ended up in the passenger foot well.

I got away with so much as Mac was very rarely there. He would issue instructions to fetch the bodies, mainly from the Heath Hospital where Hanks and I had formed a good relationship, he seemed to like me and thought I was an amusing breath of fresh air. He would then leave me to dress the bodies, Hanks sometimes helped, moonlighting from the hospital, with his embalming fluid earning him a fiver a corpse. I put the bodies in the coffin with a winching machine that had seen better days, the alternative was trying to get Hanks (who wasn't a lover of work), to lift with you. So using the winch, dressing the bodies and then moving them into the chapel of rest was all my job and I just got on with it. I discovered I was actually rather good at it! I had always been the same, encourage me and I will move mountains to get it right.

I began to realise that I was in a privileged position when the father of my school friend Nigel Chater became one of our next clients. For me there was little emotion, I don't know why; was it nature or nurture? I think it was just indifference really. I had not developed the mental capacity to understand, I was green, knew nothing about life and was devoid of thought about any of it. Sounds bizarre but definitely true. In Miss Jones' eyes, Mac had got it wrong again, Mr Chater had died as a suicide and his face was ruddy from the car's carbon monoxide fumes. Mac had used

29

whatever gowns he had in stock and had therefore dressed him in a red gown that made the man's red face shine out even more. Miss Jones was not amused! It just about summed up their relationship really, they never had a good word to say about each other but put up with each other as it suited them. Maude was always the victor of course, she had too much experience for little old Mac!

It was about this time, when I was seventeen, that the hormones I had been keeping under wraps began to rear their gorgeous head. One afternoon, when in the lounge with Mac's daughter Debbie, I was aroused as she spoke to me and I suddenly realised that something quite new was going on. I'd had a couple of girlfriends before, but this was something quite different, it was deeply sexual. Debbie wasn't particularly attractive, I just think that I was feeling the feelings for the very first time – bizarre, although nothing happened of course and certainly not on the premises.

Being young and headstrong, I was particularly perturbed one day when Mac, who had looked with disdain at my black drainpipe trousers and jumper, informed me that I would be going to Rhiwbina Village to see his tailor and be measured up for a funeral suit. I had such mixed emotions, I was thrilled that he had decided to spend some money on me (he was a bit Scottish, Mac) but terrified that the trousers would be flared which would not do at all. After all, one had an image to keep up didn't one? It couldn't have been much worse.

Brian Lacy, the village tailor, was the original mincing Mr Humphries, tape poised to measure the inside leg. I knew that after coming out of his shop, the flares would take off with a passing breeze. Mac couldn't grasp why I was so miserable about it all. He had just spent some of his hard earned money; I should be grateful. I imagined all hope of romance with Mac's daughter disappearing down the local river as the flares swished from side to side. I felt everybody was looking at me, well thinking about it wasn't that why I had become a funeral director in the first place? Strange emotions continually went through my head, typical I guess of the youngster in his first job. I did occasionally wonder what my peers were doing, certainly nothing so enthralling and unusual, and as I found out over the next eight years, rewarding and long lasting.

The local crematorium was an interesting place, if only for one character, Mr Les Tidball on the organ. He was, oh I guess at least a hundred and eighty years old, and had been through several World Wars. It always looked as though he might keel over if we closed the chapel door too loudly. He really did look on his last legs, and of course his organ playing skills were never stretched beyond Crimond and The Day Thou Gavest (I calculated after I left funeral directing that I must have sung Crimond about two thousand, five hundred times during my career). But the one thing about dear old Mr T was that he had a wonderful wandering eye. It was his left one and it used to go all over the place, particularly when he was speaking to you. Amazingly though, it seemed I was the only one that had noticed it and I used to bring him into conversation just so I could cop a load of this wonderful sight. I mean never mind Ripley's Believe It or Not, here was our very own freak in Cardiff, dear man. So, what with Mr Tidball on the organ, wheezing away in stereo (him and the organ I mean), the continual pace up and down the crematorium steps of various coffins, and the catafalque going up and down more often than a bride's nightie, it was a busy old place. Also people there knew my Dad, as he was on their regular list. Dad always regarded a funeral as a good excuse to get out of the daily grind and have a social and in Wales of course, there was always the possibility of a good bun fight afterwards. In fact, not only did Mr Tidball know Dad, but I worked out pretty quickly that the crematorium superintendent did as well and also the cremator operators. "Keep Mr Davies on a low gas John, Alan Penrose is on his way!"

31

Slowly as I became more au fait with things, Mac entrusted more and more to me and as he didn't have the finesse that I was to later find in my Bristol mentor. He was more than happy to farm out the rubbish work; the old lady dying in her bed late at night, three floors up, weighing twenty stone, or arranging the funeral of a guy from Grangetown with no known relatives. So, I was given a little elastic and before I knew what was happening, I was arranging my first funeral in Caerphilly, on my own and me being only seventeen.

I soon twigged that Mac wasn't really cut out for the job he had taken on. He fussed a lot in front of the family, always appeared flustered (partly due to his red face) and was never as diplomatic as he could have been. I had only been with him for three weeks and we had taken an open coffin home to a house in the deepest part of the Welsh Valleys where "bringing Dad home" was an old tradition. I hadn't gone on the take home, but I turned up on the day of the funeral with Mac and the other bearers, thirty minutes early to seal the coffin and carry it out to the hearse. It was the first time I had done this so I was more than a little intrigued to see how it all worked in practice, I'd heard stories of coffins upended to get around corners, now I would see for myself what actually happened.

We turned up at the house and Mac immediately surprised me by not going in first and introducing himself to the family. Instead, he let us all wander in through the open front door, into the drawing room where the coffin lay on small wooden trestles. All four bearers hung around the coffin looking at each other, none of us knowing what to do, and then in came Mac waving one of those modern Yankee ratchet screwdrivers. It seemed incongruous and unnecessarily invasive. Mac puffed his cheeks out.

"Right" he said, "I'll go and see the daughter next door. Come with me Tim." I followed, intrigued and observant.

"Hello" he announced. "Anyone want to see him before we screw him down?"

There was a deathly silence. No one spoke and then the daughter wearily bent her head and slowly began to sob.

"I'll take that as a no then" Mac said cheerfully, and marched into the front room. He replaced the lid and began (rather noisily I felt) to fasten the screws into the coffin. I don't think it helped that he had rested the box of screws on the lid itself so that with every turn of the ratchet, which made a sort of slurping noise every time it went up and down, the little box rattled and shook like a pair of dentures. It was a scene I would never forget and one that had a lasting and profound effect on me.

I was observant enough to understand even at such a tender age that it wasn't what you said, but how you said it. Mac wasn't cut out for this job, I decided that there and then. It was then I realised a golden rule of business; it doesn't matter what is going on, however unholy the chaos, what actually matters is the client's perception. It is a rule I have never forgotten, and boy did I need to know it sometimes!

Mac was a bit of an oddball to work with. There seemed to be few instructions written down, it was almost as if he was making it up as he was going along, come to think of it perhaps he was!

After four months, Mac spoke to me as I left work.

"I can't pay your tax" he said. "I also can't afford to pay any Stamp. I'll pay you in cash from now on."

Now, I may have been a little naive, but my Dad had always taught me to make sure all payments and receipts were above board, then you didn't have to have sleepless nights. This wasn't a system that was going to work and I told Mac straight away. It didn't go down well at all, but he wished me well and we shook hands and that was it, career over before it had even begun. What was I going to do? Since the curtain was pulled back I'd been enraptured and enthralled, how could I carry on?

Chapter 3

"Evening Sir – Derek Here"

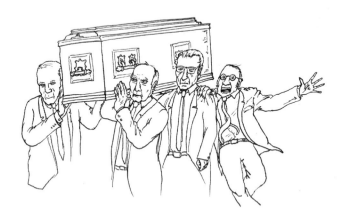

The South Wales Echo was a paper I didn't ever read, but my Dad always seemed to be scanning the obituaries and attending funerals in the Cardiff area. I didn't ever discover whether it was customers he had managed to poison with his potatoes or just old friends, but one night he carelessly tossed the paper my way and said "Why don't you look for a job in here?" He said it so casually I picked up the paper and within two minutes was reading "Husband and Wife wanted to work in funeral home in Wales area, must be car driver and flexible." Well never one to allow the lack of a wife to set me back, I got to work.

The 1950's Adler typewriter in the hall had always been good to me, the only boy in the school who attended typing class (there were twenty-five girls all to my self, I was no fool). I enjoyed writing lists on it and generally messing around. Now was the hour of truth, me and the Adler had to produce a letter convincing the potential employer to grant me an interview.

I sat and mused, this was my chance to show how good I was with words. A chance to sell myself, well I had always been good at that. The letter went through several drafts, each of them previewed by Mum, I gave it my very best shot.

I was perhaps a little economical with the truth; I didn't say I was only eighteen, I didn't say I was unmarried and I didn't say that I had only been in funeral directing for four months – okay, I was *very* economical with the truth! And then we went on holiday and I forgot all about it.

We arrived back from the Lake District to find a letter, with a Birmingham post mark, inviting me to come for an interview. I had already missed the interview, it had been whilst I was away! I telephoned and spoke to a sweet lady who agreed that I could still come for an interview, and gave me the address of the employer – Hodgson and Sons in Handsworth. Mum, despite having checked my letter, was concerned. She forced me to phone and explain to the MD that I was unmarried and only eighteen. I picked up the phone with trepidation, feeling that I perhaps shouldn't do this, although in my heart of hearts I knew I had slightly misled in my letter. I asked to speak to Mr Hodgson and this booming voice said "Hello Timothy". I explained, and babbled a bit. His response was totally unexpected and from the heart. "Well come up with confidence, I haven't see anyone I have been impressed with yet!"

So, come up with confidence. I was ridiculously so, and I was heading for Handsworth, like a dog with two tails I believe the phrase is. My Dad drove me, we stopped off at Frankley Services and I changed into my best suit (well alright it was my only one). So, complete with three piece, including pinstripe waistcoat and fob watch, I announced myself at The Oaklands Funeral Home looking like Bertie Wooster with acne. Handsworth appeared a rather cosmopolitan area to me Dad looked around the shops inspecting the price of bananas as he used to on all our foreign holidays, come to think of it must have been like a holiday for Dad, there was not a white face to be seen anywhere.

An incredibly short elfin-like lady, aged about thirty (I later discovered this was Sandy, who I had spoken to on the phone), immediately put me at my ease. She made me an awful cup of coffee and asked me to wait just outside a door which stated in large capital letters 'THIS DOOR TO REMAIN CLOSED AT ALL TIMES'. It was the beginning of the Howard legend.

I honestly don't remember much about the interview with Howard. I remember him asking me why I wanted the job and I remember waffling on and on and on. I think even he was surprised. But you see this was one of my skills, in radio work, you always had to be ready to talk if the tapes ran off the spools or the cassettes jammed and it was something I was very good at. Starting a conversation had never been a problem for me, the difficulty was stopping. In that respect I guess I must have struck a chord with Howard and the interview did seem to fly by. I wasn't shown around by anyone and was strangely vague when my Dad asked me how it had gone. I think I mumbled "Well this was only my first formal interview, I didn't quite know what to expect."

There was no particular stress about whether I got the job, as I had only ever applied for one job before and got it. There had been no second interviews, no waiting lists, no letters, no psychometric testing; bizarre really when you come to think about it. I waited a week and then one fine morning a letter plopped through the letterbox with what would become the very familiar purple type on light purple paper. Yes! I got the job! It was £70 a week (don't laugh, it was good money at the time) rising to

£100 a week after eight weeks training at Roy Preddy's Funeral Home in Bristol, after which I would be installed as manager of Caradoc Price Funeral Home in Dowlais. It was all too much, before I knew it, Mum and Dad had contacted friends of friends and arranged for me to stay at Winterbourne, just a few miles away from Mangotsfield and with a Christian couple called Maureen and Adrian and their daughters Pam and Wendy.

Bristol couldn't come quickly enough for me. Many years later, after I had long since forgotten such detail, my Mother reminded me that after dropping me off in Bristol on a Friday night, ready to start work on the Monday morning, she had cried all the way back to Cardiff, a good forty minutes in the car. A couple of months later when she had got more used to the idea she cried just to the Severn Bridge, then after a year, she was quite glad to see the back of me. Normal family relations had been restored, I was returning home with washing and problems and wanting both solving; the washing was straightforward, the others less so!

Mangotsfield (the name says it all really) boasted a post office, a florist, a Spar and a funeral directors. It was not a happening village as they say. Mornings at my lodgings made it all worthwhile though, on my first morning, Pam, Maureen's pretty fifteen year old daughter came down for breakfast in her bra and knickers. She was scolded by her Mum; "Go and get dressed dear, Tim doesn't want to see all that first thing in the morning!"

"Oh Mum" said Pam "It's only Tim!"

Of course Tim didn't have quite such a problem as she might have thought and these were very happy days, spent in the love of a warm and completely insane family as they grew up. There was the aforementioned Pam (15), a rather more discreet Wendy (17), and Emily (only 3 and the apple of her father's eye). Maureen was rather like Ria in "Butterflies", hopelessly scatty and her cooking and timekeeping mercilessly teased by her husband Adrian and the girls (and I was learning pretty quickly too!). I lived in a small bedroom upstairs and kept myself to myself, I struggled with being away from home at first, but adapted well to learning my craft and enjoyed most days.

I reported to the funeral home and met one Derek Paul Tyler, who was going to be my mentor for the next six months. Derek had built himself a growing fiefdom at Mangotsfield, which really was the worst place in the world if you were eighteen with hormones. It didn't exactly have much going for it. But looking back now I can see that meeting Derek Tyler was the single most important employment matter in my life. Everything from now on would be "because of Derek". He was tall, immensely handsome and carried himself with great dignity. Typing such words much later on makes me realise how lucky and fortunate I was to end up there. I could have ended up anywhere and might not have thrived. I thrived under Derek. And whilst we had little fallouts and fights I remain immensely grateful that he took the time to show a young idiot the ropes and keep his patience. I don't know how he did it at times! Derek was clever, hard-working, neat, tidy, organised and commanded huge respect. He was my first mentor and I am dearly grateful to him for being that. So Derek, thank you, a million times over.

At Roy Preddy's, Derek lived on the premises. There was a lounge downstairs, separate from the funeral office and a bathroom upstairs between the two bedrooms. So in many ways Derek had a good deal, but so did the company as all the managers were expected to be on call every night, with one night off a week and each weekend, with one weekend off a month. In return for this devotion to duty, they received the premises rent free, a good deal all round.

Up from the lounge was the kitchen where we all met around the kettle for morning coffee. The only other full time staff were Mary Brittan who answered the phone, rattled out all the typing (an age before computers) and dealt with the million and one detailed enquires that passed through the doors of a funeral home on a daily basis. There were doctors visiting to fill out cremation forms, relatives visiting the chapel of rest, flowers arriving for up to twenty-five funerals a week, coffin supplies being delivered and stacked, coffin orders being produced for the funerals to come, body measurements to get from the mortuary or coroners court; it was all incredibly hectic and Mary was very efficient. There was also dear old Roy Vincent, who had worked for Preddy's for two years when I got there, he did all the odd jobs that were necessary for the business to run efficiently.

The premises were rather run down and in need of an upgrade. Howard had spent £25,000 straight away on essential repairs, but it remained a crumbling, damp old funeral home, the chapel of rest was in a lean-to out the back!

One bugbear was Derek's Mum, a bit of a nightmare really. She had been drafted in to wash up in the house, but decided when we had drinks, what drinks we had and generally kept order whilst sticking her unwanted oar in far too frequently for my liking. You see she interfered with what I was doing and I found it all so unjust, just part of my training I guess. If I washed the hearses when it was cold, then it was a silly thing to do as people would slip over (all the better for the funeral home I reckoned!) and my writing was never neat or clear enough for her. I seem to recall lunch was never quite enough for a growing boy (bear in mind that the average age of the bearers here was fifty-five) and was always eating (another fault, she told me). But she didn't break me.

Unlike Steve Wood. He had been recruited just after me and would constantly be told off by Derek for the typical youthie things, driving the hearse too fast, or messing around in the coffin shop with the staple gun. The staple guns were used to fasten the side frills into the tops of the coffins. However, if you pressed the trigger they would shoot staples across the room at a rather alarming speed. We had staple gunfights, impersonating Clint Eastwood, crouching and hiding behind coffins as we took cover. We (okay, I confess, me more than Steve) used to change the cassettes in the cranky old tape player that Derek had wired up to the light switch in the chapel of rest. It was a daft thing really, all it meant was that while shifting coffins around in the chapel bays, we could listen to the music we wanted to, rather than Derek's fabled organ music which really was rather depressing. I reasoned that people were upset enough as it was without wallowing in it and a bit of Human League or The Jam wouldn't do anyone any harm. Of course we always took the tapes out when the clients came for a viewing. Until one day. To my death bed, every time I hear the opening chords to "Twist & Shout" I will recall with horror the day Steve had left his tape in. I opened the door, pulled the light switch on and pulled it off in my hands as the opening chords blasted through the chapel air. Ah, the folly of youth!

We also dressed up in gowns, hid behind doors and jumped out on each other, none of this was particularly original, but it was all good fun. Roy Vincent was also very easy to work with, much of the time he was a little nervous of Derek (in truth we all were), but he lightened up quite a bit while I was there and joined in the games too after a few months.

Although Steve and I were a bit silly, not too unfocused though for a couple of teenage/twenty somethings, and Roy was a big child really, we got on with the job in hand, with the underlying knowledge that we were part of a very important company. There was a wonderful family

41

atmosphere about the place. Derek was a control freak and this meant that he ran a very tight ship but one we were all proud to be sailing on. Yes he had his faults and it was a strict routine, but it was one that I would be all the better for once I got to Wales.

My coup de grace though was managing to get the chapel bays confused. I was showing a family their late uncle, "he looks so well" they said. This may have seemed a rather bizarre thing to say, but it was mainly because the last time they saw him he had his mouth open, dribbling (we had sealed it), he was bent and contorted (now he was lying down), etc, etc. The small problem was that I had managed to show them the wrong body! I didn't mention it, didn't think it would have helped anyone. I would wager a bet that most people that have been in the funeral profession for anything over a couple of years have probably done the same thing, mistakes certainly do happen.

And so this is where I learnt my trade. I dealt with the typical situations in funeral homes, these were to become part of normality for me for the next eight years. Coffins going into houses that didn't quite fit through the doors, bodies coming out of nursing homes in the small hours without waking the other near death patients, filtering ashes into various receptacles at the crematorium, seeing coffins disintegrate in the tremendous heat of the cremator furnace and the skeletons dissolve, mopping up pools of blood at crime scenes. And as well as all this trauma and coping with it (more of that later), arranging in fine detail the paperwork, administration and telephone calls that were all necessary for the business to run. It truly was an eye opener and now, behind the sacred curtain, I soaked this all up. I was a ready and eager student and still in my teens.

And then of course it all went wrong. Howard failed to agree terms with Caradoc Price. A potential acquisition was now, not in the offing. I was led to believe that the owner had been dragging his heels and the takeover was off! What was going to happen? Well here I fell on my feet, Derek had obviously given a good report on me. Steve Wood had recently defected to the Co-Op, Derek kept referring to him as being better off there as they did things at a hundred miles per hour, he would be right at home there! And it felt better all round.

We had an interesting team; Roy Terry, the stately hearse driver who came in most days (when he wasn't working on the Western Daily Press); Norman Darch, a rough salt of the earth type who came in early to fasten down coffins and get them ready for the hearse (it kept him out of the house his wife said); Jack Brown, a thick set, coarse guy who I never got on with; Roy Vincent, a class guy, and chief limousine driver, and then there was Ron Pedlar.

Ron was a gift for any writer, he was just so excitable, clumsy and funny. Most of the time he didn't know he was being funny, which of course made him even funnier. He was extremely nervous and in awe of Derek and just used to get things wrong. Imagine Frank Spencer in a pallbearers uniform and you have Ron. Ron wasn't allowed on burials as these were considered far too complicated, with much lifting between gravestones and up and down grave kerbs, the chances of things going wrong were greatly multiplied. Derek had worked out that if he was kept to cremations only, then little could go wrong. All Ron had to do was to stand at the back of the hearse and be one of the four that carried the coffin fifty yards into the crematorium chapel and placed it on the catafalque. Not much could go wrong with that Derek reckoned, and in the main he was right. But when Norman was on holiday and Roy Terry couldn't get time off from work, then we all got moved up two places in the line and this meant that Ron was back on board for burials! I have to tell you that in all the funerals I ever attended and conducted, I never, ever saw a bearer fall in a grave, but Ron came the closest, twice! And he did it with wonderful Ron aplomb. Just as the vicar was intoning the Ecclesiastes *"In the midst of life we are in death, for who do we succour but to thee oh Lord"* from the corner of the grave came "Whoa! Whoa!! Whoa!!!" The sight of Ron's arms flailing and grabbing hold of Roy Terry really was a classic comedy moment. Ron never let you down, he was true value for money. In fact it got to the point where the two Roys, Norman and I were so pleased to see him on a funeral that we would hug him like a long lost friend, honestly it made our day!

We were at Aust. A village nobody knows expect those with keen eyes at the Severn Bridge (it is of course the place of the old bridge, rarely used these days). Ron had, through other bearers' bad fortune, managed to persuade Derek to take him on a burial and there we were standing at the back of the hearse about to take the coffin inside the church. The family had already gone in and were waiting for us.

"Thank You Gentlemen" Derek said. This was the standard only ever spoken words at a Derek Tyler funeral, and they simply meant proceed to the next stage. The next stage was drawing the coffin out of the hearse and lifting it all at the same time onto our shoulders. I was at the back with Roy Terry, Ron *should* have been at the front with Roy Vincent. We drew, we lifted and Derek said (as only he could) "Have you all fallen out with Roy then?" Ron had decided to join us at the back, so we had three at the back and dear old Roy struggling and puffing and wheezing all on his own at the front. It doesn't sound particularly funny now, but because it was Ron and the way Derek said it, we all got the giggles, Derek included. I still cannot fathom how the coffin was carried into the church reverently, because three of the four bearers were struggling to contain themselves so much that the wreath on the coffin was shaking, not a good moment for dignity! I wonder if the family ever noticed?

So, I started a "Bring back Ron on burials campaign", if only to increase the amusement factor on quiet days. Things were good, I got used to Derek' style, he was very smooth, totally unflappable and quite funny really. When he walked in front of the hearse down the road it was clear who was in charge. He delighted in marching out in front of the hearse in full tails, carrying his top hat and gloves, delighted even more in pointing a disapproving finger at an articulated lorry he felt was going a little too fast past his cortège. He was precise with his paperwork, the families loved him. In so many ways, though he was not a good trainer, he was a brilliant trainer because I learnt most of my skills through sheer osmosis. And the cards fell nicely... Derek had to go into hospital to have his ingrowing toenail seen to and this meant four weeks off, during which time I would get to run the operation with the ever reliable Mary Brittan by my side. Bosomy and a bit of a vamp, Mary had taken a bit of a shine to me (funeral wise I am talking), she and I ran the place for that month (well actually she probably did and I ponsed about in front of the hearse thinking I was chocolate).

Derek Tyler was a class act, made for the career that he carried off with such presence. Imposing and deeply handsome, he must have been over six foot two, olive skinned, wore a lot of gold jewellery and he had the old ladies eating out of his hand! He was my first mentor, my guide, my saviour. He was still arranging and conducting funerals in 2016 and will probably be carried to his grave with the arrangements of the next funeral in his hand. He seemed so old to me at the time (I was eighteen, he was thirty-six), but he was very much the right person to learn things from, no doubting why Howard had sent me there to learn my trade. Initially I thought it was because of the proximity of Bristol to Cardiff, but at such a tender age thirty miles could have been three hundred really! I was homesick, uncertain about many things as well as launching into a home and career move that had not been given great thought.

45

Derek had worked for Roy Preddy for a number of years and as Derek had got more experienced, so Roy went down the same path that Howard's father had, and I suspect a good number of the funeral directors in the UK since; he liked a drink or two, or three in fact! And that fatal flaw allowed him to manage cock-ups on a hitherto unbelievable scale! I never met him in all the months I was there, but I felt I knew him. All the bearers were unanimous in their criticism of him; a panicker, a horn hooter in the cortège, a faffer, loud; really all the qualities you would be looking for in a nightclub bouncer, not in a calm and dignified funeral director. But Roy wasn't stupid, he realised he had a pearl in Derek, so before selling the business he secured a future for his bright and sparkling manager. In the year following acquisition by Hodgson's, the newly acquired funeral home of Roy Preddy managed to not only do the 450 funerals forecast, but in fact 525, freed from the shackles of Mr Preddy's shambolic management! I discovered all this and more at the first ever Company Conference in 1984. I couldn't wait to go of course. It was all I was living for and I was wound up by John Taylor to prepare a speech that was all the things it really shouldn't have been…

The first funeral I was entrusted to conduct all on my own for Preddy's was an elderly gentleman's burial at Doynton Parish Church just outside Pucklechurch in Bristol. I remember wearing Derek's second best tails and top hat, although I used the trousers that I wore to drive the limousine. I was as nervous as you could possibly be, but the Two Ronnies (sorry, Roys) made it as easy for me as they possibly could and I will never forget them for that. Coming back I was on a high, the funeral had been fairly brisk, no hitches and it all seemed to go down well (no pun intended). I was expecting a well done from Derek but that was not forthcoming, only more criticism from his Mum, par for the course by now and like water off a duck's back, but I remember it as a real red letter day, this had been my show and it had all gone well!

Not long after this I decided I would splash out and order a brand new tailcoat and black velvet Crombie overcoat (I still have the overcoat today although it is a little tight around the chest). There were two main suppliers in the funeral magazines which by now I devoured avidly (sad). One was a firm called Lyn Oakes in the Midlands and then there was this wonderful advert with a dolly bird with a Dolly Parton figure, for a firm called Brook York & Co. Beulah York answered the telephone with such a high voice I wondered whether the phone had developed a problem, but she was kind, sweet and so helpful. I was to buy clothes from her for the next thirty years.

I quickly got used to the daily routine, Canford Crematorium was our local and it was not unusual to be there four times in a day. My main claim to fame is that all the time I was in Bristol, I went through Westbury-on-Trym village probably in excess of five hundred times, yet never once did I stop to buy a postcard, pint of milk or newspaper as we were always in a funeral cortège. I am staggered at the number of people I have met from Westbury-on-Trym and I can always say to them "I've been through your village, it was just before Canford Crematorium on the very steep hill." Can't say I missed very much, it must have been pretty hard work carrying any shopping back up that hill!

Derek was very funny. Neat and tight with words, he used to enjoy mocking the Co-op as they were always in too much of a rush, they were slapdash and everything he wasn't. We all enjoyed the day we arrived at Canford to find ourselves in a backlog, as the Co-op had not only arrived late, but their tailgate had jammed. Now bless, this could have happened to anyone, and if any funeral director had ever been in need Derek would have helped out, but we were on our own funeral and couldn't actually do anything, apart from sit back and enjoy the huge farce unfolding before our eyes. There really is only one way to get the coffin out of a hearse and that is the back, but in their desperation, the Co-op tried very hard to get it out of the drivers door in haste as they knew that twenty minutes was their allotted time, otherwise they would be back to the end of the queue. I naively said "Could we help them Mr Tyler?"

"No. Let them struggle" came the sweet but devilish reply. They did of course fail miserably and were last seen trying to get a crowbar from the cemetery diggers office around the back to force the tailgate open. Thankfully they had the sense to leave the family in the limousine around the front. Still, most amusing for us!

Derek had an excellent working relationship with the vicars, he had them eating out of his hand. First and foremost he was a wonderful diplomat and ambassador for the firm. Freed from the shackles of the disastrous Roy Preddy, this was his show, there was never any doubt about who was in charge and he ran it extremely well. People are often asked who in cricket they would have to bat to save their life and they answer Geoffrey Boycott for his technical brilliance and reliability, I can safely say the same about Derek for funeral directing – he would be my man, time and time again. I liked Derek very much.

Occasionally we picked up business in South Bristol, which entailed a trip across the city to lands unknown. The new fangled crematorium there was in sharp contrast to the last fading days of Arnos Vale crematorium where burials had taken place since 1765 and re-opened graves were a song and dance to put it mildly. The way burials work is that most graves are new. They are dug next in line by the cemetery authorities and therefore there is a whole new expanse of green at one side of the grave. Graves that are re-opened after many years are something else. We could have sold tickets to watch us manoeuvring our way through the headstones and kerbstones trying not to fall over with the coffin.

On the rare occasion we had a re-open at Arnos Vale, Derek got understandably twitchy. Bearers were watched very carefully in the previous few days before the funeral and at the merest hint of a cold or sniffle, Derek insisted they wrap up well else Ron be called off the substitutes bench to create an unholy fiasco. You see with Ron it wasn't just his clumsiness, it was his dignity, or lack of it. It was not unknown for him to get chatting to the vicar about the local rugby scores that weekend. It certainly didn't help when he met the proprietor of HG Harris Funeral Directors at Staple Hill, as Austin Sheppard used to play prop forward for England and Ron would collar him to talk about crooked feeds, squeezing against the tight head or lifting in the lineout. It was all a wonderful sideshow which kept me entertained, especially when the afternoons were cold and the coffins heavy. There were two sections at Arnos Vale, one appeared to be some sort of creepy overgrown jungle, where lost tribes of Amazons could appear at any turn. Throughout the whole time I was there, we probably only buried two people in that section, yet it remained a part of my memory that will never fade.

Cemetery chapels were never warm and welcoming places, even crematoria that had been built and run by city councils, were functional places, sterile and unloved. But cemetery chapels were always an afterthought, placed slap bang in the middle of the cemetery, often with little or no heating, you half expected Bela Lugosi to rise out of the crypt and bite you. The scene was like something out of a gothic horror movie and I used to dread funerals held at such places. In part because of the cold (I have never liked being cold), but also because funerals were a performance, and it was a bit like putting on a production of Richard III in a local church hall with a set built by boy scouts, it just didn't fit in with my sense of drama and style. Oh no, cemetery chapels were to be avoided at all costs!

At this time, Howard was beginning to make his move, clearly incredibly astute and a hard grafter, he had worked like crazy for eight years to get his father's funeral firm out of the huge hole it found itself in in 1975.

His father, Paul, by most accounts a dreamer and a drinker, had managed to lose most of the company money, and as the surrounding area had seen many houses demolished, its own funeral numbers dropped from a round a thousand to about 350. The overheads were still very much the same and he just went around in a vicious circle. Never having enough money to replace the vehicles (the removal van apparently had old coffin plates welded over holes in the floor) and after calling a rather cheap building firm to mend the holes in the roof, he discovered that all they had actually done was nick all the lead off the roof! Slowly but surely, the staff began to lack confidence in him. Paul approached Howard to see if he could raise some money for the business and then in a turnaround a friend told Howard he should buy it, as he was the one who knew how to run it. He got an increase on the bank overdraft, sketched out an acquisition plan on the back of an envelope and Hodgsons started off on the road to fame. So much of this was now company folklore but it was all neatly sketched out at the 1984 Company Conference where I made a great statement, but not a good diplomatic move, when I announced I would be prepared to go the ends of the earth for the company, such was my emotion and ambition at that age!

Howard had bought the business in 1975 (I was eleven then). He worked for four years to pay back the bank and then embarked on a series of acquisitions of small funeral homes, initially Crowther Bros in West Bromwich, the first of what would shortly become over five hundred in a fifteen year career. So, in 1982 Howard had bought Preddy's, Hodgson's sixth acquisition. Mr Preddy got a load of cash to restock his wine cellar and Derek got a boss younger than himself, but with the panache and drive that appealed to such an organised man. Thinking back on it, the Jaguar XJS, the long hair, the dark glasses and the oh so snappy suits had something to do with it, but there was substance to Howard. The story of how he saved his father's funeral home had become legend within the fast growing company and Howard himself had already acquired a revered status when I joined the firm in October 1983.

I remember the first time I saw him, he deliberately said little to me, his Jag had pulled up in the drive in Bristol; he was on one of his famous whistle stop visits where he would check five hundred details and prepare a hit list report. His dark glasses and long hair just won me over, I fell in love really. It wasn't a sexual thing, it was just awe inspiring, I remember Harvey Ewart telling me that he would have crawled over broken glass for him back then. Years later many of the managers said they would have done so as well, he just had it, an attraction and a leadership quality that made people want to follow him. It is the same stuff that Shackleton and Hillary had, often fairly indescribable, just class and commitment, he won loyalty and deserved it, despite his failings (of which we all have many). I remember being very impressed one snowy morning at Preddy's when Derek had been up early digging the hearse out of the snow that Howard had rung to check all the funerals would go out on time. It gave me some insight into control and management at an early age. He probably didn't know it at the time but he was my mentor and teacher as much as Derek.

I guess the bottom line was that Howard had actually done it all. He had been at the sharp end, conducting funerals at Hodgsons until the end of 1983, so he knew what it was all about. My father respected and valued Howard based on the little he knew of him, a man who had made his money through his own hard work, you could never fault Howard for that, it was true. As Howard pursued other funeral interests he was quoted as having conducted over ten thousand funerals in his time, I say good for him and a big "Bravo", he had built a business from pretty much nothing and revolutionised the industry. He had the right to be proud! People hated him for that and yet they could have all done it, but Howard had the X factor, no doubt about it. Yet in many respects Howard wasn't any different to any other son who has bought his father's business, he was just determined to ensure that things would be run his way now and the business would start making money. Howard had a drive and ambition to be feared. Many years later when I met over 800 funeral directors in the pursuit to purchase their businesses I can count only about five who impressed me with a similar drive, most were Nowhere Men, they were people going nowhere fast.

Google "John McManus" and you will find many things; a rock singer, an American attorney at law and a Nepalese sherpa, but you will find no trace of the man that always totally disarmed Howard and left him short-changed. Everyone knew him as Johnny Mac, he was working class down to his boots and had been bus driving when he joined Howard (shades of 'You were working as a waitress in a cocktail bar…'). There was something so laid back about Johnny Mac it made you love him even more. He was meant to be the area manager overseeing Derek and therefore one away from Howard, but whilst I was at Bristol the changes went around again and JBT (more of him later, oh much more!) became Derek's boss and Johnny Mac went back to controlling funerals and the famous dipsomaniac Arthur Hamer at The Oaklands Funeral Home.

Johnny Mac was as Brummie as they come, much later when I owned my own coffee house in the centre of Birmingham and used to serve the rock star Dave Hill from Slade, I noticed that they had the same flat vowel approach to torturing the English language. Johnny was a good man. Totally unflappable, just what Howard needed I reckon and used to smile with amusement how he used to get JBT totally worked up with only a few choice words. Johnny used to reply in his Brummie twang "Orlright Oward, I'll deal with it" and there was nothing much Howard could say. I think it really rankled him.

I only occasionally spoke to Johnny Mac, and although I liked him a lot, I had quite some difficulty in understanding him at times. But Johnnie appeared to be very relaxed about everything, it was almost as if he held the phone in one hand and a reefer in the other. Come to think of it…

Chapter 4

Car Washes, Lip Salve & N-for-Nuts

It was December 1983, I am writing this in September 2021, almost forty years later. What a lot has happened since then. Just as I was getting into the swing of things, I heard from Derek that Howard had agreed to purchase SA Evans in Hereford, and I was destined to be there by May of the following year. I am unable to describe how excited and terrified I felt, but I managed to keep it all inside (most of the time). In many ways this couldn't have worked out better, I had five more months to soak up all I could at Derek's feet and then move on to my own show. I was a little apprehensive, I had no idea what the future held, but I didn't spend much time planning, I lived for each experience and for each day.

The name SA Evans meant nothing to me. I looked them up in the Funeral Director's magazine and was unable to ascertain much, apart from their address and phone number. I confess that as the weeks flew by I got more and more nervous. It was all a little surreal, was I really going to be entrusted with this funeral home all on my own? How would I cope moving house yet again? Would I have any more luck romantically than I'd had in Bristol? (Fat chance I guessed) – what on earth would the next few months bring?

SA Evans was a firm just waiting to be taken over. A small rural concern in the city of Hereford, it had been run into the ground by the son-in-law of Arthur Evans, John Worley. The company had been plodding along in its own casual way when Worley decided to sell it. He was incredibly secretive about the whole affair. At an early stage when writing to Howard, he took a photograph of the outside of the premises and then cut out the sign showing the name of the business. He was certainly a little odd. Evans' main claim to fame had been in 1982 when they arranged and conducted the funeral of Jimmy Honeyman Scott of The Pretenders. Ken James, one of the employees enjoyed telling me about all the wacky types who had visited the chapel of rest in the days leading up to the burial. All the types you can imagine, said Ken, including a very young Chrissie Hynde. And apart from that, not much else.

The firm was to all intents and purposes run by June Hemming, in her mid-forties and unmarried, who did the same job Mary Brittain had done at Preddy's. Then there was Richard John Smallbone, in his late sixties, who was looking forward to a few quiet years before retirement. In addition and an important part of the business was the family run car hire firm LT Baynham & Son, who had worked with Evans for three generations. John Worley had two hearses, but no limousines and, because he wasn't running the firm efficiently, he frequently had both hearses out at the same time, requiring the hire of two limousines and the attendant staff from Baynhams. Terry Baynham, the proprietor, had recently died at a very young age. His widow May, her son Grant, and Pip Jenkins ran the firm now and were at Evans premises daily, with cars, staff or more often than not both.

It was only when researching this book I discovered that when the acquisition happened Howard had spoken to Grant & Pip in the office at Evans and informed them that, after three generations, their services were no longer required. As Grant Baynham told me "He informed us whilst looking out of the window, I seem to remember". And that in a nutshell was Howard's downfall, just a straightforward lack of respect and understanding for the common man.

In a way it was foolish because Baynhams were good guys, they had worked hard to keep most of the funerals even slightly dignified whilst John Worley, the Basil Fawlty of the funeral world, created chaos all around. In any event, we would need them after the takeover for when families ordered extra limousines, or when we required additional bearers. Baynham's were just down the road from the crematorium, so it was easy for them to pop up there and give us a lift. It didn't take a genius to work out that in a small market town like Hereford, it would have been good to have guys like the Baynhams on our side, so that our view could have been defended every night down the pub; after paying so much for a funeral business's goodwill, the least you could do was to look after it! So, it would have made far more business sense for Howard to have been frank with the guys but also polite and a little more upbeat. Now, so many years later I can understand why they were more than a little disenchanted with operations post Worley.

In some ways I am glad I didn't know of Howard's rudeness when I started there, perhaps things would have been different in how I'd dealt with them. But I always enjoyed dealing with the Baynham guys, they were totally reliable, very smart and charming to work with, all qualities you are looking for in a funeral home. The three mainstays of our bearing duties were Grant Baynham (more about him later), Pip Jenkins and Steve Cartwright. They were hard working and loyal, and although they were very, very kind to me, I always felt they were putting up with me really. I can't blame them, thinking back I am slightly horrified of how I might have come across. And yet, it was the arrogance and the naivety of youth. Young people are like this because they have not yet had the 'diplomatic' fuse wired into their brains.

I arrived in my dazzling new company car, well actually it was a grotty old Ford Escort with a small hatchback. It had been Derek's at Bristol and this was my first experience of Dead Men's Shoes. Howard had a policy of hand-me-downs, like children we would be given the cast-offs of those above. So, armed with this new status symbol I returned my red Vauxhall Cavalier to my Dad (I had bought it from him for £750) and strutted into town.

I was enthralled that I had been the subject of a recent head office memo, which went something like this:

> We are delighted to announce that Graham Hodson will be taking charge to assist Mr S Scott as Assistant Managing Director; Mr JB Taylor will remain Director in charge of the West Midlands, with Mr John McManus Senior Manager in charge of Derek Tyler (Roy Preddy) and Mr T Penrose for SA Evans (Hereford). Mr John Mould was to remain Manager at The Oaklands and Mr David Bonham was to be Director of the East Region – in charge of Mr Cliff Summerscales (EV Fox & Sons) and Mr A Hunt (SA Bates).

Well, puffed up cheeks or what? My little world was complete! Here I was, nineteen years of age and not a trainee manager, not an assistant manager, but Manager. I was in charge and I loved it, my show was about to hit town.

At one stage SA Evans had been a funeral home ahead of its time. The facilities were a lot better than Roy Preddy's. There was a small greeting area, which had a couple of chairs in, this led through to the bearer's clothes room (with ashes cunningly stored in the cupboards above) and then on the left the chapel of rest. There was a garage and through the back was the mortuary, preparation area and a tall white fridge with capacity for four bodies. There were two large coffin stores off this area and they all linked back to another garage where the Hodgson limousine would be housed. Previously all their limousines had been hired from LT Baynham, but things were going to change and that would be the first. It was a very good setup downstairs and this was repeated upstairs. A small kitchen area, three offices, one where John Worley planned his misdemeanours with his assistant, an arrangement room and (I never fully understood this when I arrived) a stock room. The stock room was quickly turned into a coffin selection room and I shared John Worley's old office with one RJ Smallbone.

The world that Richard John Smallbone lived in was a very easy and controlled one. Entrenched in his office, behind a solid walnut desk with it's overflowing ashtray, he was the chief funeral arranger for SA Evans. Known as John, this would have been confusing but everyone called John Worley, Mr Worley. He lived in constant fear of Muriel his wife telephoning to issue some shopping instructions or to enquire exactly what time he was to be home. Theirs was a very structured and unstressed life, but with the sale of the funeral home, John Worley's departure and the arrival of one Timothy James Alan Penrose (only forty-five years his junior), his life was to be turned totally upside down and his blood pressure was to be turned totally upside up (is there such a phrase?)

John (I never heard anyone call him Richard all the time I was there), was about five foot nothing, he arranged the funerals and quite frankly, rarely did anything else. He was against the takeover from day one, but then I don't suppose you would blame him. The first words he ever uttered to me were "Hello Mr Penrose, I was hoping to get your job". With the acquisition, John's daily duties changed; he became limousine driver, coffin fitter, occasional funeral arranger, always a bearer, grave marker and general dogsbody. He would continually make remarks like "Another gallon of petrol for Mr Hodgson's jaguar" when I sold a better coffin than the standard one, a practice he stopped doing after I admitted it irritated me! John was always huffing and puffing under his breath and although he coped very well, he must have wondered what had happened to his tidy and organised life. We used to take the mick a bit as well, he used to ring the obituary notices through to the Hereford Times and right at the end when the telephonist would say "Could I have your name please?" he used to reply "Smallbone, S M A Double-L B O N-for-Nuts E." We were in fits, I could hear June starting to fall about in the adjacent office and it was one of those things that was even funnier because you were anticipating it, a bit like a Laurel & Hardy prat fall.

Of course John was not used to wearing a top hat and tails, and the first time he did he looked so ridiculous I didn't know what to say. Ken James muttered "penguin" out of the side of his mouth and quite frankly I could see the resemblance. John was in it for the salary and the stability, he was not a showman and never had any wish to be. At this time, it was standard Hodgson practice to walk the funeral from the funeral home, walk it to the house and also away from the house. We were the only funeral directors in Hereford doing this and I felt it was a very classy touch. I informed John that he would be expected to do the same but was not prepared for the embarrassing consequences one mild winters day.

Walking in front had become a practiced black art during Derek's training, but he had taken it one step further. When he wished to get into the hearse, instead of stopping, like all the funeral directors did in Bristol, Derek had a coup de grace. He stepped slowly to one side, allowing the hearse to continue onward, he opened the door whilst still walking (quite a circus act, I can tell you) and then got into the hearse, with the cortège never having to stop at all. He was quite the Phileas T Barnum of Bristol. It was as smooth as silk and I loved it! I did it the same way of course, and drew a diagram to explain to John exactly how it should be done. Looking back now, goodness knows why I bothered, but it seemed important to me at the time, as these things do, and I was determined that John Smallbone was not going to let the side down.

He got to the point of stepping inside and slipped on a patch of ice. He held onto the door, was dragged cursing for about ten yards before being hauled in by Ken James. Filthy dirty, wet, cross and pride exceedingly damaged, he never walked a funeral again. Looking back on it now, John had gotten a pretty rum deal. He had probably worked quite hard getting Worley out of his monumental scrapes. But Worley had rewarded him by selling the business for loads of money, then some nineteen year old upstart had come in and changed the way everything was done to get his Hodgson pound of flesh, it was pretty tough on the old boy really!

After this incident I started acting a bit more sensibly towards John. He couldn't ever let go of his animosity towards the strict reporting styles and controls that Hodgsons had put in place. But all the improvements, new vehicles and far less daily chaos came with a price, you couldn't have everything! John and I got on well, he was good at the job he was doing and very efficient.

Looking back with hindsight (which I failed to purchase off the shelves at frequent intervals) I would have dealt with things differently, but I was making decisions as a nineteen year old. I was focused, driven, always looking to make daily improvements and run the tightest ship possible. No one needed to manage me, I was more than happy pushing and managing myself. At times I didn't take into account the staff's needs and their own personal, daily issues. Such is the bane of youth! I was so lucky in landing in Hereford where frankly any living body would have been better than John Worley. That was a massive break and it made me. It was sheer luck and I milked it for all it was worth.

There were many times these dear people got me out of scrapes. One Friday afternoon I totally misunderstood one family and booked the wrong church, and on top of that forgot to book the cemetery. Thankfully John picked up on this and didn't let me look a complete fool, for that I am very grateful!

Another time dear Ken answered the phone late one winter's night, I had rung to confess I had taken a wrong turn down a deserted lane and got the car completely and utterly stuck fast in deep snow. He came to the rescue late in the night, got his car down to the blockage and pulled me out amid grave sacks flying, probably cursing under his breath. He was charm itself and must have thought to himself that he was dealing with a first class prat! He was very good at concealing his true feelings on a number of ripe occasions.

June Hemming did all the admin, letters, phone calls to the vicars and when the guys were out on a funeral, did all the arranging. June was about four foot wide and four foot high, absolutely lovely to work with and lovely to me. If ever there was a case of inner beauty and charm winning over traditional beauty this was it. She lived alone with her Mum as her Dad had fairly recently died, yet she could not have given me any more support than she did in that first year while I was trying to get myself sorted. Part of me suspected that she would be on my side as, like John Smallbone (S M A Double-L B O N-for-Nuts E), she had rather got to the end of her tether with Mr Worley, they were trying to be a dignified firm of professional funeral directors and Worley was managing to foul everything up at every turn of the hearse driver's wheel.

June was very efficient and also wrote beautifully neatly, this was an important part of the administration duties, as once the details of the funerals had been put into the arrangement form, they then had to be written up into our big blue Day Book. The Day Book controlled everything that the funeral home did. If anything came in or out of the funeral home it got ticked and initialled in the Day Book. All removals of bodies, removals of jewellery and subsequent noting of where their things were got recorded there, it was a vital controlling record and one that we revered.

It was a couple of months before I discovered that June had a secret admirer. Occasionally, perhaps once a month, we received a phone call from David Stephens at Clifford. David was a builder by trade, in fact a wonderful craftsman. He worked wood beautifully with very skilled hands. David also carried out funerals, this was part of a local Hereford tradition where the local builder was also the local undertaker and even today it continues in small rural villages. I recall tales of nursing homes being visited at night for a removal by the local builder, and upon arrival discovering the van was actually half full of concrete mix for the following days work, so Mum had to be left on the pavement whilst this stuff was taken out and put back in after the body had been loaded. I didn't ever see the premises at Clifford so I am not suggesting for one moment that this is what David did! He was a lovely, rural character who had the most magnificent Dennis Healey eyebrows. They moved up and down when he got excited and this normally directly related to the amount of money the clients had paid for their funeral. We saw David monthly or thereabouts as he would hire our hearse to make it a posh job. We enjoyed seeing him and used to make him cups of tea while he was waiting for the hearse to be loaded up.

June married David at the age of forty-five, in pure white and with a dignity brides many years her junior would fail to muster. June made a magnificent entrance awaiting the man with the twinkling eyebrows that was to become her husband for a tragically short period of time. David was diagnosed with cancer only two years after the wedding and he went, buried in one of his own beautiful solid oak coffins with brilliant brass handles to an untimely and early grave. Poor June, but always a battler she no doubt gained comfort from all her WI friends and wonderful church support network. She was a complete one off, so talented and so much a part of my success at Hereford.

There was also Ken James, possibly Territorial SAS, but then so was everyone you met in Hereford. If you were fortunate they all claimed to be the second guy on the embassy balcony during the Iranian Embassy Siege in 1980. Ken collected the bodies, fitted the coffins, drove the hearse and was a general gopher. Ken was dearly kind to me. I have never managed to work out why. Thankfully, he was a fully paid up member of the "John Worley is completely insane brigade" so I must have seemed a breath of fresh air to him. We very quickly had new vehicles, I got the funeral home scrubbed and polished and all our new procedures meant that all the funerals went very well. Perhaps he enjoyed such a world of rules and discipline. Ken had a dear girlfriend Lorraine and she was also very sweet and easy to talk to.

I think everyone in that building had been glad to see the back of John Worley. It hadn't helped that the week before the changeover, he had driven the hearse on a large police funeral, fallen asleep at the wheel and mounted the grass bank just outside the police station. The wheel had been wrestled from him by Graham Holman who was still suffering frequent flashbacks. I felt that this had probably been last chance saloon for most of the staff, they'd had a skinful!

We also had a cleaner, Rose (good job we didn't get married as she would have been called Rose Penrose) and she was delightful and very sweet. I recall that she was a single parent with a young son, whom I never saw, called Ryan. She wrote me two incredibly sweet letters whilst I was there. I found them a while back, she wrote so beautifully and was again a very kind person, calling me Mr Penrose! Ye gads!!!!

With this crowd of staff, what John Worley did was anybody's guess! Well, actually it wasn't, because by the sounds of it John managed to pull off the most amazing cock ups. This was probably one reason why he had decided to sell, he had run the family business down as far as it could go, at least that's what he thought. In the first year Howard managed to lose a further twenty-five to thirty funerals, but then he had already factored this into the huge amount of readies that he paid John Worley for the business.

Worley was as mad as they came. Stories that came thick and fast over the next few months were difficult to believe, he was like Mac only twenty times worse. He had fallen on the business as son-in-law to Arthur Evans and worked very hard over a ten year period at running the business into the ground. He then decided to sell it to Howard (this was a recurring pattern over the next ten years). Even now it beggars belief what Worley did, arriving at the funeral home (or shop as he called it) late and due to go out on a child's funeral, he loaded up a dirty hearse and took it fully laden through a car wash, apparently the attendant's face was a picture. He was known for liberally applying lip-salve to his lips during the graveside committal and once introduced a family to a bald vicar not wearing his toupee one windy day "Here's Rev Fleming, I didn't recognise him with his hair off." He also took his little Jack Russell dog with him one day when he went to arrange a funeral at a lady's house. The dog ended up attacking the lady's cat and Worley had to lock it in the car. I mean you couldn't make it up, people just wouldn't believe you, but it is all wonderfully and fantastically true.

Much of what John Worley did wasn't daft in itself, just the way in which he did it. He was renowned for his lack of thought when dealing with clients, one memorable occasion I was able to see this first hand.

One day a little old lady arrived to collect her husband's ashes, which was a fairly common occurrence. Mainly the ashes were scattered in the garden of remembrance, occasionally they were interred in a casket (JBT at head office liked this, you could hear him rubbing his hands together on the end of the phone at the extra sale) or sent back to the funeral home to be collected by relatives. John came downstairs with me, took the lady into the staff room, climbed a step ladder and opened up a cupboard. He proceeded to sort through the last twelve months of ashes, stored in various polytainers, plastic urns and wooden caskets, piling them high on top of each other on the floor and occasionally handing them to the widow saying "Hold this one will you" and "Here he is – oops no, sorry, wrong one". I was aghast. No one had ever given me a master class in how to hand ashes over to a relative, but I figured there and then, John Worley would probably not be able to write a training manual about it all. So between Mac and John Worley how grateful did I feel about Derek Tyler. His was an ordered, steady office and we did occasionally have fun! This show in Hereford was now my own and I had to make or break it with this crowd.

But the best was undoubtedly the weirdest. In the chapel of rest, there was one small bay which could be closed off by a pull curtain. The bare little bay had a pretty naff tiled floor, which made it easier to clean up any spillages. Above the coffin, lit by a lamp, was a rather unremarkable painting, certainly not by any Dutch master. When showing Howard around, John Worley had explained with typical Worleyian logic "Oh and when you get the customers in here, you put the light on above this painting and it *really sends them!*" Put this with all his many quirks and you have probably the most idiosyncratic funeral director I have ever had the pleasure of working with. Ken James did rather a good impression of him, which amused us all greatly in between funerals.

And then there was Graham Holman, an intriguing character who couldn't do enough for me but was always seen as a massive crawler. All the part-time guys were either retired police officers (Graham had been an inspector) or ex-firemen, who were in the main rather frail. It was a constant source of amusement to me that these were the people called upon to lift upwards of twenty-five stone atop their shoulders through a packed church, weave their way through an undulating churchyard and lower it into a fourteen foot hole. Thankfully the days of the Health and Safety were not with us, I dread to think what happens now, I really haven't a clue how they would manage!

Graham was a hard worker, eager to please and specialised in taking names at the funeral. He would turn up early, set up a stall and take the names from people as they entered the church. Once home after the funeral, he would type up the report and we would then send it to the family; Mr & Mrs G Davis representing all the staff at Jenkins Haulage Company, etc. Graham drove a green Panda car, which was lovingly christened Kermit. Months later when he replaced it, the new vehicle became affectionately known as Kermit Mark 2 or shortened to KM2 on the garage orders. June was always amused that he referred to me as "Mr Penrose" and then "Just getting there Sir" was an oft heard comment from the bearer's room, very entertaining.

And then there was Walter Thomas who appeared to be about 150. Walter looked a little like a Chelsea pensioner without the uniform and was charming and stately to everyone he met. He also always called me Sir which was so deferent and very sweet. It was only later that I discovered he and Graham Holman did not hit it off. Graham had a rather inflated sense of his own importance and Walter was working class. Well that was all right by me, but Graham used to make comments like "Look at him, he's falling apart". Then later in the week, Walter would quietly button hole me and ask me if I felt that Graham could carry on with all the health problems he'd been having. Oh yes, there was rather a rivalry there. So this rag bag bunch of elderly pensioners were soon to be put through (I kid you not) coffin bearing training in the side garage in order to make absolutely sure that each movement would be as choreographed as I was used to in Bristol.

I enjoyed the environs at Hereford. Gaol Street was a little back street just off the main run into town. We were just down the road from the police station and right at the end was the most wonderful newsagents/ tobacconists. It was run by two guys, one about twenty-five stone with a sparking moustache and the other a dapper five foot two Granville look alike, they ran the shop between them in a very funny fashion. The shop was crammed full of different types of tobacco and so many newspapers. I dropped in occasionally and was always referred to as "Young Mr Evans". Across from here was Widemarsh Street, which led onto the main centre of town, and here things hadn't changed a great deal in fifty years. The market day was still important to Herefordians and everything in the town seemed to be centred on this. There were also plenty of Welsh people living there, which pleased me no end. I found people were fairly relaxed and not as wound up as they had been in Bristol. Again it was sheer luck I had ended up there. It would have been a very different story if I had gone to Merthyr Tydfil as originally planned. Such is life with its twists and turns. Sometimes you arrive at a fork in a road and inevitably you make a decision to go one way rather than the other. My Hereford fork was a brilliant twist of fate and this set the tone of my "Golden Balls" existence.

Chapter 5

Running SA Evans

*"You can't just book it and expect
me to be there you know!"*

Graham Hodson (more on him later) was there then to oversee the
transition from Worley chaos to Hodgson chaos. He commandeered
an office, sat with his diary and worked through a check list (this was
to eventually become my job three years later). I was in his office one
afternoon, after the takeover from John Worley, when we received a call
from the coroner to move a body from a tower block in the Whitecross
area of Hereford. I was very young and inexperienced and was to go out
on this call in charge, I was only nineteen.

We arrived to find not only police, which we had expected, but also Hereford Fire Brigade in tow. They had both been called to the incident. The entire tower block had been taped off and scenes of crime (those people in the white boiler suits that you see on the telly), police detectives, regular coppers, ambulance men, and now sadly not needed firemen that looked smoky, dusty, wet and exhausted. All would soon be clear. Charles Faulkner, an elderly pensioner had suffered a critical heart attack whilst smoking, the cigarette had caused a fire and his whole body had been burnt up. Previously I had dealt with a carbon monoxide suicide, but that was a bit cleaner than this. Here we had a blackened corpse, hot, smelling and still in his fireside chair in front of a still broadcasting television. My first job was to turn it off as "The Wombles" had just started and the song "Underground, overground" didn't really seem to suit the moment. There were eight firemen in the room, the chief of police, and Ken James, who had driven the removal vehicle, and me in my three piece suit.

"Right everyone out except me and James please guys" I commanded, hoping I sounded more confident than I felt. I tried to block out the image before me and focus on each small movement one bit at a time. We eased the burnt flesh into a body bag and placed this in a huge polycarbonate shell (which must have weighed fifty kilos on its own) and struggled down in the lift and over to our transport where we took the remains to the County Hospital. The morticians were light and breezy, there was something about dealing with such tragedy that made this sort of approach essential if you were to cope. They were practical and helpful and understanding. This really made a difference to me on this baptism of fire.

Once back to the funeral home Graham asked me if everything was all right. I answered very casually "Oh Yes", but the burnt smell on my jacket and the look in my wide eyes must have told him that I had dealt with quite a moment. That afternoon made my name locally. It didn't take long for the local police to consider to me as unflappable and to be relied upon for getting a body out of anywhere at any time. Over the next eighteen months we took bodies out of rivers, car boots, suicides in outhouses (mainly hangings), drains, farmers shot, youngsters drug overdosed, it was a slick and professional job that we executed all fuelled by adrenaline. I was in the thick of it, in charge and not even out of my teens. I also discovered I was very good at retaining my emotions and being able to logically decide what the most important thing to do first was, then the procedure we would follow until the deceased had been taken off the promises. I often wonder where all this came from and I guess it was part nurture but also me taking a great big grip of myself and deciding if I was going to be immersed in this world then I was going to be the best I could possibly be. The most important aspect was to never panic, to retain a calm exterior and deal with each matter logically. It was a good decision. I was in a way doing it for myself, a matter of personal pride to be the best.

Only three weeks later we were called back to the same flat to discover that the widowed Mrs Faulkner had had a heart attack, died and not been found for three weeks. It was the height of summer. Again Ken joined me in the journey up and down the tower block's lifts. It was clear to everyone that the body had lain there for far too long in warm conditions. To explain; when such a death occurs bodily fluids will seep out of the corpse and this will attract flies, the flies lay their eggs and maggots hatch. Maggots like dead flesh, so will gorge on it and over a very short period of time, a living human being with thoughts, desires and talents becomes a haven for thousands of maggots all crawling amongst each other vying for the best bit of flesh. When you are called upon to remove such a body and take it back to the mortuary it is crucial to suspend disbelief and put your feelings in a box. Otherwise it would not be possible to cope, either physically without vomiting or mentally. It was something you got used to, but in every case like this, the stench of flies and maggots took weeks to get out of my hair and brought home the fact that this was not a particularly glamorous job. But it was just part of the role, you never knew, when the phone rang, what you were going to find at the end of it. In some ways part of the excitement. But back to dear Mrs Faulkner, she was clearly as into watching TV as her husband had been and whilst University Challenge was a little more erudite than previously, we decided to put up with it for time as the TV plug was covered in maggots. It was all right with Bamber Gascoigne saying "Fingers on Buzzers" but seemed to be beyond the surreal as once we started to lift the dear lady he intoned "I'll have to hurry you". Another day in the weird world that had become completely normal.

Often the phone would go in the middle of the night and disturb my sleep. "Hello Mr Penrose, it's Hereford Police here, we've got a body in a car in the Black Mountains". They used to sound so excited! Only once did I let them down, albeit briefly. I took a call at about three in the morning for a suicide in the boot of a car at Pontrilas. I told them I would be there in forty-five minutes, all I had to do was to get changed, meet Ken at the funeral home and drive up from Hereford City Centre. I put the phone back on the receiver and looked longingly at my bed, ooh, just another five minutes I thought... the next thing I knew, the phone was going again, it was the same guy but it was now an hour later! That was the last time the phone stayed in the bedroom, I put it outside on the landing where I had to get out of bed and be up on my feet. It was the sort of mistake you only make once!

There was something undeniably exciting about being on police call or Coroner's work, it is well described by Barry Albin in his book *Don't Drop The Coffin*. The police in attendance, the police escort, the scenes of crime officers, the feeling that you are the centre of attention and that you are the master of the whole circus act. It is a totally unique feeling and one I will never forget.

In those days sudden deaths were dealt with in one of two ways. In larger towns and cities there was often a "Dead Box Man" who collected the bodies of sudden and unexplained deaths in a discreet black van, these were the suicides, murders and accidents. In more rural places, they were dealt with by the funeral directors on a rota basis. Removing the body for the coroner did not mean that you would necessarily conduct the funeral, but it was useful to pass a card to the family at the time of removal, as if you were called out in the middle of the night and moved the body for the coroner then you received £5 only. This was upgraded to £30 if your firm then went on to conduct the funeral. It was a clever and workable Howard incentive and caused some heated discussion at company conferences! It would be an exaggeration to say that as bodies were being cut down from overhead beams the family would be presented with a business card… but not by much.

One morning we were busy preparing for the days funerals when we received a call from the police station to attend a scene at the local Speed Plus Dry Cleaners in Widemarsh Road, Hereford. I have never forgotten the name to this day. It was about ten past eight. We were only ever given an address, and hadn't a clue of what we were about to find. When we arrived we realised it was something a bit special. The Dry Cleaners at this time in the morning? We were escorted to the rear of the shop where the towels were laundered, and there hanging from the RSJ cross beam in the roof was the body of a man in his mid thirties. I will never forget that he was still swinging, making an eerie creak at the end of each swing, it was just like a Hitchcock thriller. All these years later writing this it seems odd. But this was a job that had to be done, so atop a ladder held by James, there I was only nineteen and cutting down a body. My only thoughts

72

were "be professional, be in charge, be calm, be organised". It is at times like this that training comes to the fore, although I suspect there needs to be a certain innate temperament to cope with such matters. Twenty-five years later I can honestly say I have never had a sleepless night or any sort of nightmare about the deaths or tragic sights that met me in all my time spent funeral directing. I do admit however that I have spent *many* sleepless nights worrying about business decisions, bank overdrafts, staff problems, money worries and battles with lawyers. Perhaps that tells you something, there must be some sort of moral there!

Post Traumatic Stress Disorder is mentioned so frequently now. Even though I was so young I knew I couldn't let anyone down, so I blocked out the emotions of these horrific moments, put them in a little box, tied it up with a ribbon and kept it there. It's ridiculous really as there had to be some sort of long term effect, or maybe not? We are all wired differently and I am lucky that it has never bothered me at all. Upon attendance I was telling myself to plan and work out what to do; who cut the body down on a hanging, who held the weight and who did what. I know that Ken James who carried out most of these removals with me was of tremendous assistance; Ken, I salute you now!

It was undoubtedly suicides that caused everyone the most internal pain. The pain was completely different to bereavement, as you had no prior knowledge of the person and therefore no 'grief of loss'. What bothered me most was the continual questioning in my mind, what was it that finally tipped them over the edge? Could someone have said something to make a difference? How must they have felt when they wrote their suicide note? In all the time I was at Hereford I only dealt with perhaps thirty suicides, but they were the hardest to cope with. I guess I was learning a lot about life as well, throw in these incidents, a few nasty road traffic accidents, deaths by misadventure and murders along the way and the whole pot pourri does become a rather strange mix which must have some effect on you. I collected bodies from water tanks, many from car boots, and one young sixteen year old suspended from the ceiling in an outside toilet with his diary just beneath him. I noted the small things surrounding each death, the note left on the table, the coiled rope around the beam, the bottle of wine just next to the shotgun, the empty pill bottle, the gaffer tape – always the tape, attaching the hosepipe to the car exhaust. All these details played on my mind and I imagined the last few moments. It was impossible not to really. I always found it most difficult to deal with the relatives on such unexpected deaths. One of the things it taught me was the perspective on everything; things may be bad, but they were never as bad as they had been for that poor, dear man whose early visit to the Dry Cleaners that day was for something far more significant than collecting his freshly laundered shirts.

One night when my parents were visiting me for the evening (Cardiff is only an hours drive from Hereford), I received a call from Bob Brown at the Coroner's Officer. Could we attend a coroner's removal as soon as possible in the Whitecross area of Hereford. I tried to raise Ken James on his pager (we were very high tech remember!) but failed. Not wanting to keep the police waiting, I asked Dad if he could come along and give me a lift, after all isn't that what Dad's are for? I buttoned him into my black Crombie overcoat, it was only about eight sizes too small and we set off in the white purpose built ambulance we had for such occasions. I explained to Dad what had to happen, although I didn't explain that it could have been a murder or a suicide. I didn't see the point, I decided I would deal with it all when we got there. We pulled up outside the house, the police took us inside and an elderly lady was dead on the sofa. She looked as if she was asleep. Clearly she had suffered some sort of heart attack and died peacefully. Right next to her was the stiff body of her Yorkshire terrier Hamish, who had died of starvation, as the woman had been dead several weeks. Thankfully it was winter so there was no repeat of the Mrs Faulkner scene. Trying to remain nonchalant, as I felt I was being closely observed by Dad, I asked Bob what would happen to the dog. "Oh could you take it as well please?" he said. So, in as dignified a manner as possible, we lay the little doggy corpse on top of the dear lady and took them both back to the County Hospital. It was the first and last removal Dad ever did with me, although I did drop in to see him in Cardiff en route to Swansea Crematorium one afternoon and he obliged by driving the hearse from our house whilst I strolled in front in my tails and top hat. It was the last time I did that though as Dad had a number of neighbours in the morning asking after my mother's health.

So, slowly, I sorted out the funeral home that Hodgson's had acquired. I remember the days and nights spent hoovering the garage, sorting out the coffin stock, polishing the hearse until you could see your face in the panels, getting right under the second deck and making sure every last little petal had been removed. I remember putting up notices like 'Be a PREPPIE Preppies are Prepared Ready, etc...' I must have been a complete pain; here I was only nineteen. I knew nothing, yet thought I knew everything. With hindsight John, Ken and June had been very, very kind! It is clear now, looking back that I needed to get out more.

There were families that were memorable. There was Mr Dubbin who appeared to me absolutely delighted that his Auntie had died. He was the only relative and was laughing and joking when he came in to arrange the funeral. I found it all a bit odd but remembered that people reacted in different ways. I thought he would pull himself together by the day of the funeral but as I walked down the path to his house he charged out of the door, put up his thumps, all smiles and with a grin all across his face shouted out "Alright Mate?" It was one of the most memorable funerals I had ever conducted. He was of course the only mourner in the limousine and the limousine driver told me afterwards he was telling "Knock Knock" jokes to him through the glass partition that he had pulled to one side and was frequently lifting his backside, breaking wind and intoning "Speak on sweet lips that never told a lie". In the end the limousine driver lost it and just laughed like a drain. Funny the things you remember so many years later…

It was about this time that Howard twigged we could make substantially more profit per funeral if we managed to sell the client a better coffin rather than the standard one, which was rather naffly called a Superior Veneered Oak (SV Oak for short on the arrangement form). Hereford had only gone into the realms of solid oak coffins when a rich farmer was being interred on private land, well not exactly, but you get the idea that it was certainly rare. The man reason for this was that selling anything else had just never been considered. The funeral details would be arranged and John Smallbone would say "We use a normal cremation coffin, will that be all right?" and of course almost everyone said yes. Well you would, wouldn't you?

So we worked it all out and got the pitch off to a fine art. I would get to the point where the only remaining detail would be the coffin, I would explain the pricing structure and would then rise from my chair in the office (this was important) and say "Now we need to select the type of coffin you would like, if you would please follow me into the selection room where I can show you around and you can do that". I learned very quickly that just saying "Would you like to come with me to the selection room?" was not a good move, as some families would just say "No". To be honest I got a little obsessive about it, and we were now selling coffins with Raised Lids (£30 more expensive), Panels (£40), a Solid Mahogany Coffin (£100), a Solid Oak Coffin (£340), and a Solid Casket (£750). I seized on this straight away and not just because we got rather a lot of commission on the sales. I was keen to sell as much as possible, to prove to myself, more than anyone else, that I was the best at this job. I quickly raced up the better coffin ladder and proudly sat at the top after the first month. Amazingly this caused a problem; I was asked if I was sure that the clients were happy with their purchases! Ye gads! I even used dear Old Wilber's *Successful Funeral Service Management* (more later) to set out the coffin selection room, as he stated, I jest not, that when Mounties get lost in the Canadian forest they automatically turn to their right. A right turn is far more natural than a left one, so I set out all the expensive coffins to the right of the room. But I was far more subtle than this, I moved the cheapest coffin down the line; if you started with this people would say "that's fine for us" and there was no way forward. So I put the SV Oak in the middle of the left hand wall and developed a smooth (but not slimy) patter that delivered a genuine argument for the sale of a better coffin.

I was sold on the idea that it was an important part of the transaction. Clients had selected every other detail of the funeral, the hymns, the limousines, the flowers, surely they deserved a choice when it came to the most expensive item of the entire funeral? In my view there was no doubting this logic, yet you never knew what was going to happen. Time and time again I was surprised by people's coffin selection and this stood me in good stead when selling the wide range of coffees in my gourmet coffee house many years later.

JBT's approach at The Oaklands was rather different. Derek had often commented that JBT was as subtle as a hod of bricks and the more I worked with him I found this to be true, but I never liked him any less for it. He used to ask clients into the 'booking office' rather than the arrangement room and openly referred to the "Crem" and not the "Crematorium". But his pièce de résistance was the selection room, where his SV Oak had a grubby side frill, handles falling off and not level and a scratched lid. People ordered the cheapest coffin from JBT at their peril! In defence of his system, if not of his morals, very few people did. Well you wouldn't, would you?

JBT was a superstar, one that I never truly fathomed in all my time there but I knew I liked him very much indeed. His major claim to fame was that he just didn't listen to what you said on the nightly report. Frequently I would put JBT on speakerphone in the office for John Smallbone to hear and John always said "You could say what you like to that man, he isn't listening to a word you are saying!" One day I decided I would try this out. On my nightly report to JBT as Derek was away, I informed him calmly that there had been an outbreak of typhoid in Hereford, we had booked thirty-four funerals in one day and that not all the confirmation letters had been typed up that evening as June Hemming had been carried off by a plague of locusts from Worcester. It was typical JBT really as he smoothly and quickly murmured "Good, good" down the phone and exhorted me to get the numbers up and work hard! JBT made his name with me that day and I will always have room in my heart for him to the day I die.

I really enjoyed the mechanics of arranging a funeral, they were rarely complicated. It must have seemed incredibly complicated to our clients, but to us it was a walk in the park, or a walk up the crematorium drive in fact. Most of the funeral arrangements started with a telephone call, where we noted details down on a first call sheet. The details of the death and appointments to see the family were noted down and stapled to a brown A4 folder, this then served as the entire funeral record until the family came in to finalise the arrangements. Most of the families were happy to come in (well perhaps that's not the best choice of words, but you get the point), and we would carry on with a detailed arrangement form with the particular aspects of the funeral noted on. We had one main arrangement room, using June's office if we were doubling up, normally you could expect to get the details down in thirty to forty-five minutes. I had been taught by Derek to gain the information in a conversation, you would say "And your husband, how old would he have been on his next birthday?" and "Would he have been wearing any jewellery on him?" It was never easy, often straightforward, but never easy. Sometimes you were very aware that a hearse was slowly revving its engine on the drive outside as the 1.30pm funeral to All Saint's Church would be about to depart and you were not yet on board. It made you be very precise about the questions you asked, very in control of the conversation and many times thinking of more than one agenda. It was dealing with that pressure that made a brilliant funeral arranger. I was rarely thrown, although there were a few times. I asked one lady a question I had asked many times before "what religion was your husband?" She replied "C&E." I stumbled my reply, pen poised, "Pardon? Is that Church of England?" I offered. There was a pause and with beautiful comic timing she replied "No, C *and* E; Christmas and Easter, it was the only time he went!"

I always remembered what Howard had taught me in the early days, "When you are with the family Timothy, you must be whatever they are but a little less." It was sound advice. I felt at ease with the distraught and weeping family where I was sombre and professional; with the matter of fact people I was a little more relaxed and tried to be as business-like as possible, and with the laughing and accepting families (there were more than you might expect) I was smiling and efficient.

I was rather unprepared for one keen gentleman who went way beyond the laughing and accepting to laughing and joking. I asked if he would like to see his mother-in-law in the chapel of rest, his answer was "Not on your Nellie, I've had her living with me for ten years, smoking my cigarettes and drinking my whisky. I'm glad to see the back of her! Haven't you got anything cheaper in the coffin area? I was thinking more of on orange box". But all my replies were delivered with the consummate ease of a professional who by now had started to see it all and did not flap. It was always entertaining and never boring, you never quite knew what the day would bring and this was part of the joy. It was so mixed and varied, I thrived in such an environment, I felt hugely successful and proud of all that I was doing. I suspect, but I am not entirely sure that the profession is still very much the same, the characters, people's emotions and the same stuff happening. Hereford now, seems such a long time ago and I still cannot quite believe I was so lucky to be in the right place at the right time.

One of the more entertaining characters in the vicar database was the wonderfully named Prebendary John De La Tour Davies. I said to Ken he had quite a mouthful for a name and quite frankly he was good value for money as he was always entertaining. It was only after I had been there for a few months that Ken let on that John's daughter was rather famous. Frances De La Tour was very funny, appearing on the television as Miss Jones to Leonard Rossiter's Rigsby in "Rising Damp". Once Ken had told me it all made total sense and I couldn't attend another funeral in his presence without hearing Mr Rigsby say "Ooh Miss Jones".

At the time I lived at Bobblestock, a new housing estate north of the city. On my Dad's advice I had bought a starter home for the princely sum of £14,500 and quickly moved into this sterile environment. There was a small garden at the front and back, but horror of horrors, no central heating! There was a small electric fire on the wall in the lounge although this could hardly warm a glass of milk. We went to Argos to buy plates, cups and saucers, sad to say I am still using some of those plates thirty-five years later, they don't make things like they used to you know! The house was just a base really, I started work early and finished late, this was to set the scene for the next four years of my life until I got married. Work was everything, but I did get nights out and occasional treats. I was looked after fantastically well by June and her dear Mum, Phyllis, several evenings a week. They shared my sense of humour and I guess they enjoyed having me around, a breath of fresh air and something a bit different. June's mum was a widow who lived on Homer Road in a lovely house called Bibury. They were both so kind and managed to keep me together as I really was missing home a lot!

I got on very well with most of the clergy. Probably again, benefiting from the fact they were all pleased to see the back of the most hysterical and yet hilarious funeral director in Herefordshire. I treated them all with the due deference they had never received from Worley and got politeness and huge co-operation in return. In most of the cases. There was one vicar in Tupsley, a small suburb of Hereford, named John Hall-Matthews and he was intent on trouble from day one. I had heard that he could be difficult, he didn't seem to like funeral directors and that he was known to be very short (not height wise, although he certainly wasn't the tallest of people) with people in general. It seemed strange to me that someone with such a personality would choose vicaring as a job, why not get a job where you didn't actually have to see people or get on with them? Yet here he was thrust straight into the fast lane of social learning.

To be fair I had due warning and so I was on my guard when I telephoned to plan a funeral service for one of his parishioners. He was a bit off (as my Mum says) from the start. "You can't just go booking the times and expect me to be there you know". I said I was aware of that, but obviously we had to be guided to a certain extent by the family. It was pointless organising a very early funeral if family had to travel from different parts of the country, so 2.00pm was often a good time. I happened to have been

81

tipped off that John Hall-Matthews liked his afternoon golf and was vary wary when suggesting such a time.

It was quite a tricky and diplomatic situation. From an efficiency point of view was wanted to run all the funerals with the one hearse and limousine. If we utilised our assets properly, we would maximise the profit and really sweat the overheads. So, it was best for us all if we arranged one funeral in the morning and one in the afternoon. This meant two funerals a day, ten a week, easy on the Evans numbers. When the busy season was upon us, we could be doing three or sometimes four a day. To do this well meant many hours preparing the funeral times with the family (as now we needed one to be at ten, one at twelve, one at two and one at four) and then many clever staff movements to ensure they all went off successfully. John Hall-Matthews frequently attempted to put a spanner in the works, but most of the time we managed to hold off from strangling each other to work together. He was quite simply unpleasant to deal with and I cannot for one moment imagine that he gave the family any sort of solace whatsoever in their time of need.

The vicar of Bodenham church was an altogether more interesting character, long since died at a young age I hasten to add, the Rev Derek Miller inspired love amongst all his parishioners, lust amongst the younger female ones and commitment beyond the call of duty. He was as smooth as silk, a fine figure of a man with the looks and manner of a young Donald Sinden. He would greet me with not only a "Good Morning Mr Penrose", but also a "Are my vestments straight at the back?" or "How is my hair looking from the side?" Eau de Cologne sweated from his pores and I distinctly remember never seeing a stray hair on his chin, here was a wet shaver, goodness knows how many hours he spent in the bathroom getting ready for a funeral! He was just an out and out showman, totally vain and cared not one whit who knew it. He was stocky without being overweight and I always enjoyed going to his church for a funeral, you knew it would be a command performance. He had persuaded all the ladies in the congregation to make brand new kneelers for the church and I have to say that there were plenty of candles, robes and hassocks at Bodenham. It ways a rich and fruitful church with few, but dedicated members.

While I was in Hereford, I reported to Derek who reported to Johnny Mac, who reported to JBT, who in turn reported to Howard. I had to ring up Derek every night with the figures of funerals booked that day and listen to Derek intoning that "Mr Howard won't be pleased" when we hadn't had a sniff of a funeral for three days. Howard had bought a bit of a turkey really. Somehow John Worley had managed to convince him that the business was doing about 350 funerals a year, but in the first twelve months we managed to puff and wheeze our way to about 280. The pattern was quickly established though, Derek would in the main leave me alone and I was left to promote my peculiar brand of management. Cobbled together with bits from my Dad and bits from books I had bought. My favourite being *Successful Funeral Service Management* by Wilber Kreiger, I went to bed with this book, it was my lover for twelve months.

Hereford was, and to a certain extent still is, a close-knit market town. I had caused quite a stir, but no matter how badly I could have run the funeral home, it wouldn't have been worse than John Worley. Now, Hereford people weren't used to the showman antics of walking in front of hearses, but we never encountered a client that complained, as it lent a touch of dignity to the occasion. We had many, many clients write many, many letters remarking on how lovely it was to see old fashioned methods employed once more. We also made a first of shouldering every coffin into the church, crematorium or cemetery chapel. We only did this at Evans in Hereford because that was what I had been taught at Preddy's in Bristol. John Worley had used a horrendous coffin trolley everywhere, which was much easier for the bearers and much less to think about, but the mere act of shouldering a coffin seemed to me to be the final act of adding dignity to the end of someone's life and I felt very strongly that we should do it at all times. It has to be said, there were times we struggled, trying to lift twenty stone onto the shoulders of four elderly men is not easy and needs to be a finely tuned process. I discovered that the key to this was to ensure that everyone lifted at *exactly* the same time, I was at the back of the coffin to give what can only be called a bump up. We walked in step, coffins are heavy things at the best of times and one step slightly astray could mean disaster, so we practiced in the garage at SA Evans until we were much more confident. This attention to detail carried on throughout the funeral home, we organised things properly, got the detail right and I was extremely good with the clients. I loved funeral directing and funeral directing it appeared, loved me. On the weekend, I went into Hereford city centre and enjoyed a ham omelette and chips with lashings of tomato sauce and (wait for it) signed for the bill and settled on a weekly basis. Could it possibly get any better? Guess what? It could!

Chapter 6

The Men in Black meet the Men in Black

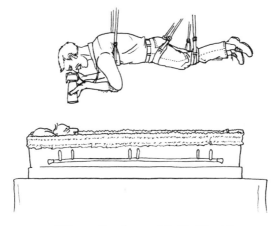

"Big smile please, Mr Nutkins!"

The Special Air Service or SAS as they became known throughout the world, exploded onto our TV screens in May 1980. Like millions, I sat in awe and stunned excitement as they ended the Iranian Embassy Siege in dramatic fashion. I was only sixteen. They sent around forty heavily-armed troopers into the building and eliminated seven out of the eight terrorists holding thirty-five people hostage in the centre of London. It was the exercise they had trained for over and over again. Many years later when interviewed as part of a BBC documentary Trooper Robin Horsfall admitted they were all ready for it and were hoping that the order to go in wasn't going to be rescinded. They wanted to show what they could do, this was going to be their day. The SAS captured the British imagination like no other regiment before or since. The iconic sight of two SAS men dressed in black hostage rescue kit on the balcony of the Iranian Embassy captivated an audience that were merrily enjoying Snooker on the BBC. The soldier on the balcony with the window-frame gelignite was John McAleese (known to all and sundry as Mac) and it was he together with a colleague that rescued Sim Harris the BBC sound recordist on the famous balcony scene.

David Stirling had formed the regiment in the 1940's and now everyone was hooked with the mystique, secrecy and excitement that was the SAS. At the tender age of sixteen, I was as captivated as the rest of them and I kept the Daily Mail press cuttings that went into great detail on how they saved the hostages and killed the remaining terrorists, save one who mingled among the women leaving the building. I don't know why I was so captivated, I had never enjoyed war or gun games in school. My grandmother whose husband, a dear kindly man by all accounts, was a conscientious objector during the war, told my brother time and time again that she didn't like us playing with guns. At the young age of about ten we continually made fun of her pacifist stance ("I want you to be soldiers for Jesus"), but our lack of interest in anything aggressive and war like must have somehow rubbed off on us from her. I guess the real reason behind my interest and some might say obsession in 1980 was the story of a brilliantly executed plan. Two years later when the Falklands War culminated in a victory for the British Forces, I was again interested beyond what was perhaps normal for my age and plastered the wall of my recreation room with the Daily Mail press cuttings. What captivated me was the planning, execution, preparation and advance knowledge, all designed to ensure that the plan went off perfectly. This trait and skill (or weakness, depending on your view) was what formed me over the next twenty years.

Little did I know that just over three years later from a young schoolboy's interest, I would be arranging and conducting SAS Trooper Al Slater's funeral in October 1984 in Hereford and being in charge of over four hundred people on the day. It was one of those moments that the phrase "arrogance of youth" comes into its own. I had no fear, no concern, and no worries, here was my stage and I was desperate to be a huge part of it. It was the chance of a lifetime. I believe the number of funeral directors in the world that have arranged and conducted a 22 SAS Regiment funeral are in the single figures. I like that. I am one of around six individuals in a total of 7.3 billion.

Al Slater had got caught in a cross border battle with the IRA. He was a rising star in the regiment and had recently been featured heavily in the BBC TV series *The Paras*. He was only six years older than me when he was killed. I asked my Dad to come with me to Heathrow airport, we collected his body from International Freight from Belfast and brought him back to the funeral home in Hereford. It was all very low key, security was fairly minimal, until a few days before the event itself.

The centre of all SAS activity was at Stirling Lines, in Holme Lacey Road in Hereford City Centre. There were no signposts to the camp, you just had to know where to go and like a famous pop star in their midst, the townsfolk were protective of the regiment. I don't know quite what Keith Edlin, Camp Adjutant was expecting that day when I drove through the security and sat in his office to discuss the funeral arrangements for Trooper Slater but if he felt I was rather young, he didn't mention it. He was courteous and supportive and I felt confident as I sat in his office discussing the practical details of this, my first military funeral.

As I sat there and went through arrangements for the family, viewing of the body, bearer party practice and service arrangements, troopers would knock and enter every ten minutes. One I remember as clear as day, dressed completely in white Arctic fatigues. It was helpful that I had been trained by Derek to expect the unexpected, so I remained calm and collected, but frankly wondering what apparition would come through the door next.

The day of the funeral brought a few last minute butterflies for me, but I had met the bearers of the coffin, fellow troopers of Al Slater. They had arrived in full dress uniform very early to fasten his beret, complete with the famous motto "Who Dares Wins", belt and dagger to the coffin. We then had to drive the two miles to St Matthews Church where the regiment had their own special cemetery in the churchyard. As I walked the hearse away from the funeral home I saw snipers on the roof of the nearby Hereford Times building. Everyone knew whose funeral this was, I was in charge, I was the ringleader, it was my show and today I felt well over seven feet tall. I walked the funeral a little longer than normal, got in to the hearse just by the traffic lights with Widemarsh Road and drank in the atmosphere of the great occasion.

I remember snatches now. The family, standing out as they were the only ones dressed in non-military garb. The huge six foot eight black pallbearer whose boots squeaked eerily has he carried the coffin down the aisle. "Bronco Lane" who attended the funeral, minus all his fingers as he had lost them on Everest. The slowness of the bearer's march and the dignity of it all. In SAS terms, Al Slater had failed to "Beat The Clock", the term given to soldiers from the regiment who die as they come back to be buried near the clock in St Matthew's Churchyard. I have never experienced anything as moving as the final moments of an SAS funeral. After all the ceremonial duties have been carried out, Last Post and Reveille is played on a bugle and the members of the regiment all march to the foot of the grave and salute. It is extremely moving and

I shall never forget it. Again, what a privilege and what luck to be sent to Hereford rather than say, Huddersfield.

Whilst I was in charge at Evans, I conducted four 22 SAS funerals. The next one, Raymond Abbots was in a way even more dramatic. He had been fatally injured during a live round exercise. The SAS are the only unit in the British Army to use so many live rounds, they will use more live rounds in a day than the average British soldier will use in his lifetime. Ray Abbots was shot in the training room at Bradbury Lines. This is the place the hostage rescue plan was practiced time and time again. Diana, Princess of Wales and her sons had been there for training, as had most of the senior members of the Royal family. It was important for them to know the capabilities of the SAS, so they would be better prepared if they ever got into a dangerous situation. That room has gone down in history, it is known as the Killing House.

Ken James and I collected his body from a side room at Hereford County Hospital, he had been declared dead on arrival. Yet again, the military machine swung into action but this time I knew what to expect; the bearing party wishing to practice with an empty coffin, snipers on the roofs, the moving salutes and the precision, it was all becoming very familiar. In the months that followed I was to conduct two further SAS funerals, with their strict planning and tight family bonds, my respect for the regiment just grew.

One was the funeral of a Trooper that had died at the tragically young age of thirty-seven from a brain haemorrhage. Now, many years on, sense has prevailed and the regiment have moved from the city centre barracks to a site at Credenhill where I suspect that the security is a little tighter than it was in the halcyon days of 1984 when I arranged Al Slater's funeral. They still keep the best part of a 747 aircraft fuselage buried in the woods in Pontrilas and frequent it to keep their hostage rescue methods up to date, but although their physical presence has been removed from the city centre you can still feel them as part of the city, they will never be forgotten.

However, none of the SAS funerals I conducted were to be as career changing or as memorable as the day a certain Matthew Nutkins walked into the funeral home and asked us to arrange the funeral for his father who had passed away over the weekend.

On the face of it there was nothing remotely different about it. I was aware enough by now that Matthew Nutkins had money, his dear departed Dad had been a director of Gilby's Gin. Matthew had a definite reputation for being a little eccentric, but nothing could have prepared me for the next ten days. It all started with the visit to the selection room, where he was to select a coffin for his Dad. He looked around with his nose in the air and I became increasingly embarrassed at the poor range we had on display. I sensed something in him wishing to spend more, there was a sort of disdain as he was looking. I seized the moment; "Is there anything you like here Mr Nutkins, or did you have something else in mind?"

He did indeed have something else in mind and asked if we had anything more expensive. This was where it all kicked off. I remembered reading about American Caskets in one of the Funeral Journals, sad to say that this was my reading material at home! I got straight on the phone to the agents in London, was this range available? Could they get it to Hereford fairly quickly? How much would it all cost? We eventually settled on a Dark Cherry Wood Batesville casket which alone was well north of £2,000. I hired a Rolls Royce hearse and three Rolls Royce limousines (one had been Richard Burton's old car I had been told) from the upmarket funeral directors Pargetter's in Coventry and purchased brand new striped trousers and tailcoats for the bearers to wear. I even arranged for the grave to be bricked, whitewashed and dressed with flowers. It was a world class act and was going to cost a world-class bomb.

Of course, ever the showman, I decided to walk the funeral all the way from the house to Hereford Cathedral, and from the Cathedral to Tupsley Churchyard. Part of this was to give the hired photographer Vic Herbert plenty of time to get the shots that had been requested by Matthew Nutkins. Vic, ever the mucker in had also agreed to take photographs of the late Mr Nutkins in his casket. So one bright summer's evening there we were the two of us (plus the late Mr Nutkins, looking rather like John Paul Getty) hunched up in the first chapel of rest at Hereford trying to get the best possible angle. First we had problems with the flash bouncing off the coffin, then we decided we really needed an overhead shot, so, ever resourceful I winched dear old Vic up on the fridge trolley and he leant over and got some rather exquisite shots to add to the portfolio. I think Vic thought I was more than a little mad, but he went along with all my proposals and we managed to deliver the goods exactly as Matthew Nutkins wanted.

I called Vic a few months ago and we reminisced. He had never forgotten that bizarre day, he told me that no day's work had ever been so interesting, bizarre or memorable. I was pleased and like to think that in a small way I had brought a bit of sunshine into his life one warm day in the summer of 1984.

I felt that despite all the arrangements we had made, I still wanted to top everything with a flourish and so, two hours before the cortège set off from Gaol Street with Mr Nutkins on board, I lowered myself into the white, bricked grave and arranged layers of flowers there for the coffin to sit on. In short, I had lost a week of my life to arranging this, their perfect funeral. It was fantastically high profile, brilliantly profitable and exactly what the family wanted.

The final bill I cannot remember, but I do know that it came to more than the purchase price of my first house on the outskirts of Bobblestock, perhaps about £15,000? It was a huge amount to spend on a funeral and I had engineered the spending, decision-making and execution of the perfect funeral! I remember that John Taylor couldn't quite believe it. A standard Superior Veneered Oak Coffin with full services was priced at £375. The finest Solid Oak Casket that the company had in their price list was £750. Even the finest Solid Oak Casket and the best of everything else from a normal set up would have struggled to hit £1,000 and here was one that had broken the £15,000 barrier! Thinking about it now, it really was rather special.

I guess that was my downfall really. Everything had been perfect and I was on a high! How do you follow that? Well it could be topped, only a week after the funeral, Michael Maxwell - Mr Nutkins's son-in-law wrote to me and wrote a separate letter to Howard. People often write to the funeral director after a funeral. I was already thrilled to receive such letters and had started to keep a personal folder of them all (even now I still have them!) I remember Derek showing me one of his more effusive ones, and by heck it was good! He told me "You can't buy these, never forget that!" He was right, he normally was, the collection and preservation of such letters became a bit of an obsession for me. Michael Maxwell's letter to Howard really did set the cat amongst the pigeons. The letter could not have been more complimentary if I had written it myself. It congratulated me personally on the planning and execution of such a classy and detailed funeral, it went into great detail about me personally arranging the flowers in the bottom of the bricked and whitewashed grave (I must admit I liked that bit!). Howard's big boob was to photocopy it and send it to his managers with a memo asking them to note it. It was not one of his more inspired moments.

They noted it all right – too right they did! It took me a while to understand why people knew who I was when I turned up at the company conference only six months later. However, they were there to bury me, not to praise me (with apologies to the dear old bard, Shakespeare).

I thrived most of the time at Evans. I enjoyed the work, I was in charge and Derek came down very rarely to see what we were up to, which suited us all down to the ground. The vehicles were spotless, the garages and stock rooms kept dust free and the admin in Tim and June's safe hands rarely missed a beat. There were occasions when things slipped through the net, but we managed to sort them out before the problem got to the family. This was the main reason for all the checks that we had in place. Before getting in the hearse to conduct a funeral, we double checked everything which ensured you couldn't drop a massive clanger.

When taking out a funeral the Funeral Director had the important funeral envelopes, in these were all the fees that needed to be paid to the various protagonists; the minister, the gravedigger and the cemetery. There was also the green disposal certificate, which was essential for the burial in a cemetery or churchyard, without this key piece of paper nothing got buried! Before getting into the hearse it was essential to check the body in the coffin against the various paperwork you were taking with you on the funeral. So, the lid of the coffin was opened, the name on the leg in indelible pen was checked with the paper label on the toe (even today I see these labels in Rymans and they give me a lovely flashback to those days). It was a very detailed system of checks, it needed to be really as there were so many things that could potentially go wrong at a busy funeral home, if you thought about it you would never move the hearse off the drive.

Gypsy funerals were another thing altogether. I knew a little bit about them, they paid cash, normally from the waistband of the elder gypsy man's belt, they were particularly ostentatious and this was good for the better coffin graph, they ordered loads of limousines and they liked bags of pomp and ceremony. Well all this sat fine with me and I reckoned that it was fair exchange, they would order a solid oak coffin, eight extra cars and I would go into my Noel Coward overdrive and give the best performance of my life.

I had already managed to make a complete fool of myself on my first gypsy funeral. We were bound one day for the village of Much Marcle, famous with me, long before its association with the evil Fred West.

Ken wasn't around to drive the hearse and I always felt a bit nervous without him. He was one of those guys that gave you confidence wherever he was. So we were lumbered with a hearse driver that didn't know the area and wasn't particularly good at hearse driving anyway. Put that with the fact that he wore pink socks, had spiky hair and most of the time his muddled head was full of alternative rock music and we had Grant Baynham, still young at twenty-four, but five years older than me. Grant was an interesting young lad, he was never really interested in the work, his head always appeared to be somewhere else, usually still at the latest gig at The Whistle and Blow in Hereford. It was only now that I was to discover how vague he was in practice. As Grant had to drive the hearse and I hadn't been to the church before, I asked him to check the route and make sure he knew which way to go. The cortège was a hearse and three limousines and it was imperative there was no faffing about with directions.

We collected the family. I made a bit of an arse of myself as I tried to load the limousines in Hodgson fashion by reading out the names of each of the occupants one limousine at a time. This was a disaster as most of them were called Smith and many of them couldn't read, so I ended up with about twenty-five chasing into the first car and the last car setting off on its journey with no one inside, it was a bit like a Whitehall farce. The bearers and drivers were chuckling to themselves at the arrogant Penrose put in his place yet again.

Whilst I was trying to load the cars, I committed the cardinal sin of putting my top hat down on the floor where a Yorkshire terrier decided to relieve himself in it. Then I bumped my head on the caravan getting out, it was turning into a Tim Penrose comedy sideshow. I don't think the family minded, they were just interested in getting value for money and well, a funeral for Mam with all this extra entertainment thrown in was a bonus and they were all well chuffed.

But it all came to a wonderful and tragic head when, with the spire of the church but two hundred yards away and the vicar within sniffing distance, we arrived at a crossroads. "Left or Right?" said Grant, giving me the Russian roulette choice. I was staggered and a horrible feeling arrived in my stomach. I could sense the family right behind us and I didn't have a clue which way to go. I could see the church, we were almost there, but…I just didn't know, so I said right.

Of course it should have been left. The entire cortège carried on a beautiful arc away from the church, never has a cortège more slowly driven left of its target and never has a funeral director been more desperate. What was I to do? It was all up to me. We couldn't reverse, and then I saw a gypsy caravan up the road on the left. "Quick" I said to Grant, "drive up there and pause for a moment and then execute a U Turn." We did, all the limousines did. When we arrived at the church, met by a rather bemused vicar who wondered exactly what was happening, I explained to the mourners I had seen the gypsy caravan and decided to go and pay our respects. I was met with total silence, and to this day I will never know if they knew. Did they?

Looking back now it's a bit like someone else was doing all these things. I can't quite believe I would have the balls or the chutzpah to carry it all off now, yet with the arrogance of youth and the disdain of anyone older than me I just went for it, time and time again. Yes, I was making it all up as I went along, but most of the time it all seemed to work out, there was a lovely innocence to me that didn't believe things couldn't be done because my Dad had never told me that. You see it all comes back to Dad in the end really. I believe your environment shapes you and although Dad was not present at school football matches, through osmosis-like effect the values, skills, passions and driven way of working has never left me. Its a thing I am most grateful for above all else and I salute him proudly now, thanks Dad!

As Evans was a very small operation (although I talked about it in rather grandiose terms), I got very close to a number of my clients. Mr Mousley was one such chap. He had arrived to bury his mother-in-law and I got on extremely well with him and his two daughters, who were very close to my age. The funeral arrangements went really well and then only five days later he was back on the phone saying that they hadn't left to go back to Bromley in Kent yet, but his wife had died and they had decided to have the funeral in Hereford. I couldn't quite believe it! Two funerals in six days, that was a record! And I remember receiving the loveliest letter from him a little later on inviting me to their house to stay anytime I wanted, what a gent!

Then there was Babs, a single lady of indeterminate age who got very close to me during her Mum's funeral. She had travelled down from Blackpool and was a dearie. I liked her and got on extremely well with her, she was fun to be with and cheerful as her Mum's death had come as a happy release. After the funeral I received the most beautiful card and a present of a table lamp for the side of my bed. She was very sweet and signed the card with a flourish that said "Any time you are in the area, come up and see me!" Hmm, I was a little shocked, I was only a youngster!

Then there was the young couple whose baby had died and they had asked me personally to carry the coffin down the aisle of the church. The family were from the SAS regiment and again it was an extremely moving ceremony. Children's funerals never bothered me and I couldn't see why they would, of course many years later and having three children of my own, I probably couldn't do what I did then. In those days it meant so little to me, I couldn't identify with children. In a way this was good for the business as I was always a safe bet to keep cool on a child's funeral and I carried out many in my first few years of funeral directing.

Despite all this success on the field of play (so to speak). I was singularly unsuccessful in finding happiness in relationships. Granted, part of the problem was that I didn't ever go anywhere to meet anyone. I worked late, was normally first in and weekends were spent with my own company. The more this went on, the more of a rut it had become. I fell in love briefly with Bridget who was a handsome (not pretty) girl from the small Pentecostal Church I attended at weekends. Bridget seemed a lot of fun and sang songs in the church in a very clear and pretty voice. I got close to her and then, one fateful night took her out to dinner, only once. I am still embarrassed to think about it, let alone write about it. I think I spent the whole evening talking about death and funerals. That was my world, I knew nothing else. I had previous girlfriends when I was in Cardiff, but that seemed light years away now. I suppose I felt I had to keep up this desperately serious image and dress soberly even when I was out at the weekend, as everyone knew I was the manager from Evans the Undertaker. Bridget rapidly found someone else younger and less depressing to date and I was unceremoniously dumped. This sent me into a sort of downward spiral as getting any female company now seemed to be impossible. It was to prove difficult for a couple of years, in the end I had to loosen up a bit, or as King Louie from the Jungle Book says "Unwind yourself".

Peter Wood was vicar of St Peter's church in the centre of Hereford and it was more than a little unfortunate that he looked like Harry Secombe. For some reason, my Dad knew him and he had arranged for me to spend the first two weeks of my time in Hereford with him. Peter and his family were lovely to me, I had little experience of living away from home and they went out of their way to do whatever they could for me. For some reason we rarely conducted funerals with Peter, but on the one occasion we did, it would forever stick in my mind as The Worst Possible Thing to happen on a funeral.

I had been trained by Derek to sit right at the front of the church, in the aisle across from the pew occupied by the main mourners. The mourners would follow the coffin into the church or crematorium and just as the coffin was set down, the mourners would then file into the pew. The art was to let a few mourners into the aisle first so that the main mourner would end up in the aisle next to the coffin, and of course be first to follow the coffin out again. During this one funeral, Peter was holding forth in quite vigorous tones (I couldn't stop thinking about the Goon Show every time I saw him) and was proclaiming what a wonderful man "Derek" was. I was a little bemused and checked my funeral envelopes, they told me that the man I was burying was "David". No particular worries I thought, nicknames were often used instead of family names, and Peter had seen the family the week before the funeral to sort out the arrangements. I was just working out what I was going to have for dinner in the evening when all of a sudden there was an explosion from the pew across from me. The widow was up and out "I'm beginning to wonder whose funeral I'm at" she shouted. Her face about three inches from Harry, sorry Peter's nose. I was up like a shot, all my training went into practice. I held her arm and apologised for Peter, he has got a little confused, Peter's red face told of all the embarrassment there could ever have been. But that was nothing, when we got back to the widow's house to find her on the phone to the local bishop with a complaint that went on and on. I have to say I can't blame her really.

The longer I was at SA Evans the more checks and double checks I put in place as this had now become rather fun. I also went to the trouble of putting an emergency kit underneath the hearse deck. I had read about this in Wilber Krieger's *Successful Funeral Service Management*. It is still around on Amazon if you're interested and rather a fun read even if you have nothing at all to do with funeral directing.

Still, Wilber Krieger had nothing in his book that would have assisted me the day we went to Madley. This was a small village in the Golden Valley. I can remember little about the village itself now, apart from the fact that its telephone prefix was 01981 although its name will be imprinted on my brain for evermore and yes, dear Grant Baynham was present again, but this time he would turn from sinner to saviour.

The funeral was straightforward, there was nothing remotely unusual about it that would have alerted me to the fact it would remain with me for the rest of my life, marked up in one of those boxes with a huge label on it BIZARRE. We had two gravediggers that we used for burials. There was John Fortey who lived way out in the sticks and didn't own a phone, so every time we needed to instruct him, John Smallbone drove out there with the measurements. I went once, but got spectacularly lost and drove around in circles in the Black Mountains for two hours as night was falling, not a form of entertainment I can recommend. There was also Les Wooley. John managed to section out the grave and applied such a finish to the walls that they looked like they had been plastered. It was such an art, fantastic and all for £40! Les, however, clearly had bomb disposal experts as family, since his method seemed to be to place a small amount of gelignite at the appropriate place and detonate. The resulting crater looked like something out of All Quiet On The Western Front. I tended to use John more than Les as John's graves were fabulous to look at and he was far less coarse than Les who used to cuss at the vicar and smoke furtively behind the gravestones. So, heading to a John Fortey grave I thought nothing could go wrong.

We got outside the church with this six foot five coffin and were about two hundred yards from the grave when I noticed that the neatly coiled webbings the coffin was placed on before being lowered were not there. I had never really clocked it before, it was something that just happened. I had not got involved, the gravedigger provided the grave, the mats and the webs, that was the deal and yet it hadn't managed to get on to one of my more famous check lists – where the heck were they? The grave was now getting closer and quickly. I whispered to the front right bearer Grant Baynham to go to the hearse and get the spare webs. I will never forget the look on his face, sheer shock, followed by a calm, measured walk back to the hearse. By now we had arrived and the absence of webs was glaring. We placed the coffin on the trestles next to the grave and I looked around hoping that perhaps I had missed them and they would suddenly appear. It was not to be. All my Derek Tyler training came to the fore as I stalled and stalled. We took the flowers of the coffin (no Grant yet), I theatrically took out my white handkerchief and polished the final floral leaves of the coffin plate (still no Grant) and then paused as I spotted an imaginary fingerprint which I then rubbed out with care and love (still no Grant) and then I saw him. I can look back on that moment and remember it as vividly as anything in my life, he appeared over the brow of the hill and looked at me and, with an awful finality, shook his head. But I ensured there was no panic, no John Worley moments, no "Ooh we have forgotten the webs", all calm and precision – a coolness in the face of certain death.

Grant arrived back, paused and then walked past me up to a tree where there was a blue car tow-rope hanging. He untied it and, with as much dignity as was possible to muster, handed me the rope with the reverence due the Turin Shroud. I then threaded the bright blue nylon rope through the front left and then the back right handles so the rope was across the coffin. We lowered and we struggled and we puffed whilst the vicar read the committal. We said nothing, no-one said anything, until I heard a little old lady in the churchyard afterwards "Oh how nice to see the Scottish Courtesy Cords being used, just right from John's Scottish heritage"... which showed me that there was never any point in panicking because if the cards fall well, you just might get out of the most unholy of scrapes.

We drove back in the hearse in total silence until we got back to the main Belmont road. Then I turned around and looked at Grant and we knew, we just knew that nothing else as amazing would ever happen in our lives, we lived to fight another day.

However, and this is a pretty big however, there was one scrape I didn't ever really satisfactorily conclude and that was when I dealt with a most delightful family from Wales who had come to bury Auntie Eddy. They were very Welsh and once they had discovered that I was a kinsman, they grew close. It was one of those funerals when quite frankly it was all a lot of fun. Auntie Eddie was expected to die and the Welsh crows were treating the whole affair as a huge jamboree. Everything went according to plan; the family instructed that we remove the rings prior to the cremation and then place them in the ashes casket (even as they ordered it I could see JBT's eyes glistening at the prospect of another sale). It was all pretty straightforward really. And indeed it was, until they arrived to collect the ashes casket. Thirty of them arrived in a coach to come and join in the fun, sorry, help mourn and take the ashes casket back to Wales to bury it in the local cemetery. I bore the casket reverently onto the coach and as I shook the main mourner's hand. He put his arm around my shoulder and started to give a little speech about how wonderful Welsh Tim had been, how us Welsh people must stick together and I was drinking it all in when I realised. The rings were still sitting in the safe in the office in the funeral home that they were parked outside. Various possibilities ran through my mind; Basil Fawlty "just testing the walls", other delaying tactics, an admission, a feigned call back to the funeral home? In a split second all these flashed through my mind and then I settled on the coward's way out, I did nothing! To this day my Father has two cheap Welsh gold rings in his safe, I mean what do I do with them?

Most of the funerals that we conducted went without a hitch, or at least we discovered the hitch before the family did which was the key! I cemented my position there, grew increasingly obsessive about the cleanliness of the funeral home, and crawled on a regular basis to JBT and Derek.

All the time I worked hard on improving everything. I was only challenging myself really, but I was continuing to drive myself. Not only did I want the cleanest funeral home, but also the most highly vacuumed carpets in the hearse footwells. I worked out that if they were vacuumed every day then they didn't actually get very dirty and once you had vacuumed those to within an inch of your life, there were always the chrome strips on the door to polish and the tyres to paint with black paint. When we had a day with no funerals, we scheduled both hearse and limousine to be covered with beautiful thick wax which we then lovingly took off to give the most glorious sheen. I had no doubt whatsoever that my funeral home had the finest fleet in the country. Things could not have been more perfect, we were at the top of our game and we knew it. I considered ordering red paint for the garage floor and drawing a white outline for the hearse to be parked in, of course with the word hearse written in large block capitals, but I didn't as we would have struggled with the hearse outside for two days whilst the paint dried. I was still working on a solution to the problem when I was moved to Dunstable (more of that later).

But what I didn't understand was that I had managed to create a mystical world where everything was perfect and I got cross if someone marked up the Day Book with anything other than a perfectly neat tick (and there had to be no overlaps on the upward stroke, otherwise I would have to tippex it out and start again). It was approaching obsession and decidedly unhealthy.

I don't know what the staff felt, frankly I was too self-obsessed to notice them most of the time, I was living in my own little dream world and rarely did my world and theirs cross. In retrospect they were all extremely kind and bore with me, I must have been quite a shock to their normal daily routine.

Chapter 7

Promotion

JBT

John Bruce Taylor was a descendant of Robert the Bruce and was as tenacious in many ways as the man who became famous all because of a spider. JBT (as he was nationally known) was Howard's boss at Eagle Star and was as loyal as the day was long. He had a wonderful habit, which was a gift to mimics and comics. As bald as the proverbial coot, he had a habit which was to extend his long arm and put it over his forehead, mainly when panicking about whatever Howard was asking him. But it was really a game, JBT always referred to him as Mr Howard and declared his business love for him at frequent intervals. Howard would never have left John in serious cack, although he used to shout at him regularly, theirs was truly a marriage made in heaven.

JBT had been bashing on about a company conference for ages. It was to be held at the Arden Motel in Birmingham and all the managers would be there with the directors and their wives, of course Billy No Mates had to take his secretary June didn't he! JBT really psyched me up for it, it was the closest thing to a cult you could imagine. We didn't have a company song, but it wouldn't have surprised anyone if we had. We would have walked through fire for Howard and it was all done very cleverly mainly through JBT who pounded away day after day perpetuating the Howard myth. The day dawned bright, I had pulled out my very best tie pin and polished my shoes till I could see my face in them, and we were off. A day of high excitement, one that was to set me on the Hodgson road for so many of the formative years of my life.

I confess to being on a bit of a high. Nothing was more important to me than work and here we were about to spend a whole day discussing it! Within minutes of arriving I met the hitherto unseen John Mould and we chatted easily and enjoyably. Johnny Mac had already ordered a beer and I could also see a small man striding towards me with bright eyes and a ruddy, eager face. This was the immortal Arthur Abraham who never ceased to be a source of amusement all the time he was with the company. Rumour was that Arthur had been a regimental Sergeant Major in the army and through a contact with Cliff Summerscales of EV Fox, been promoted to Assistant Manager and was now to be Manager of the newly acquired Wilson Forrest & Long in Fleetwood, Lancashire. There was no doubting Arthur's enthusiasm and willingness to obey orders which had clearly been drilled into him during his time at the Western Front, but he didn't seem to fit with my idea of a competent, quality funeral director. During lunch I heard him holding forth about how traditions differ in different parts of the country, his Yorkshire voice echoed around the dining room "You see lad, the first thing I say when I get to the house on the day of a funeral is come on, where's the black pudding!" For the rest of the time I was to see him at the company I could never quite get out of my mind him saying this. He surpassed himself while I was at Head Office by requesting "some of those SS20 forms". He did of course mean P45 employment forms, they were this christened for the rest of the time I was there. He had a bit of non class and style about him, did Arthur. His way of dealing with people was in the true tradition of all sergeant majors made famous by Windsor Davis; he shouted at them. It didn't seem to help much I felt.

Arthur turned up at the conference with Richard Lang, a tall gangly lad with an American accent, a white suit and (ye gads!) long hair! With one look JBT told me what he thought of that straight away, the guy would be out on his ear before very long. Richard's father had just sold the company Wilson Forrest & Lang and I heard from Mary a couple of months later that I had been earmarked to take over the firm instead of Arthur. Derek had told Howard it was too early (bless him for this) and they had sent Arthur Abraham instead.

For the company conference I had dressed in my best double breasted suit (they really were all the rage then) and by now had grown my hair from a straight crew cut to the most awful ratty tail long hair which quite frankly must have looked awful. I suppose I was trying to look like Howard even then! How desperately worrying!

The conference was for me fascinating, we had an introduction with reports from the various regions, JBT stood up to speak and Graham Hodson didn't, which rather surprised me. After a few workshops in the late morning Johnny Mac held one on how to run better Garage Orders and I scribbled away feverishly like the newly converted cult member that I was. We had lunch and then came back into the room where it had been rearranged for the 1984 Company Conference awards. Just before the awards, Joe Jordan a famous Birmingham gynaecologist spoke, I remember his warm way and neat humour. He looked at the garage orders on the flip chart and said "I mustn't keep you too long, as I see you are due out of the garage at 3.30pm".

I guess at some stage it is nice to look back on the fact that you won Best Manager of the Year Award and Best Kept Funeral Home in Hodgsons all those years ago, but unfortunately my haircut was not one to be proud of. June came with me to the weekend and I was thrilled that she was happy to accept the cup with me as well, after all she had worked just as hard as me for it! I suppose the awards didn't endear me to anyone there, as they continued to think they were dealing with an upstart that really should have had a haircut before turning up.

By November of 1985, it was predestined that I would receive a promotion. Evans in Hereford ran well, the Hodgson systems were in place and working, we were regularly in the top three of best coffin sellers in the entire company. The Derek style of dealing with clients paying "Hello my dear I am just ringing to see if everything is coming back to normal after the funeral" worked as well as it had in Bristol and my ability to maintain an almost zero debtor list endeared me to Howard if not to my fellow managers. I had been very fortunate, another guy the same age as me, John Mould, had got a job with Howard and worked out of The Oaklands Funeral Home. He had the rough job, the thin end of the wedge, the short straw. Howard was always there, watching like a hawk. I was allowed to make my mistakes without Howard or anyone of any note permanently looking over my shoulder. And so, what with the Nutkins funeral, the SAS and no outstanding accounts (and don't forget whilst we are at it, the Manager of the Year Award, the Company of the Year Award and the Best Kept Funeral Home Award) my course was clear, but I hadn't been any better or brighter than dear John, just fortunate that I hadn't ended up in Birmingham.

The whole point of economies of scale was that all funeral vehicles would be centralised and most funerals, if not all, should to be carried out using the one hearse where possible. I understood the economics and the financial benefit of it immediately, but we only ever struggled at SA Evans when we conducted seven funerals in one day (bear in mind this was a rural area so our hearse was well travelled that day). If you were clever in planning, you tried to arrange one funeral ending near where you wanted the next one to start, and you sent bearers in separate vehicles to meet you at the crematorium just to lift in for sixty seconds and then go off to do another job. The permutations were enormous and had only been pushed by me at Evans when we had delivery of a new hearse from Birmingham. At that time, my dream of a perfect Hodgson empire was rather shattered as the hearse was filthy dirty, but it held in the glove compartment jewels beyond price as Caernavon said. The jewels were historic garage orders, instructions for the staff and vehicles in the Birmingham area. It was directly from this that I got the jargon and nuggets of transport wisdom that allowed me to show that I knew exactly what I was doing, my garage orders were more exact, detailed and professional than anyone's. They involved such complicated permutations that at times even I was confused and I had written them; To Crem in KM2 for 3rd A Job, To Crem Only In Ambulance for a Lift in, Return and collect deceased Davies from County Hospital, Park Ambulance around Back, Meet at Cemetery Chapel for Lift in and Wait, Swap Hearse Keys with... and so it went on. It was fantastic, almost something out of Boy's Own and I loved it. It was very clear by now that I needed to get out a little more.

Probably the two most complicated manoeuvres I managed was a coffin swap. This was where we went on the funeral with two coffins, but the second one was hidden underneath, and only brought up onto the display shelf when we had finished the first funeral. It meant we did not have to drive the hearse back to the funeral home to collect the second coffin.

We could pop the coffin up, drive around the block and get back to the crematorium just as the family arrived for the next funeral.

And then there was me taking the family back in the limousine, and meeting up with the hearse in a lane somewhere in the Herefordshire countryside. Both of these ruses worked extremely well as they shaved minutes if not hours off the schedule and meant we could cram even more funerals in to each day. I was caught out once when waiting in a lay-by, I stepped out in front of the hearse to call him in. I got in, only to discover it was in fact being driven by Dawe Bros, the local competition. No one was amused and I can still see the startled look on the Hearse Driver's face to this day.

Late one night just after I had carried out the reports with Derek I had a phone call from JBT. "Mr Howard wants you up at Head Office" he said in a loud and commanding tone. Now, Head Office at this time was in Kingstanding and somehow I managed to get to Kings Heath (direction had never been one of my skills) and I rolled up at Kingstanding at about 9pm just as Graham Hodson was going home. Howard met me, didn't turn a hair at the late hour and explained what I was going to be doing from Monday. The funeral home of SA Bates was a poisoned chalice and proffered to me whilst I was only twenty-one.

Dunstable sat in the heart of Bedfordshire, just a short hearse drive from the nearest crematorium at Luton. It was I immediately felt a heartless town. So different to what I had left and so impersonal. Luton had become a London overspill and displayed all the cosmopolitan tendencies typical of such a place. Mini suburbs leading out of the city that were run down and on the verge of falling down. Impersonal shops and large quantities of city folk that were not prepared for the country yokel from Hereford about to work his magic on the local funeral business.

SA Bates was in West Street. It was a firm that had been acquired in 1982. It had been run by Alan Hunt who had frequent run ins with David Bonham and Howard. It came under the jurisdiction of David in the East Region as it was only forty-five minutes away on the motorway. Just twelve months after SA Bates had been acquired, R Metcalfe had been acquired, fifteen miles away in another county, at Berkhamsted. In addition, there was a branch office at Tring a few miles away. This was due to be re-opened and re-branded, I was put in charge of dealing with this and managed to mess it up. Tring being the place famous for the Great Train Robbery so many years ago out of Cheddington sidings.

Now this was to be my mini empire, presumably Howard expected me to have the same effect on the business as I had on SA Evans. So, leaving June Hemming, Ken James and John Smallbone in Hereford I went with the words of June ringing in my years "You have worked so hard, you really deserve it!" I felt she was right, of course, but what a tragedy was about to hit the stage!

I had little time to plan, I was to leave straight away. I packed a case, said goodbye to June and left for the loneliest night in a motel I could ever have imagined. I was well away from my comfort zone and as I dropped off to a heavy sleep that night in the motel in Luton I dreamt of promotional success and not of the nightmare that was about to engulf my world. Even as I drove up through Luton, I suspected this was going to be a difficult challenge. I was young, no support structure, no huge experience and I was going to be watched by a Regional Director that was not my greatest fan. You couldn't blame him I suppose, all those memos from Howard about how brilliant I was, well here was the chance to cut Timothy Penrose right down to size!

Arriving at Bates and Metcalfe, they averaged about eight hundred funerals a year, more than double what I was used to. The secretary was

110

pretty useless, Moira, a vamp that apparently had chased Alan Hunt away with her come ons. The other staff were Andrew Ketteringham, a young eighteen year old who had no get up and go and looked permanently bemused, his Dad who reminded me of Ruth Lawrence's Dad astride a tandem, Tim Durrell who was a cockney spiv type lad, Wally Cox and Keith Fleckney.

Keith was my John Smallbone and I should have been clever and witty enough after eighteen months of working with the old buzzard from Hereford to have worked out exactly how to play things. He was actually very similar to John, he had also had a mad boss, Ron Metcalfe who had slowly but surely started to get even more eccentric as he got older and left the running of the firm to Keith. Keith had been more than hassled by Alan Hunt, didn't like Howard and was fairly hacked off with the Hodgson system. If I'd been smart I would have played to Keith's strengths and got him on my side. If I'd been smart I would have leant on his considerable experience in the industry and built on that to provide a firm foundation. But I was twenty-one. I wasn't smart. I wasn't clever. I wasn't all the things I should have been to a firm so clearly in trouble.

There was no doubt that Keith was a good man. Like so many funeral directors, incredibly caring about his families, often to the point where he failed to see they were in business to make a profit, not just help people out. It was a difficult balance, of course you had to be good at your job in order that your firm made money, thrived and then went on to better things, but it was always important not to lose sight of the reason why the business was started in the first place!

I blame the BBC myself. About that time, there was a series about Customs and Excise starring Peter McEnery. The character he played was Harry Caines, a forthright district manager for the customs and excise. He ran a very tight ship, I loved the series and modelled myself on him. To admit it now is cathartic and probably more than a little embarrassing, but it was the influences that turned me into the type of manager I was. I distinctly remember his comment to one of his staff "I'm not open to argument on that!" I used it at Tim Durrell one day when he failed to show any urgency at turning the limousines around before the next funeral. I was impressed by Harry Caines, he got results and that was what I wanted. I desperately wanted results, not only to prove to David Bonham that I was up to the job (he made no secret of the fact that he thought I wasn't), but to prove to myself that I was made of the right stuff and that Bates and Metcalfe would prosper.

The drive from Dunstable to Berkhamsted was interesting and always full of incident. We passed Whipsnade Zoo and Henry Cottons, the golfer's old private house, it was a lovely, picturesque ride. I enjoyed it even though I had the troubles of the world on my shoulders. I worked extremely hard at the timings, ensuring we made the return from Luton Crematorium in enough time to get the empty hearse to Berkhamsted for the next funeral from Metcalfes. But that was only aspect of an enormously complicated job and of course I wanted it all to be perfect. With that narrow attitude I didn't stand a chance. It would be so easy now, with the benefit of experience and hindsight. Dragged out of my cosy little world at Hereford I had been plunged into a soap opera, a sit-com and a Hammer Horror movie that was not to have a happy ending.

Chapter 8

Wrong graves and slippery slopes

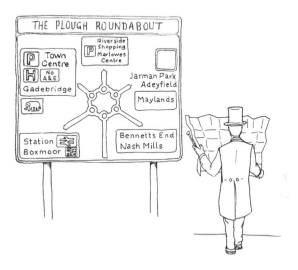

In the short time I was in Bedfordshire, I had some lovely moments. The middle 1980's were years when many people were just not used to going to their local parish church and therefore when confronted with the fact that someone would have to officiate at the funeral, were rather stumped for a choice. In Dunstable we made it all very easy. Officially as funeral directors we had to inform the parish priest of the death of an incumbent and ask whether or not they would be available to conduct the funeral. This worked very well in Hereford, but in Bedfordshire people just didn't know their vicars from Adam (if you pardon the biblical expression). We often had to contact the local vicar who wouldn't really want to conduct the funeral service, and cause us all sorts of grief when trying to arrange a suitable time for our system. So we turned to Reverend David Cooper.

Cooper was a class act, clearly a failed thespian he insisted on the same procedure for each family. Locally he became known as the Martini vicar (any time, any place, any where...) and quite frankly at £16.50 a throw (this was twenty-five years ago remember) he was doing rather well. His personal best at Stopsley Crematorium in Luton was apparently twelve funerals a day. He brought sandwiches with him to eat in the crematorium office as he was often scheduled to be there for most of the day. Why was he so good? Well, he loved it, he was even more a showman than Penrose. He would never speak to the family before hand, but as the coffin came out of the hearse onto the bearers shoulders he would intone:

"After this it was noised abroad that Mr. Valiant-for-truth was taken with a summons. When he understood it, he called for his friends, and told them of it. Then said he, I am going to my Father's; and though with great difficulty I have got hither, yet now I do not repent me of all the trouble I have been at to arrive where I am. My sword I give to him that shall succeed me in my pilgrimage, and my courage and skill to him that can get it. My marks and scars I carry with me, to be a witness for me that I have fought His battles who will now be my rewarder. When the day that he must go hence was come, many accompanied him to the river-side, into which as he went, he said, "Death, where is thy sting?" And as he went down deeper, he said, "Grave, where is thy victory?"

Cooper would always insert the deceased's name into the last sentence with great drama.

"So he passed over, and all the trumpets sounded for William on the other side."

It was quite fantastic to watch. Then he would then turn, lead the coffin in with me following behind, enthralled in the hands of such a professional. He was amazing, and the act continued in the same manner, he never followed the family into the garden of remembrance, that was their time on their own he always used to say during the eulogy, but little did they know that this was because he was back at the front of the crematorium chapel again on the next funeral intoning in the same way *"After this it was noised abroad..."*

Whilst it was easy for us and a fine fiscal situation for Rev Cooper, one couldn't really fail to feel sorry for the parish priest who had to deal with the mundane stuff on a day by day basis. Yet when the crunch came the family had hired an expert funerals service officiator with no thought of being in his debt so therefore no dreary Sunday service to attend the following week.

But we worked in tandem, both giving the most fantastic professional performance worthy of the £16.50 fee for him, and us deserving of our fees. You see funerals are nothing to do with the dead, they are for the living and you only had one chance to get it right. It is the equivalent of a Royal Shakespeare first and last night. In my opinion this is what many funeral directors missed, they just didn't get the plot. They worked hard at the nuts and bolts of the business but they did not have the finesse, the style, and the panache that was needed for a truly great performance. And for me as a young twenty-something year old, it didn't matter how many mourners were at the funeral, six hundred or just six (and bear in mind that the average number of mourners at a UK funeral is twelve). I was not performing for anyone else but myself, they were my standards and they had to be the highest of the lot. There was always something that could be done slightly better or a little more efficiently, you never stopped improving. It all sounds a bit anoraky now and I guess it was, but it has always stood me in good stead for all of my businesses.

There was one vicar whom I didn't get on with and this caused innumerable problems for me whilst I was there. Rev John Tabor of Northchurch was simply the most obnoxious man I had ever come across. Doubtless he thought of me as pompous and overbearing, he seemed to despise me for my age and there wasn't much I could do about that. He had written to Howard (rather cowardly I had thought) and said that I walked up the crematorium drive like a strutting peacock! You get the idea. To his credit Howard had spoken to him and suggested that I went round for tea one afternoon and show him all the letters I had accumulated in my career to date. But Tabor wasn't having any of it. He spoke down to me when I arrived and didn't want to see any of my letters. So an uneasy truce took place between us and we both went about doing our jobs as best as we could, it was not a pleasant situation. I guess this should have forewarned me to be very careful, to use Derek tact with these sort of people, to butter them up and use the old flannel just like Derek had, but I'd had it very easy at Hereford. I had been welcomed with open arms. Only one letter difference in the name, but those arms were not so welcoming here in Hertfordshire and every time Tabor and I met, we both sensed the chill between us.

Just as in Hereford, we were working in the most glorious of surroundings; Buckinghamshire, Hertfordshire and Bedfordshire had some of the most beautiful countryside. Due to the location of the three offices, it was not unheard of to pass through all three counties on the same day, sometimes on the same funeral. However for sheer hilarity, Hemel Hempstead was one place we were always keen to go, particularly if it meant a funeral cortège going through the magic roundabout. That wasn't its real name of course, it was the roundabout at the end of Two Waters Road, just before the centre of Hemel. The roundabout had no less than eight possible exits! The rule was simple, you could enter and exit anywhere you like and taking a funeral cortège through there was not a journey for the inexperienced or faint hearted. It was a miracle we got through intact. Of course Derek Tyler, ever the showman and control freak would have walked the whole lot through, barking orders as he went, but I didn't have the balls for that, plus I valued my life too highly! It was a hoot though and one wonderful memory during difficult times.

We attended Stopsley Crematorium, West Herts Crematorium and occasionally ones further afield. Luton was made for quick ins and outs, twenty minutes a service and built for a slick operation. Once again, like Canford there was the occasional over runner, but no French farces such as the Co-op stuck with a coffin in the back. Most of the time I was conducting funerals I was in a surreal world. In Hereford, always in control, I was planning what I was going to have for dinner in the evening, writing out a shopping list in the hearse, working out how much milk was left in the fridge, the sort of thing that seasoned funeral directors do day in and day out. Here I was constantly panicking about what was going wrong with the business and why I couldn't control it to the level I had in Hereford. I had concluded (wrongly) that it was something to do with the distances between the two offices, but that wasn't true at all, I was just too inexperienced and David Bonham, my immediate boss, was unable to spur me on to greater things. In fact, whenever I saw him I just got lower and lower.

Although I was only at Dunstable for ten months, I still managed to bury a body in the wrong grave. I am forever thankful that when it came down to it, my client didn't seem particularly fazed and the vicar of the churchyard could not have been more helpful. I am not proud of the following, but it does go to prove the point that panicking never achieves anything and a cool and logical approach to thorny problems is undoubtedly the best way to achieve a satisfactory solution.

Richard Barrings was a delightful chap who had contacted us to make the funeral arrangements for his mother. He was upper crust, spoke with a cut glass accent and I was extremely impressed and a little bit in awe. Everything on the funeral had gone according to plan and we had just lowered the coffin when Barrings turned to me and said, "I am *awfully* sorry to make a fuss Mr Penrose, but I think we have put Mummy in the wrong grave." I was such an old hand at this game now, that things rarely fazed me, I recall muttering a thank you and that I would discuss it further with him away from the graveside. Indeed Mummy was in the wrong grave! Of course, as funeral director, I was responsible and all the while we were returning the family in the limousine I was wondering how on earth I was going to sort out this monumental cock up!

I telephoned the vicar when I got back to West Street. I carefully explained the situation, scandalously bunging most of the blame onto dear old Roy Hawkins who had dug the grave and therefore marked it. I can only claim a feeble defence that I was a desperate man with a mission to survive! The vicar however, was pretty unfazed "What's the procedure Mr Penrose?" I went into great detail about an official exhumation and the necessary Exhumation Order that was only obtainable from the Home Office. "Oh bugger that" was his response, "it's my churchyard, come out early tomorrow and swap them around".

And so it came to pass, that early the next morning (feeling more than a little like Burke & Hare), two bearers, Mr Barrings, a sheepish Penrose and the Rev Henderson oversaw the rather undignified slippery removal and re-burial of Mrs Barrings ...and no one else ever knew! Houdini Penrose had struck again.

Yet all the time I never seemed to be able to catch up, either with my paperwork on the funeral, my never ending run around with the staff, or getting even slightly in control of my personal life. I was only at SA Bates for a short time, but it felt never ending. And I had bought a house in Dunstable! Oh dear, not the best of moves. During that time I cannot remember doing anything that did not revolve around work. I had made no friends (we can't unfortunately count the crematorium assistant Sam) and I was just stuck. Thank heavens I was given an out, or who knows what would have become of me?

I overslept for the only funeral I would ever conduct at the world famous Golders Green. I was woken by Wally Cox "Morning Mr Penrose, are you coming on this funeral or not then?" Cut to Wally belting down the M1 with me getting changed in the passenger's seat, thankfully we didn't have a coffin in the back as were due to meet it at the crematorium. Fortune smiled on me a number of times, but not enough and I was starting to lose it on a weekly basis. I had asked my dad to come up and help me one weekend to get up to date with banking forms and such, but all along I felt it was not in control. With hindsight, if I had been to a larger funeral home first then this would have been a breeze, but there was already so much anti-Hodgson feeling and I just didn't have the diplomatic skills to deal with it. Looking back now, I can see how I should have dealt with it, but that's easy now – hindsight is always 20:20.

Wally Cox was a legend. Unflappable, immoveable, still the same, Wally had seen it all and was not going to change his habits for a young upstart like me. But he was easy to manage and just got on with it, it made my job a lot easier. Wally carried a knife with an old bone handle around with him everywhere. He used it to cut his sandwiches, take out stones from his shoes, screw the coffins down and cut the string that tied the mouths of the deceased together. Wally's all-purpose knife brought a rare smile to my lips every day. If Wally is still alive he would be 112 by now.

Most of the time I spent at Dunstable I was near to total panic, I was trying to run it exactly the same as Hereford.

Only five weeks after I got there Moira left. I had to find a replacement. I chatted up a girl called Yvette who worked in the local supermarket not the classic way to recruit new people I discovered. She was only about eighteen, but too slow and young, although bless her she was very keen to be helpful. Then I went to the other end of the spectrum and employed Rebecca. 'Twas a total nightmare. She was sweet and as honest as the day was long, but had no sense of urgency or drive. Help! Where on earth was June Hemming when you needed her?

It might have been different if I'd had two Wallys and a June rather than a Moira or Rebecca, but I didn't and I struggled from day one. Remarkably I did managed to run almost all of the funerals on one fleet. I insisted that Berkhamsted phoned in and booked the funeral on my Day Book so that I could control the fleet, but as I tried to sort out the staff, the funeral home, my seventh house move in two years, my world rather quickly began to fall apart.

Yet, all the time things were going wrong I managed to give an outward appearance of normality. I still stuck to the rules religiously. I was a hard task master to Tim Durrel and Andrew Ketteringham in particular, feeling in my ignorance and youth that the best way was to be hard with the chaps and I could always pull back later. I was still conducting funerals in the same way, walking in front to the house for a little while, away from the house and the same upon arrival at the crematorium. I was also doing my "Luvvy Darling Bit" at the house. It worked like this; I would knock on the door upon arriving at the house and ask everyone to remain inside, usually everyone tried to get out when the funeral director arrived. Then I would ask them to all go into the lounge or drawing room and I would begin thus:

"Good afternoon ladies and gentlemen my name is Timothy Penrose and I will be conducting the funeral for you this afternoon. We have arrived in plenty of time, so for the ladies amongst you if you would like to take a seat now, please do so. In a few moments time we will be moving the funeral cortège off the drive at about 3.12pm and arrange to arrive at Luton Crematorium at 3.25pm in plenty of time for the funeral service to begin at 3.30pm. In a few moments I will return with the names of the ladies and the gentlemen that will be travelling in the first limousine, I would be grateful if you would please follow me to that car. I will then return and load the second limousine in the same way. When the loading is complete then I will walk the funeral from the house as a mark of respect for the deceased. One last thing, and I have often noticed this is forgotten – does anyone have a key so we can get in when we return?"

The last bit had been added as I'd shinned up too many drainpipes in my tails now, and wanted to avoid it happening again! Thus speech made, I tended to be in control of proceedings. I had more than one elderly lady saying loudly "Isn't he young?" and I suppose that I was, absurdly so, but those thoughts don't tend to cross your mind at the time, you just get on, plan your way and carry it out.

To his credit, Howard did recognise that things had been getting on top of me and instructed that I should have an assistant manager. I appointed one Harvey Ewart. Despite never having interviewed for a member of staff before, I found myself liking his quiet confidence and felt we would

121

get on well together, and we did. Harvey came from Sunderland and was around double my age. Harvey's claim to fame was that he had embalmed Sid James the Carry On star and this fact along with many others endeared me to him. Harvey said when they were embalming the star, they could all eerily hear his dirty throaty chuckle! I guess part of my downfall was the fact that Harvey got on extremely well with David Bonham and I didn't. David still felt I was a little upstart (fair enough) and I found him rough and ready and lacking in style (which was something I had always responded to). It was all doomed to failure but I have no-one to blame but myself. Well I could blame someone else, but it would be totally unfair.

I just wanted the world to stop turning for a few weeks and I would then naturally catch up. But this was never the case and despite late nights and full weekends (I had given up entertaining the idea of slipping home to Cardiff for the weekend by now) I was never up to date. And slowly, but very surely not only was the funeral home falling apart, but so was I.

On my departure, Harvey was given a promotion to Manager and he quite rightly took it with both hands. There was always an uneasy truce between Harvey and me, I don't know why, but there was. I certainly didn't hold him to blame for my misfortunes at Dunstable, I had brought it upon myself, but I did feel a bit sorry for myself, it was probably an age thing!

It all came to a head with a mistake. I took a call from a competitor, Neville's Funeral Service, to provide them with a limousine for a funeral and forgot I had booked it out in my fleet already. It was the second time I had done it and I knew there would be problems. When I then had a visit from David Bonham to discuss the situation, he discovered that in my panic to get things right, I had not declared two weeks worth of outstanding accounts, effectively ending my career at a stroke.

Outstanding accounts had always been such a part of my success at SA Evans. I was astounded to discover that other Hodgson firms had up to twenty outstanding accounts at any one time. At Preddy's, Derek often had none, or two or three at most, and this from a firm whose policy was that anything over seven days from the funeral was outstanding. One of the remarkable ways that Howard had managed to accumulate cash so quickly had been on his strict policy with debtors. Looking back on it now with the benefit of hindsight it was absolutely the right policy. And because I had grown up with Derek's system, it was the only system I knew and therefore I followed it to the letter. On more than one occasion I was at zero outstanding accounts when Derek was at one and I was as pleased as punch.

To this day I won't remember what got the outstanding accounts up to twenty or so, I guess I had just taken my eye off the ball and everything had slipped. But I was proud of myself for having the balls to get two accounts in that had been written off.

One of these outstanding accounts I had inherited from Alan Bates and basically it was because the family had no money. I discovered they had never claimed the death grant they were eligible for, so managed after a period of eight weeks to get the money from the government to settle the £350 debt. I did feel proud of myself I have to say, so proud that I told JBT that I had claimed the £25 discount as they had a recommended letter (I made this up) and then went out and bought the family two convector heaters which they badly needed. I often think of them and wonder what happened to them, did it make any difference? Where are they now? What about the children? I guess I'll never know.

And then there was David Wilkins, who refused many times to pay. He always had a reason and stopped answering my phone calls. So one night at about 8pm I decided I was going to get this money. I dressed up in my tails, top hat and black gloves, drove the hearse to Linslade Avenue (an address I remember to this day!) and sat outside the house. I had placed an empty coffin on the top deck and sat outside for twenty minutes. Sure enough, I saw a twitch at the curtains and Mr Wilkins looking totally bemused. I really do think he thought we had dug his mother-in-law up. Looking back now it seems totally audacious, but he came out, we negotiated a discount for cash and he paid me there and then! It had worked and I had got the result I had wanted. It wasn't a method in the funeral directors' journal and indeed I have only ever told a handful of people about it, until now that is.

Chapter 9

Demotion but Salvation - Don York, the Master

I received a letter, fairly polite under the circumstances, issuing me with a formal written warning, but with a note tagged on from Howard that if I got on with things, then I could put it all behind me. In a way, although I had massively failed I was relieved and went off for two weeks holiday when at last I saw the outside world through something other than a black hearses windscreen. Dad didn't say much, he didn't need to, he knew I had worked as hard as I could. But I had not been clever about the work and I had misled the company at the death, everything had just got on top of me. I was free from that world for the moment which was all that mattered, I honestly think if I had spent one more month there I might well have driven myself completely insane. I had certainly got to the point of running around in ever decreasing circles. I had no close friends or allies. I should have been more clever in the way I got Harvey to help me, but I was too young, too wet behind the years (despite all that had happened at Hereford). It was only now I realised how much the team, albeit a bit eccentric and off beat at times had contributed to the success of Evans and the smooth running of the funeral home. At Hereford I had little time for socialising, but at least I got out occasionally and always on a Saturday. I had no stability in Dunstable and it had become a bit of a living nightmare.

The news of my demotion, I am sure came gleefully to many of the other managers. Penrose taken down a peg or three at last! For too long I had built up a cocooned world for myself, believing that it would be perfect. With Bates and Metcalfe I discovered a whole new nasty, world that was hard work and didn't run as smoothly as I was used to. I guess I had totally set myself up for a fall.

I still owned a flat in Dunstable, worth about £36,000, although truly I was never there and would have been far better kipping down in the funeral home and saving the money. On a normal night I would get home at about 11pm and then get back into work the following morning at 7am (although towards the end I started oversleeping badly) and my existence was pretty grim. Dinner consisted of a pie for one warmed up in a microwave and orange juice from a carton. Perhaps I should be grateful I was teetotal at this time, if I hadn't been, I probably would have blown a huge amount of money on booze to drown my sorrows. Mentally I had fallen apart but had now been given a chance to get things back together. Humiliated? Yes, but of my own making. What happened with the benefit of hindsight was the best thing that could have happened and I am eternally grateful

126

that Howard (clearly seeing the bones of genius inside me!) did not dump me totally but gave me another chance.

It all sounds so depressing now and even twenty-four years later I find it difficult to write about, I suppose because it is of one's failings and not success, and it reminds you of what you should have done all those years ago. But it is part of life and many of the lessons I learnt all those years ago, late at night at Dunstable I have never forgotten. Life is crammed so full of "could haves", "should haves" and other such ridiculous statements, I hadn't and I hadn't big time. How the mighty have fallen!

One thing I now regret is that whilst I was at Head Office much later, I chanced upon a proof of the Stock Exchange prospectus for Hodgson Holdings. Howard floated the firm on the Unlisted Securities Market in June 1986 and in the prospectus, there were details of the directors (of course) and rather unusually the senior managers. I was, at the time the proof was drawn up, one such senior manager, but of course by the time the document was finally approved and circulated in its rather natty shade of deep midnight blue, I had been expunged from the text! I had been there as bold as brass as a twenty-one year old Senior Manager and I had been so proud! Fifteen years younger than any of the other senior executives in the document, I just didn't quite make it into print.

When Howard floated the company on the USM it was valued at £7,500,000 a small figure by today's standards, but an enormous sum then. He was the second quoted undertaker on the Stock Exchange, JH Kenyons had floated three years previously but their pre tax profit returns and aggressive acquisition policy were nothing like Howard's. In his offer document, Howard had forecast pre tax profit of £725,000. In the event he managed to deliver £850,000 and the city were thrilled and enthralled in equal measure. Likewise Howard loved publicity and in this is he was outstandingly clever. He played the press for all it was worth. He was good at it and got many column inches due to his Jaguar XJS, fedora, snazzy overcoat, long hair and dark glasses. In the early years of being a public limited company, Hodgson Holdings returns had been excellent. As time went on, people believed the spin and kept on generating inches of press to a firm that was rather quickly losing its way.

It never occurred to me as strange at the time, but in all the weekly directors meetings at Head Office, not once was a budget presented and compared with actual performance and financial matters were rarely discussed. One of the reasons for the downfall was the lack of clarity in numbers and performance. This was clear all along for those who were prepared to look, but we weren't encouraged to look. It was as if the elephant was in the room and no one wanted mention it. Howard was certainly clever and had worked his knackers off to get the firm to where it was, but taking the company up a rung on the ladder meant new skills had to be employed and many of the staff just didn't have them. It was as simple or as difficult as that.

In 1980 Howard made a quantum leap, in a secretive and last minute Dutch Auction, he had purchased the hundred year old firm of Ann Bonham & Sons in Northampton. Cyril and Dennis the owners had not always agreed on how to run the business (it was said they even had different doors to come into the funeral home by, they loathed each other so much) and eventually concluded the best way forward was to sell the business. They had insisted that Cyril's son David was to be a director of any company that acquired the firm. Of course Howard being the impetuous guy he was acquired not only Bonham's but also a young David Bonham. Scruffy, not particularly well educated and not that interested in hard work. He'd got quite a promotion, and it hadn't gone down at all well with the staff he used to work with.

Bonhams was highly respected in Northampton, they dealt with all the funerals of local dignitaries and it was quite a thing for such a large firm to be sold at this time. Howard confessed much later on, in a meeting that I had attended, that once he knew he had bought the firm he thought, "Help, what am I going to do now?" It was certainly a major move at such a stage in his small company's development.

So David, exalted to such a high level, moved away from arranging and conducting funerals to working with Howard on developing a region. He became responsible for SA Bates in Dunstable with the infamous 'I like my beard and I won't shave it off' Alan Hunt. Which left Cyril and Dennis' peer as the only working director in Bonhams.

It was to this esteemed funeral home that I was despatched in order to earn some hard life and big funeral numbers lessons. This was a monster of a business but running like clockwork with a very settled crew. It was a crew, I discovered after a few weeks that knew exactly what they were doing and all worked together tremendously well to assemble thirty-five to forty funerals a week, ten times the amount I was used to. They had techniques which were completely new to me and scales fell from my eyes on a regular basis. It was an absolute breath of fresh air. Head of all funerals and general patriarch was someone who was pivotal in my rehabilitation. He threw out a bridge for me to walk across and prove that I still had a future at Hodgsons. This was Don York.

Donald A York was a bit of a legend in Northampton. Linked with Earl Spencer (I always thought he had a regal bearing about him) and their family funerals, he was a dear, dear man who was one of the good guys. It was Don who took me under his wing and showed me how it was possible to run a business that conducted a huge number of funerals. They had been bought at approx 1,800 funerals and were still doing 1,650 two years on from the acquisition. Don was very anti-Howard and against the takeover and you could see why, but all that was secondary now. Don was a huge crutch to me when I was at my lowest ebb at just twenty-one and was in serious danger of losing the plot. We were a good match me and Don, as Don enjoyed the social aspect of arranging funerals and the chatting to the vicars, but wasn't remotely interested in administration and the hard detail that goes towards arranging a funeral properly. So, we developed a pattern, Don would be propelled downstairs into the arrangement room to get the basic details. I would phone the cemetery or crematorium, arrange the death notices, flowers and make sure that the letters were typed properly. I would ensure that coffee was made at regular intervals and that Don was looked after like the elder statesman he was. Working with Don was fabulous and fun, he was a real character. He had the most extraordinary stutter, which delighted someone like me, and I perfected the impression to standing ovations from the coffin fitters during their tea breaks.

I had always enjoyed people's idiosyncrasies when I had been a schoolboy, I had often received the cane for my excellent impressions of Choco, he could never say his R's, so strange how the tools that went missing in the lesson were the Micrometer and the Reamer, sorry Mr Phillips but you're probably dead now so it's not a problem or Steve Williams giving the rugby team yet another bollocking. Don was the latest to give me such class material. Most people's stutter fall into two categories, they either have a blocking stutter – this is where they block on a particular letter and say Ppppppppppppppp and then the rest of the word eventually, or another type of stutter, where they can't actually get the start of a word out and then explode once they do into the word.

Don of course, being a one off, had one all of his own and it was magnificent. It mainly happened when he was hassled or stressed and it used to come out as follows "*Ahahahahahahahahahha Wassiname*" it was a true peach and even now twenty-five years later I have never heard anyone with a class one like that. In addition to all this Don was very, very kind. Don was the reason I managed to rehabilitate myself, I was encouraged and taught in equal measure. I scratched Don's back and he scratched mine, we were an unstoppable team. He was married to Doreen and likewise she was kindness itself, to be honest I was a bit thrown by it all. But it was all most welcome and just what the doctor had ordered.

Don had a daughter called Linda who rather bizarrely worked at the opposing firm of S Wilkinson in Northampton. She and Don always had a chat during the day, they would swap notes on who had got who's funerals, how busy they each were and what the other funeral directors were up to. And in a further twist, Linda's husband Steve Summerfield worked at Bonhams as their main limousine driver. Steve was surly and we didn't ever grow close, but he wasn't as miserable as Rob Robinson who always drove Hearse Number 1 on the A Fleet. Rob was short, incredibly thin (how he ever contributed towards lifting a coffin I shall never know) and was always negative about everything. The relationship between hearse driver and funeral director is critical, it is the focal point of the whole funeral. The hearse driver leads the cortège and has to use his considerable skills to time everything correctly. It is important to arrive just at the right time, particularly when crematoriums are involved. I never liked hearse driving, in my early years I was always happier either sat in the bearer's seat behind Derek or following dumbly afterwards driving the limousine. I had been very fortunate to have a brilliant hearse driver in Roy Terry in Bristol; always on time, never, ever fazed and as cool as a cucumber. Then at Hereford, the sharp eyes and ears and military mind of Ken James, both totally different, but both fabulous exponents of the black art. Now, although Rob was very good at getting the cortège to Milton Crematorium or the churchyard on time, there was no buzz about him or prestige I suppose. That all changed one morning when there were only the two of us at the funeral home and we received a call from the coroner. Rob drove the hearse of course and I sat alongside him. When we got to the house, we were a little taken aback. There were police swarming around and just like Cagney & Lacey in America, reels of yellow tape saying "Police Line Do Not Cross". There were also those familiar figures dressed in white one piece overalls, the Scenes Of Crime Officers. This was going to be a murder or a suicide, probably a murder and probably a messy one.

For those people that were not passing at the time Rob and I carried the stabbed body of an elderly lady out of the house on an American Stretcher, they could relive the moment as the Northampton Chronicle & Echo ran a picture of us on the front page that evening. Somehow after that things changed with Rob and Me, we got a bit closer, it was a little strange how it worked out, but I was happy we had broken one barrier and I have included the article below.

Man's body found with chest wounds

By Jeremy Phillips and Terry Morris

FIVE men and a woman were being interviewed by murder hunt detectives today after the body of a man was discovered in a Northampton house.

Police were called to the rented terraced house in Gray Street after a tip-off last night.

It was later confirmed that ███████ had died from chest wounds. He is believed to have been stabbed.

A post mortem was being carried out at Kettering General Hospital today by Home Office pathologist Dr. Peter Andrews to determine the precise cause of death.

Formal identification of the body was made today by

Neighbour ███████ said three men shared the house in the town centre area of Northampton.

The first she knew of the death was when a terrified man in his thirties called at her home and asked to use the 'phone. He dialled 999 for an ambulance. Minutes later another tenant from the house arrived and called the police.

███████ said: "As far as I know the dead man had been stabbed in the chest in a back bedroom.

"I don't think the dead man lived there, he wasn't one of the tenants. I think there was some sort of fight."

Police interviewed two men in her home for about an hour before taking them away for further questioning.

The six were being held at Campbell Square Police Station, a quarter-of-a-mile away from the house.

"It is very noisy next door — I've often complained about it," said a shocked ███████

The landlord is believed to be ███████ who lives in ███████ He was at his home today, but said: "I have no comment to make."

He refused to talk about whether he went to the house last night.

The body was not removed from the house until 10 am today.

A uniformed police officer was standing guard outside the house this morning.

Detectives have set up an incident room at Mereway Police Station and the inquiry is being led by Detective Superintendent Tony Buckmaster and Detective Inspector David Armiger.

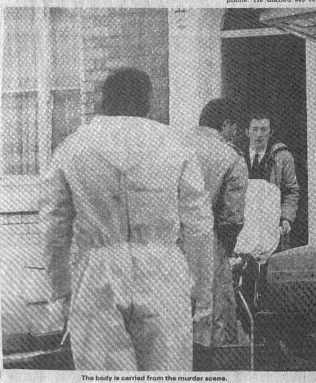

The house where the body was found.

The body is carried from the murder scene.

I make the papers again in Northampton with my "Columbo" trench coat

We only occasionally saw the rotund figures of either Cyril or Dennis when families had specifically requested them, but a cheery older chap called Derek Capel conducted most of the funerals. Derek was in his mid-forties, which of course seemed ancient to me then.

Just as Don didn't care to be out and about (we discussed at times whether he would know one end of a hearse from another), Derek hated to be in and if he was conducting funerals all day every day, was as happy as a pig in muck. Derek was a perfectionist, he kept his car in such perfect condition, apparently he'd carpeted the garage and hand polished the engine block every week. There was a rumour going around that when he took it to a local dealer for a part exchange on a new vehicle they'd chased him off the premises as they thought he had been with Jeremy Beadle and Game For A Laugh. I was never sure if this was true or not and didn't dare ask, but loved to think it was as it suited him perfectly. He was dear and kind to me though, and was a good friend when in actual fact I'm sad to say, I still didn't have many.

The girls in the office were suspicious of me. Mandy was rude to me and young Sarah flashed her knickers at me one afternoon, of course being pathetically inept as far as the female sex was concerned it led to nothing! Also there was Jenny, a round bubbly girl who had been there since the year dot and was in charge of the huge amount of administration needed in order to run the funerals. I really liked Jenny and she made my landing in Northampton a pleasure and pain free. She was fab to work with and I missed her when I left. I suspect that computers are now employed, but we were all very efficient and there was rarely a hint of a cock up. The Bonham management information leaked like a sieve and they all knew why I was there. They had grown up treating Don with disdain and here I was looking after him like he was my Dad. I worked hard at Bonhams, really, really hard and tried to make everything as simple as possible for

Don. He got the prize work, I got the donkeywork to do and it suited me down to the ground.

Don had an admirer – Mrs Brain. Don's wife Doreen knew about her, nothing went on you know, but Don used to get quite nervous when Mrs Brain's name was mentioned if Doreen was in earshot. This propelled him to Five Star Stutter, a sight for anyone, particularly on a Monday morning when we were trying to book in thirty-two funerals.

At Bonhams we had fun. There was a chap that worked there called John Siney. I never understood how or why, but he was an assistant manager, and everyone appeared to be rather tickled by this. John spent most, if not all of his life in the large coffin shop that was used to fit out the coffins. John could be in there for up to fifty hours a week, he always appeared to have orders he hadn't quite completed. We used to wind him up by keeping back the orders until he had just got the last coffin on the shelf and paperwork in the ready pile, we would thrust orders for another thirty-two in front of his face. There was something comic about John, I could never quite put my finger on it. He was rather lugubrious, he didn't smile much and was mocked a bit by the lads. He always looked so miserable in top hat and tails where as I of course looked handsome and debonair (well it was always good to have confidence!).

I was nine months at Bonhams and I guess it was probably the best period of my life so far in terms of business, success and getting on with people. I was away with the fairies, always smart, committed to getting the best possible performance out of myself and enjoying tremendously working with Don.

And just when Don and I were getting on so well, it was decided that I would move! It had been deemed my rehabilitation was complete and I was forced to leave Don and move on. I was totally torn. In many ways I was elated, it was a big step in my comeback and I realised that Howard had been very kind, or maybe he just wanted another mug prepared to work long hours in Luton? I will never know! Anyway whilst part of me felt pleased, I was saddened to leave a funeral home whose working pattern I knew and where I had managed to become an important part of the team. I was respected and liked by the main protagonists, Don couldn't speak highly enough about me (he didn't always see my stutter impersonations on a daily basis) and was genuinely sad to see me go. He was fulsome in his love for me and I for him, for I still regard him as having rescued my career. Of course it also meant that Don would be back to dealing with the stuff he didn't like which was not good news. It was a lovely time at Bonhams and one I still have nothing but fond memories of.

Whilst I was at Bonhams, going back every weekend to Cardiff, I met my future wife. My mate Jeff Gosden had an unhealthy obsession with Star Trek and told me he was going to take his new girlfriend back to his flat and watch his Star Trek videos. I gently suggested that if she wasn't a fan then perhaps he could take her out for dinner. The poshest place I had ever gone to was the Fox and Hounds at Llancarfan. So it was agreed we would go as a foursome, Fiona's flat mate Ruth would come and make up the numbers. I don't remember much so long ago, but I DO remember Ruth ordering some rare fish and being excited when we went through a large puddle with the words "Can we do it again?!". I had found my best ever friend, my soul mate, my business partner, my lover and my wife. Goodness knows what she thought of the perm, braces, and double cuff shirts, but she managed somehow to look past all this and we did make a great team, even if it took me six months to officially ask her out to be my girlfriend. Ruth and I wrote to each other regularly. I had found my soul mate which was a quite extraordinary make up of nutty and regular.

She was, I became to understand and know, far more than what appeared on the surface.

In we married in 1988 Cardiff and true to form I had organised two complimentary company limousines for the wedding in midnight blue. We went to Mickleton in the Cotswolds for our honeymoon and then decamped to my flat in Sutton Coldfield.

Then one afternoon JBT phoned and in his inimitable style informed me that I was to go to London to help bed an acquisition in. Hodgson Holdings had just purchased the largest firm ever. Ashton Ebbutt was situated with a head office in Clapham Road and various satellite offices throughout South London and into Croydon. It was a monster of a firm and conducted approximately 2,200 funerals from all its offices. It was also a bit bizarre because when Howard had been an apprentice funeral director and fallen out with his Dad, he had been sent to Ashton Ebbutt to work. Now, the young rascal had returned to acquire the entire firm. So, the plan was, that I was to go down, stay in a damp and slightly creepy house the firm owned and help Harvey Ewart with the acquisition hit list. I was torn, there was more possibilities of excitement here, but I was actually well settled with Don, had got used to a life outside of work and had actually started going to bed before midnight!

But of course, down I went to Croydon and Clapham and got stuck into the work that always needed doing on an acquisition. Much of it was straightforward, although working with Harvey was very uncomfortable to start with as he was now senior to me, and no-one had ever made this clear! Yet again I was the roving single man out and about with a mission to organise old and decrepit funeral directors into a slick machine. I remember the enormous coffin workshop where all of the group's coffins were made and despatched, and the property under the Croydon flyover, which was so unwelcoming and unpleasant to live in. The continual hassles between Harvey and myself, both vying for position in a non-position place and the extreme hassle of trying to run funerals, hearses and ambulances picking up bodies all over South and Central London.

We never managed to get it right, it was a little like those plate spinners you see at the circus. They get three or four of the plates spinning so well and then have to go back to the original ones to stop them falling off. It didn't help that the company we had just purchased had the most appalling staff, paid all the bearers in cash, and that most of the vehicles were very close to falling apart and badly needed replacing. They fiddled some of the embalming so that the clients were charged £50 yet it only cost the company £10, as the mortuary technician would do it in his spare time. So, my time there was not joyfully spent.

Ruth and I were seeing each other regularly by now, so I went home to Cardiff on any possible weekend and we met up there. She was in the middle of a nursing degree and we would meet to go out for lunch on the Saturday, church on Sunday and then I would have to drive back up to London ready for work on Monday morning. They were heady romantic times, although I felt that I wasn't coping at all as well as I had been at Northampton. I missed Don's stabilizing influence and all the fun people I so enjoyed working with at Bonhams. I also missed my own bed, I was now staying wherever was the best place to be, and living in funeral homes (or above funeral homes) is not the best recipe for a settled life!

Living in London was weird. The traffic drove me nuts, I could never quite work out hearse timings and all the paperwork was different to what I had been used to. The lack of friends and family began to get to me and I dreaded most days as there would be renewed battles with the staff at the latest branch I was going to sort out.

But it all came to an end soon enough and I was then despatched to the next acquisition that Howard had made, James Bradley & Sons in Manchester. By now I was making a name for myself as a trouble-shooter of all things funeral related. I suppose part of me was very proud. I felt I was at the sharp end, but didn't have the maturity or the insight (you rarely do at such an age) to be able to deal with it properly and ensure I made not just a name for myself, but also a good name. I was a nomad, with no regular boss, no one to report to or motivate me and I dreadfully missed Don York. I was desperate to get back to Northampton where I felt safe and secure, even if the two young girls, Mandy and Sarah in the office clearly disliked working with me as much as June.

Just before I left for Manchester, it was decided that I would go to St Albans and help Harvey Ewart out with a new acquisition E Seymour & Sons in Marlborough Road. Harvey was now entrenched in Bates and Metcalfe and had been asked by Howard to get over to Seymours and sort them out with my help. So, the tables were rather turned and there was an uneasy truce as we settled in together. The takeover did not go according to plan, we had inherited two guys who had got into a bit of a rut and they decided from day one that they were not going to clean any other car but the one they had always cleaned. Jim cleaned his hearse and that was that. Pete cleaned his limousines and they were not going to change for anyone. It was so ridiculous, the firm was near bankruptcy, the ones we were buying at this stage in the company's development often were. These guys still had jobs with a company that was actually intending to invest some money into the firm for the first time in thirty years. But they were adamant and resigned, and proceeded to take us to an Industrial Tribunal, where quite frankly I was thrilled that they lost, and lost well. It was an unpleasant experience, thankfully I wasn't called upon to give any sort of testimony, although I was in court all day as Jim gave his sob story of takeover from a horrible firm in Birmingham.

Alan Bradley who owned James Bradley & Sons in Manchester was another dear gentleman who had clearly been an excellent funeral director and cared greatly for his families. He was not a good businessman. His special needs son arranged all the funerals and then they were left in piecemeal form for a chubby, cheerful chap called Reg Knighton to sort them out. Tommy Bradley was really a case and he knew it. We couldn't quite comprehend that an operation running approximately eight hundred funerals a year (and therefore turning over about one million pounds per annum) could rely on Tommy as first port of call. Alan was never there, either swanning around at the local golf club, or drinking at his private club. And with the drivers, Derek Ogley and Norman Jump, it made a rather strange collection of Mancunians. It really was another level in the bizarre.

This was strong Coronation Street land and a few of the bearers were personal friends with some of the cast, quite how this helped us organise the funeral business I shall never understand. Much of the waste Alan had incurred running the business was because he was a very weak business man, he allowed all his staff to drive home a limousine for the night, it was a perk of the job. Well in all the silly 1980's excesses from Head Office much later on nothing would beat that. Of course it was fairly predictable that when they had their flash Mercedes replaced by 950cc Ford Fiesta many of them would complain. From having a softie like Alan running them to Tim Penrose, David Byrne and Graham Hodson things didn't exactly go down well, there was indeed mutiny on the high seas. There was clear opposition to the only measures that would save the fifty year old firm from bankruptcy.

Tommy Bradley's full time job was to arrange all the funerals that came through the door. There was but a little problem, Tommy suffered from Tourette's and this would probably not have been a desired requirement for someone in this position. Because of his condition he also had a fascination with the number 67 and would repeat it incessantly. Here we had an owner who was completely away with the fairies, a funeral arranger with Tourette's, a host of characters which were like extras on a bad B-movie and then dear old Reg Knighton, who amused us all with his desire to get on with everyone and his hatred of Alan.

Alan had started on the road to rationalisation and economies of scale. He had bought a firm off Robert Greenall in Heywood, he had a manager running it and supposedly booking the funerals though Bradley's main office, just as we had in Dunstable. Bradleys did about 800 funerals a year and Greenalls about 250, but Norman Jump would just book the funeral and tell us when it was. The effect of this meant the Bradleys drivers were out on their funeral at exactly the same time as they were needed for the Greenall funeral. So, hearses had to be hired, drivers had to be hired, it rotted the profit on the two funerals combined and was a complete shambles. But Norman had been doing things his way for five years and he wasn't going to allow a Hodgson takeover to stop him. He carried on regardless and wound up the Bradley office staff terribly.

Alan also had an office in Hyde and Wythenshawe, a particularly exotic part of South Manchester where the funeral home had shutters on its windows. Cremation Law states that a doctor who certifies the death of a patient has to arrange for another doctor from a different practice to confirm the death and check for signs of foul play. One of the doctors that used to come in to sign second parts and collect their £22.50 fee in cash, known I regret to say as Ash Cash, was a charming, avuncular jolly man. There was something cosy and cuddly about him, he was just really a very nice man. Perhaps something to do with his beard, although I do remember that at the time he seemed to be around our funeral home an awful lot. I probably saw him twice a week for three months. Once he asked me over for tea with his wife as he knew I hadn't any relatives close, or friends come to think of that! I was very fond of Dr Harold Shipman. He was indeed a very cheery fellow. Of course at the time we had no idea what was going on behind the scenes. I understand according to most trusted records he killed over 250 of his patients. Just goes to show you never know…

David Byrne arrived, an army background, but very little get up and go about him for a military man, although his boots were bulled to within an inch of their life and he crawled to Mr Graham as much as possible, he was a friend – a friend that is until the 1987 company conference.

I had done everything for David, I mean I really had. I put together the garage orders, I sorted out the staffing of them, and I made sure all the funerals were in the Day Book. All he did was to swan around making sure people knew he was in charge, and as much as I got on with the guy, I couldn't help feeling he was taking me a bit for granted. So, just before the company conference he asked me for some help in writing a speech about the takeover of Bradleys, how Hodgsons had transformed the business, that sort of guff. I could have written it with my eyes closed, and duly prepared a piece for David to read before the assembled great and good, including stockbrokers and investors, at the fabled Arden Motel. Part of me had always been a practical joker and despite all the death I had seen, I hadn't lost it!

As David got up to deliver the speech, I remembered that for a laugh I had put in his speech "And one man is the epitome of all that Hodgsons have done to Bradleys, that man, a hearse driver when we arrived, now an assistant manager, a man who has pulled himself up by his bootlaces and proved that anything is possible. Remember the name ladies and gentlemen, because he will be a force to be reckoned with in year to come – that man – please stand up today, is *"Alan Biscuit Barrel Reid"*.

There was a deafening silence… I look straight ahead, I wasn't going to be the first to laugh… and then, just as when we had the missing webs fiasco in Madley, no one said a thing. The moment passed and no one knew. Until now of course.

Manchester was notable for other things too, I stayed there for three months bedding the acquisition down and sorting out the troubles. David commuted from Barnsley and I lodged in a lovely hotel in Glossop with the proprietor Mario looking after my every need. He cooked me lovely pork steaks in gorgeous sauces in the evening and my breakfasts were always happy affairs. I buzzed back and forth from Clayton, Hyde and Wythenshawe (often seeing the good Dr Shipman) and was generally very happy.

At the company conference in December, there was a rumour going around that I was going to be moved, I had done well again and there were more acquisitions in the pipeline. I couldn't quite believe it when I heard from Howard himself that I was going to go home. He had bought four funeral directors in Cardiff and I was going to go and sort them out.

The four offices were really two businesses. The offices of William Ham and Augustine Stone in Canton, Cardiff made up one business. The second comprised of Rees William Forse and the up-market DJ Evans Forse & Co in Whitchurch, just down the road from where I left Whitchurch High School only three years previously. It didn't seem real. The combined firms would run about 1,400 funerals from Cardiff, here was the chance to practice all I had been taught by Don and Co in Northampton. I do take some credit for the purchases; on an off chance I told JBT about DJ Forse & Co hoping they would be available for acquisition. Lo and behold they had just spoken to Great Southern Group about an acquisition, our timing was perfect. I calculate that we made the first telephone approach in October and had our feet under the table in Cardiff by January. I had returned home.

If you are expecting a fairy tale ending look away now, there ain't one! It just didn't flow. Derek Tyler came down and helped out for a few weeks, I tried to sort out the fleets but Lynn Forse and I never got on. I thought we would, he knew my Dad and had often asked after me, but the change over for Lynn was too much. Perhaps retribution for my Dad's frequent comment that he was so named because he would 'force' them into their coffins.

I was an ideal target for him to vent his spleen, he was an unhappy bunny and wasn't going to have me in his funeral home any more, despite the fact he no longer owned it. Could it have been any different? Possibly. But perhaps the die was cast the moment I stepped through the door with my right young thing look on, all cock-a-hoop and keen to run the fleets on as few hearses as possible.

As naïve as I was green, I got a phone call about three weeks after we had bought Forses and Stones, from JBT. "Mr Howard wants you up here in Head office, he needs you as his personal assistant." We were all aware we were involved in the rise of a quite extraordinary company, it turned out we were right and that Howard through sheer force of nature had transformed if not the funeral business in general, the media's perception of it and what was going on behind the scenes in terms of acquisitions and rationalisation. I couldn't quite believe it! Another promotion, and only weeks after the Cardiff one. Little did I know, and it took me a few years to realise, I had actually been sidelined. But I did manage to flourish in the place I was dumped, over the next few years. I was, in fact to become Howard's personal chauffeur and gopher, and I loved it!

Freckles, a Windsor Tie and Big Ears - TP aged 8

My first top hat and tails at the age of eight. My mother who organised many shows for the local Boys Brigade has a lot to answer for - still severely traumatised many years later. Words fail me.

Cricket mad - My form teacher James R Ball front left,
Adrian Jones centre, - I am centre left holding a bat.
I was not very good at using it effectively in the middle.

Not my finest moment, yet this led to me leaving school and we did make
Radio 1 Newsbeat on the same day as the local South Wales Echo.

My brother (left) and I at a war cemetery in
the channel islands circa 1974.

The Oaklands Funeral Home - now sadly demolished but
here looking exactly as it did in 1983 when I ventured
up to Birmingham for my Hodgson interview.

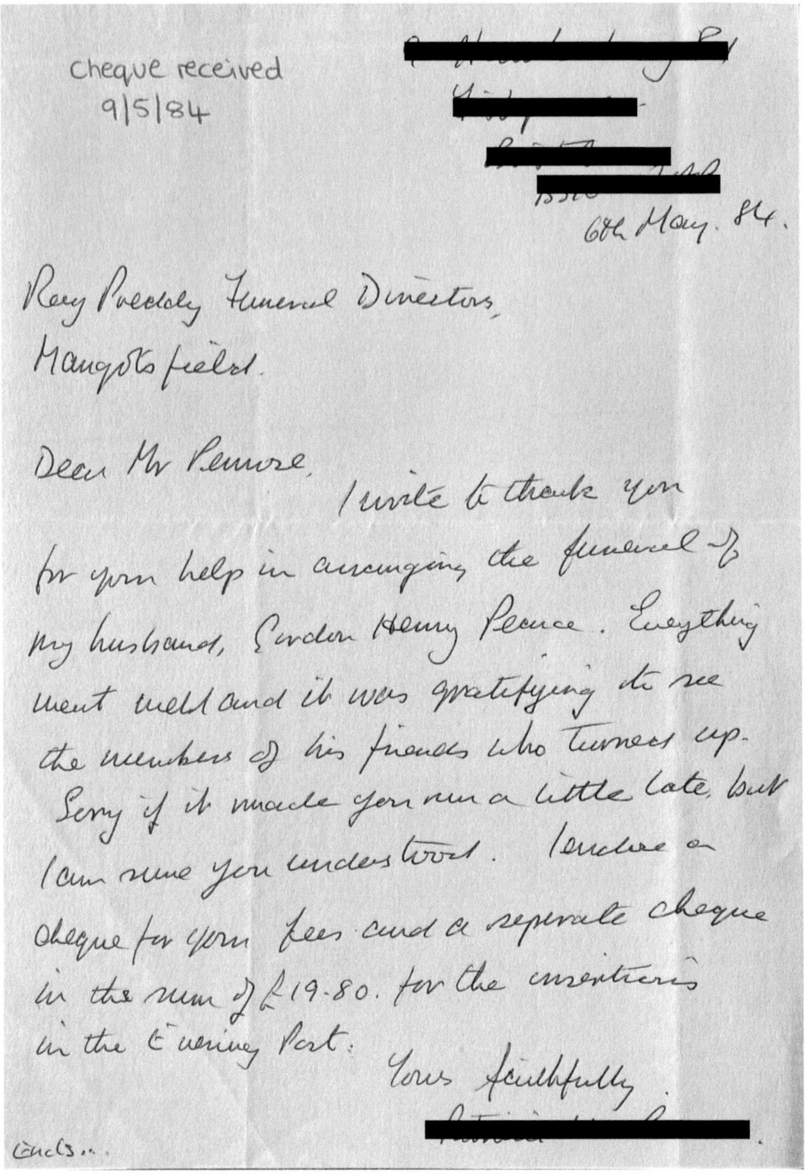

Cheque received
9/5/84

[redacted]

6th May. 84.

Roy Penrose Funeral Directors,
Mangotsfield.

Dear Mr Penrose,
I write to thank you for your help in arranging the funeral of my husband, Gordon Henry Pearce. Everything went well and it was gratifying to see the numbers of his friends who turned up. Sorry if it made you run a little late, but I am sure you understood. I enclose a cheque for your fees and a separate cheque in the sum of £19.80. for the insertions in the Evening Post.

Yours faithfully
[redacted].

Encls..

My first ever personalised thank you letter - "You can't buy these" said Derek Tyler. My file of several hundred thank you letters from families are amongst my most prized possessions.

A brilliant "caught in a moment" photo from 1984.

The Midlands Region - with Top L-R: TP, Bob Lewis, John Mould.

Bottom L-R : John McManus, John Bruce Taylor, Derek Tyler

I take charge of Mr Nutkin's funeral in August 1984.

Old men really shouldn't shoulder such heavy coffins - Grant Baynham back left sporting his usual punk hair. I get to not lift but supervise.

Hereford Cathedral in all its sun parched ground glory.

I decide to walk the entire Nutkins funeral from Hereford Cathedral to Tupsley Churchyard, it's a good couple of miles but I am young and there's no-one waiting at home.

The men in black - a privilege to serve them.

December 1984 - I am awarded the "Manager Of The Year" from Howard Hodgson.

The SAS say "Thank You" - quite a moment.

From: Captain K Edlin, Adjutant

DO-102

22 SPECIAL AIR SERVICE REGIMENT
STIRLING LINES
HEREFORD HR2 6HF
TELEPHONE : HEREFORD 57311 Ext 282

Mr T J A Penrose
S A Evans Funeral Directors
23 and 24 Gaol Street
HEREFORD HR1 2HU

17 December 1984

Dear Mr Penrose

Thank you very much for the way in which you conducted the funeral of the late ██████████. The arrangements you made were of the highest standard and the funeral service and committal were conducted with dignity and respect. My thanks also for your co-operation preceding the service.

Yours is a service that we do not wish to use frequently and I am saying that in a nice way. When it is necessary it is reassuring to know that such a fine service is available.

Yours Sincerely

K Edlin

Pristine, in line manicured graves of 22 SAS Regiment in St Martin's Churchyard in Hereford.

The 22 SAS regiment section at St Martins Churchyard in Hereford

All set for a 22 SAS regiment funeral.
From left; Lou Probert, TP, Ken James.

Ruth saved me in 1988 from a solitary existence
- she remains my inspiration.

It is now November 1990 and I have decided to conquer the world of Coffee Houses (the folly and arrogance of youth!)

Most children paint their father a picture of trees, animals or homely scenes. Anna Penrose aged 9 displaying a family trait.

December 2021 - I return to Hereford and discover SA Evans very much as I left it thirty-six years previously.

Chapter 10

Top hat and tails to filofax and red braces

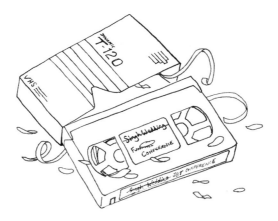

Initially I couldn't quite believe I had made it to Head Office. I had been to Handsworth before, for my initial interview and then a couple of times whilst I was at Hereford, firstly to collect a new hearse and then to collect a new private ambulance. I have to say on the first visit I wasn't too fussed to at be at the great headquarters, but on the second and third time I was on my mettle and keen to make a good impression. An old girlfriend I knew from my Cardiff days had written and on hearing I was due to go up to the then HQ suggested I would be crawling to Howard's office and showing him my new Grenson shoes whilst flashing my new Crombie overcoat. I had been told they were the best that money could buy! It wasn't quite like that, but it certainly had elements of it. I was more aware of my surroundings and of the influence certain people could have over my career. By now I had got into clothes quite a bit and possessed more than the one three piece suit that I had worn to my Howard interview. I was keen to dress in my very best suit and wear my new tiepin which I thought made me look rather like Howard, ah hero worship was a sad old thing…

I had on both occasions come back from Handsworth with tales to tell and stories to recall, this time I was going to stay, but they had by now moved the Head Office from Handsworth to Kingstanding and then to Sutton Coldfield.

Sutton Coldfield lies north of Birmingham by about eight miles. It is an affluent area and I guess part of the reason for the move was that Howard lived just down the road in Roman Road, Little Aston. Not far from him was Doug Ellis, chairman of Aston Villa and various other millionaires, it was, as you might imagine rather a plush town. Hodgsons had by now taken a lease on a non-descript office block bang in the centre of the town at the head of the Gracechurch Shopping Centre. It was three floors, but we only occupied the top floor to start with. I had often addressed envelopes to 3rd Floor Plantsbrook House and now here I was, I couldn't quite grasp the reality of it and what it would all mean. I would soon find out!

At this point I need to make a heartfelt confession and embarrassing though it might be, I freely confess that on my first day at Plantsbrook House, freed from the shackles of top hat and tailcoat I wore my snazzy stripy suit, a red tie, red socks and pink braces. You have to remember this was the late 1980's, the stock exchange had been revolutionised, Big Bang had occurred and yuppies were everywhere. I wasn't one, but I like to think that I was, besides I was above funeral directing now wasn't I? A free agent with licence to thrill!

I made friends quickly with the dragon Beryl Smith, whose reverent tones of "You will be in the naughty book" used to send shivers down my spine at Hereford. I discovered that she was actually a very sweet lady.

Beryl had joined Howard in 1979 and had overseen the administration from two hundred funerals to the current total of 12,000. Hers was indeed a name which sent terror into the heart of many a young manager. Now here she was looking just a bit like my granny. It was hard to take her so seriously after that. She chain-smoked through all the meetings I was ever in with her. She was an old fashioned administrator, a good line manager and an important person to have on your side. She resided in an office that was rather an upgrade, it had glass walls around it and she controlled the finances from there. I also met Velma Yapp, who had joined Howard just after me in November 1983 and I discovered a lot more about her family and her home situation. These were now real people not just voices at the end of a telephone. Velma was entrusted with Howard's personal stuff at Head Office as well as the wages run. She was lovely, fair, sweet and such a hard worker. Velma was always interested in you personally and spared time to chat and get to you know you a bit, is she still there, now working for Dignity after so many years, surely she is due a retirement now?

JBT had the delightful Ann working for him. Ann was lovely, but as Brummie as they came. John had no trouble understanding her, all those years of practice arranging funerals at Handsworth in the booking office, sorry, arrangement room made him the translator of many a black Country brogue. But everyone else often didn't have a clue what was going on, we would nod politely and then get into holy huddles near the office photocopier trying to work out what Ann was actually saying. There were many moments of high farce and misunderstanding, including a fruitless trip to the Dry Cleaners to collect JBT's suit that actually turned out to be something totally different. Well it made the day flow a bit and Ann worked with me on new forms for JBT, he liked designing new forms as it always gave him a sense of knowing what was going on. Ann and I worked together well, but there was always a sense of dread if she was speaking to you alone as to what you were meant to say.

Property wise I was rather confused. I had originally bought a house in Hereford after three lettings, which I sold when I moved to Dunstable. My property claim to fame is that I actually bought two properties without ever setting foot in them. Mum and Dad (bless them) were entrusted to go to Dunstable and have a look for me. Linden Close was an unhappy home for ten months and upon final arrival at Head Office in Sutton Coldfield, they spotted a flat in Four Oaks, the posh part of the town and I bought it for £36,000. So at least I had a base and I had a girlfriend, the first since I had been seventeen, so quite a shock to the system. Remember I met Ruth on a blind date and we got on tremendously well. Quiet but firm, I thought I had blown it one afternoon when I merrily showed her the chapel of rest of DJ Evans Forse & Co. Ruth was nursing on the cardiac ward in the University Hospital of Wales having achieved a first class degree in nursing. The coffin I just happened to show her unfortunately had been the incumbent of a bed on Ruth's ward up to the day before. An inauspicious start, she merely commented "Oh I didn't know he had died" but she persevered, we enjoyed each others company and even though I was desperately slow in making any sort of move I think we knew from fairly early on that we were going to be an item.

There were very few people working at Head Office at the time. Beryl Smith on admin, Velma Yapp on wages, Howard on, well Howard, Graham Hodson as H's right hand man and JBT blustering his way through the nightly reports, typhoid, locusts etc. Our finance director at the time was Stephen Heathcote, but he rarely came into the office. He attended meetings as necessary but he was there infrequently. I was given a desk and told to start working with JBT on compiling Vehicle History Sheets and Stock Sheets, it wasn't exactly stimulating stuff but also looking at Garage Orders and commenting on how the fleets could have been run faster or better, honestly!

I liked Stephen. He was always so kind to me, I must have looked a bit of a nincompoop in my snazzy tie and stuff, but he was always very chatty as I made him coffee when he was waiting for Howard to come out of a meeting. He was partner at Heathcote & Coleman Accountants in Birmingham City Centre and many years later when running my own business just down the road from him we met and reminded each other about such times.

I was still obsessed with reading the latest Funeral Magazines, I had tried to order the magazine "Funeral Director" from the newsagent in Winterbourne where I went for the papers on a Saturday, but all they could offer me was Practical Woodworking or Fly Fishing, it seemed that no-one had ever asked for the magazines I was now requesting. But in my spare moments I got hold of a few back copies from Howard and then glory jewels when we acquired James Bradley & Sons. And it was in the classified ads section at the back of one of these magazines that I saw there was an advert for desk and office signs. These were all the rage in the mid 1980's, they displayed your name and title and were really rather posh. I persuaded Howard to order them for all the directors and we bought about eight, they all had two each, one for the door and one mounted on a wooden plinth they could put on their desk (which thinking about it was a bit pointless, because most people having got into the office would know whose office they were in). Anyway, I got approval from Howard, sorted out the purchasing of them and arranged to have them put on the doors and in the offices. Immediately we had problems. The signs on the door kept falling off. We put them back on time and again with double sided tape and then blue tack, but it was always the same. They would stay there as obedient as anything until just the moment when someone you wanted to impress would knock on Howard's door and the sign would fall off. For a while I mastered the art of knocking on Howard's door with one hand and holding on to the sign with the other, opening the door, introducing the guest and then closing it ever so gently. Of course it would all go horribly wrong when Howard would then burst out of the door demanding coffee and biscuits. On more than one occasion the sign actually fell into the pot of coffee that was being carried into his office. In the end we gave up on them, I would like to think that someone, somewhere will chance upon them and wonder "what was all that about?". And I would merely comment "Indeed."

Working at Head Office, I met Marianne, of course. Marianne Hodgson (formerly Marianne Katybyan) had burst upon the manager's eyes when she attended the December 1984 Company Conference in a rather tight leather suit and an explosion of blonde hair and make up, sort of a young Joan Collins. It was probably her French accent that appealed to the younger managers. All of a sudden I was in a situation where I met Marianne weekly and then it became daily.

Marianne had her own business, really posh clothes with huge price tags on at a shop called Just Imagine in Streetly, just a stones throw away from the family house Edenwood. The house was palatial, set in the private Roman Road, I remember being totally enthralled the first time I saw it. And then slowly but surely I became a sort of Howard gopher, I would turn up after breakfast, take the boys to school, pick up the boys from school, take Marianne to friends, drive the XJS, oh trying stuff all of it! On more than one occasion Marianne opened the door to me in bra and knickers, it was probably something to do with being French. And the way she said my name, do you now if it hadn't been for Ruth I think I could have been falling in love? I suppose at the time, Marianne would have been about thirty-six and I was in my early twenties. I was a young and naive boy, pretending to be worldly wise on the outside, but quite frankly not having the first clue when it came to love and all that!

I frequently drove Howard's boys to and from Solihull School. There was Howie (he was probably about twelve) and Jamieson (Jamie, about six). Howard had lost his first son Charles in a swimming pool accident whilst on holiday in Thailand at the age of three. They were very sweet boys with cheeky grins and very well spoken. On more than one occasion I had breakfast with them and Marianne, as they weren't quite ready for me. Buzzing back on the M42 was a great laugh, the fastest I got up to in Howard's XJS was 128 mph, I must have been crazy but I was young and enjoying what I was doing. I remember I used to enjoy being at the traffic lights in Sutton Coldfield as I used to hope that people would recognise me, but then I remembered I hadn't actually have any friends outside of Hodgsons, the cult was starting to take a hold of me.

I liked both of the boys a lot, although Jamie was very young, Howard junior was very handsome even at a young age and although he didn't talk much, when he did, he had a suitably classy accent. That's what you get if you pay good school fees you see.

By now, I'd had an upgrade of car. My light blue Ford Fiesta had been replaced by Beryl Smith's old Red Rover 216i. It was a lovely car. It was the car Ruth and I took on honeymoon in August of 1988 and it drove beautifully. Only twelve months later I was upgraded again to a Rover 8 fuel injection. I remember being a bit miffed it wasn't a Jaguar, this was my sole aim whilst I was there, such are the targets of youngsters at twenty-three! But the Rover flew. I quickly managed to accumulate nine penalty points, all for speeding and could see that if I didn't change my driving habits I was going to lose my licence.

Major acquisitions were on the cards, although I wasn't privy to such information. I had managed to carve out a bit of a niche in looking after Howard's post, taking his calls and dealing with many of the things only he would have dealt with previously. One of the fun jobs was dealing with press cuttings from the newspapers and getting them mounted into posh books which sat in the reception area. It was here I first met Howard's very good friend Ashley White, including bow tie, his marvellous graphic skills and his sidekick Tony Tiffany, carefree, very funny and someone who became a dear friend. So, I dealt with many loose ends and got down to the work, I felt I was at the centre of everything and this pleased me.

Howard knew what he was doing, he was freeing himself up for the major acquisitions that were to come, leaving Tim to fill in as gopher, although most days I got to drive his XJS and this was certainly one of the best parts of the job.

I became a jack of all trades really, with the benefit of hindsight not the best thing to be. JBT was still dealing with acquisitions at this stage, quite frankly why I shall never know as he had about as much diplomacy as Idi Amin. You needed this in heaps if you were trying to persuade these old stick-in-the-mud funeral directors their future lay with Hodgson Holdings.

Howard's modest office was right next to the door and woe betide anyone who decided they could leave before him. Most days I left at 6.30pm or later, it didn't particularly bother me as I had no one to go home to, I lived a pretty solitary existence really, which is why many boring and tedious jobs were lobbed my way. Even on the weekend I would come in and catch up on stuff, enjoying the peace and quiet without the phones ringing.

It was on one such weekend that I met John Slim. John was a journalist for the Birmingham Post and was working with Howard ghost writing his autobiography. John was dapper, bright-eyed and a lot of fun, and whilst I had infrequent dealings with him, I realised he was going to be one of the good guys. He fawned a bit over Howard (but then who didn't?) and was always being told that Howard was late for a meeting or Howard had cancelled the meeting, but he was always unfailingly polite to me and most amusing to talk to. The autobiography didn't ever get published, but I met John many years later after Howard had resigned as Chairman of PFGHKI, only months after I had opened Hudson's Coffee House in Birmingham. John had a coffee and chatted to me about Howard's demise and what I thought he was going to do now. I was so caught up in Hudson's I could hardly think about the world I had already left far behind, but it was as always lovely to see him and we had a very happy half hour together.

So I made myself at home at Head Office. We had a number of different people on reception, who were made to work slavishly hard by Howard on all sorts of stuff. By now there were acquisitions being announced weekly and it became my job to order the stationery, send the funeral home the stuff, talk the manager locally through the hit list every night and generally make sure the business was being assimilated into the Hodgson style. They were pretty heady days and I enjoyed it without a thought of Cardiff and the excitement I was missing there. Little did I know it would be two years before I conducted another funeral, even then it was the funeral for my Grandfather in late 1987.

It was strange, yes I missed funeral directing, but I felt I had progressed much further than many of my peers. I was always learning different things, had access to the great man himself and knew most of what was going on in the company. I still believed that one day I would make the position of director and was enthusiastic with every project I was given. I was keen to make my mark and enjoyed the new world I had discovered in the West Midlands.

Nobody except JBT was entrusted with the Holy Grail at Head Office, the nightly reporting of funerals the individual funeral homes had booked and had to be phoned through every night without fail. He had devised an unbelievably complicated paper system; at its head it had an A2 form drawn up and broken down into small square boxes with two lines going across them showing individual funeral homes with the running totals of figures they had done in the year and the last years comparison. Of course the form was forever being redesigned as we acquired more businesses and this led to further confusion. Don't ask me why (I never fully understood this black art all the time I was there) but he would end up with two most important figures; first, the **OLD DOWN** and secondly the **NEW UP** and somehow they would balance. I had been involved in copying this and adding small amounts of detail for weeks on end, but I would have had more luck in deciphering the *Enigma* code than having a modicum of understanding of how to compile this sheet. One memorable evening when JBT couldn't be there for a nightly report (he must have been abducted by aliens, as for Howard to allow JBT a day off was un-heard of) the job of compiling these sacred figures fell to me. I spent most of the previous week planning for the auspicious day. I started taking the figures early and with sharp pencils, ballpoint pens and tippex to the fore, I was sat in JBT's office feeling like I was chocolate and at the head of Mission Control. I cleared up all my normal daily jobs very early and with a deep breath started compiling these hallowed figures. It seemed to fall into place, the West Midland region was easy as there were very few of the offices that I wasn't familiar with and I ploughed on through the Central and Eastern Regions, up to The North. All the time I was like any good bank clerk balancing as I went, as I realised that trying to find a mistake once I had got to the end would have been nigh on impossible. I started to get excited as the last regions phoned in their figures and must have started to relax, which in hindsight was fatal. After two hours on the phone, I was thrilled to discover I had balanced first time!

It was only the following Monday JBT explained to me I had missed about forty-five funerals somewhere and the figures was completely wrong, well at least I had a go! Have to say I was never entrusted with the figures again, it remained a dark and mysterious secret all the time I was there. ...or maybe that bottom figure had to be taken away from the top figure underneath the one that... I have to say I can still see the form today in my minds eye, still see the small columns and the names across the top; Hodgson (Oaklands), Kingstanding, Crowther, Hamer, Bonham, WG Ward, SA Bates, SA Evans, Roy Preddy... memories of happy and uncomplicated days.

Much later as John's sheet got so complicated that Professors with degrees in Egyptian Hieroglyphics were being called in to sort it out, we progressed to a system using the rather clever computers at the time from IBM. We purchased an AS400 Main Frame Computer, some massive beefy thing which sat whirring away in the newly appointed IT manager's office, Mick Harris. We were all in awe at the start, we knew many of the things which had been done with pen and ink could now be computerised, but few of us knew how. When the moment came, we realised after all was said and done, that we had actually just replaced JBT's rather eccentric, unwieldy but incredibly efficient system with one that had no heart or style and still gave us the same numbers. And of course, we still had to write them down in the first place! It was a sad, sad moment when JBT's famous figures form bit the dust, he had created a real one off, a special system and I for one mourned its passing.

When the AS400 had been ordered it was heralded as a huge step forward for us. All of a sudden, all the paper that had been sitting on people's desks could be entered into electronic formats and not into bound ledgers. Part of the issue was that we were all unclear exactly what problems the computers were there to solve, it certainly felt as if it was a purchase that was being carried out for no sound reason.

I suppose this step forward signalled the downward turn for JBT. I remember seeing him when he announced he would be retiring, he seemed to be thrilled, I guess he was always looking for a quiet life and here was one about to hit him just when he wanted it. Perhaps in some ways, this sparked the decline in the crisp, no nonsense reporting that JBT had always done so very well. He was never subtle, but gave you the power to get on and do it, he left you alone to deal with things and didn't interfere.

A horrendous system of tiered management was about to be heralded in, where no one got anything done because they were too busy covering their own backs. Of course that is a bit of an exaggeration, but not by much, we had managers who seemed hell bent on making sure they were covered, and dropping other people in it seemed to be done as casually as opening the mornings mail. it wasn't JBT's style at all and I missed him.

JBT had managed to get his wife a job while he was at Head Office and she carried on when he had retired. Joan was very sweet, a terrible gossip, tall and angular, I always thought a rather strange shape for a lady. Joan joined JBT in arranging funerals ("Joan's booked two this morning already" he used to shout as if the other branches could actually do anything about it!) at the Handsworth branch of Hodgson's.

When the fax machine was brought in from Ingalls only Jeff Hickman knew how to use it. He had come across from Ingall Industries and had retained his respect and rather nice Jaguar car. The said machine was the size of a 1970's duplicating machine. We stood in awe amongst the huge behemoth amidst us. None of us had a clue. It really was foreign territory. That was the day Jeff went up in everyone's estimation.

It was about this time Howard decided to spruce up the company's image and decreed that all the hearses and limousines would be midnight blue and this would be complimented by Portland grey livery for the chauffeurs. The female receptionists got to wear a midnight blue skirt and top, but with the most hideous cravat you were ever likely to see, it was just like those worn by naff building society staff. It was really pretty grim unless you had a model figure and Joan, bless her did not, she was after all fifty-five. Anyway, Joan with typical Howard comic timing was the first person nationally to wear the whole kit and caboodle. I cannot forget the horror that greeted me as she flounced out of the coffin selection room and bounded into view, it was a bit of a nightmare moment really. Many years later when JBT had retired I still met Joan from time to time and she was ever so sweet, but as was the case in those days, they were still obsessed with talking about Howard and what he was up to, whereas I had had to move on by then!

The grey livery was in actually fact a particularly good move, they matched very well with the midnight blue hearses and limousines, but trying to get it to suit all the different shapes and sizes we had acquired was, as many banks and building societies are still finding, quite a black art. We had Maureen Spooner a lady at the Clapham Road branch of Ashton Ebbutt who had clearly ordered a Portland grey skirt several sizes too small for her. Maureen reminded me of the famous wrestler Mick McManus on World of Sport, she was a strange shape and no doubt the tailor had had rather a challenge. Why she had done this was anyone's guess and it didn't make for pleasant viewing, and this was the same all across the company. No one had the foresight to control the ordering of uniforms to ensure people got stuff which actually fitted them properly, it wouldn't have cost too much to have had them all personally measured.

Remember Alan Biscuit Barrel Reid and the Company Conference in 1987? That wasn't the only company conference that managed to somewhat damage Howard's reputation. The following year, JBT had been entrusted with the task of recording all the TV appearances Hodgsons had made over the last twelve months. These mainly consisted of Howard in fedora, Howard in snazzy suit, Howard in long Crombie overcoat, Howard in XJS... you get the idea. However he was brilliant at giving the TV exactly what they wanted, here was TV material. The thought of dear old Michael Kenyon, our major rival, being able to give anyone an inspired interview was beyond the realms of any possibility. It was just not what he did. His was a world of discretion and calm, Howard's was a world of the opposite.

So, it was a good idea initially to put all these together and show them at the company conference, presumably Howard reasoned that Pontefract in East Yorkshire (where Howard had bought EV Fox & Sons six months earlier) didn't have anything as modern as TV. Ever conscious of the budget, JBT decided to use a friend of a friend who recorded weddings in Holyhead Road, Handsworth.

Holyhead Road was the most cosmopolitan area of Birmingham and it really was a case of spot the white man. Going up a very creaky set of back stairs above an Indian takeaway didn't somehow feel right, when I got to the top of the steps and met Raj, I felt I was in the depths of some rather home made technology. I think it was the rather casual way he lounged around on the sofa amidst a pile of pirated Indian Porn Movies that made me feel I wasn't quite at the cutting edge of video technology. It didn't fill me with confidence for the company conference as I dropped all the tapes to Sonny, Raj's brother. I had carefully noted down the order in which they should be recorded onto the master tape and went back three days later to collect the (by now) rather hazy second generation copy.

No one checked the video of course, I collected it and JBT waltzed off with it like the prize in a rather shabby village hall raffle. I mentioned to JBT I hadn't checked it, perhaps suggesting he should, but as usual with JBT he wasn't really listening as the shouts of "John, John!" ("Coming Mr Howard") came from Howard's office. I thought no more about it, my job was done, I had endured the two trips to Handsworth and collected the video from cheery Raj who announced it "All perfect, mate!"

The day of the conference dawned brightly. We had directors from ANZ Merchant Bank, Capel Cure Myers, the two non-executive directors and (I never quite understood this) the famous Birmingham gynaecologist Joe Jordan (not to be confused with the Scottish footballer). Howard did a good build up on the tape, but I was rather switched off. I knew the length of the tape was seventeen minutes, so snuggled down for a quiet forty winks. I was briefly roused by the introduction of Howard's Way, the soothing clarinet concerto was always nice to listen to, I stirred myself and enjoyed that part. Just as it got to the end of the excerpt there was a flurry of colourful confetti and we watched (if that is the right word) about three seconds of some anonymous Asian wedding before neatly returning to the next Hodgson TV performance.

I do not know whether Don De Groot from Capel Cure Myers had already made his investment decision on Hodgson Holdings, or whether this was a defining moment for them to confirm that they had been impressed. No doubt someone somewhere knows the truth, in all honesty I do not. But secretly at the back of my mind I would like to think they carried on investing, thinking they had surely imagined it all in a mad dream. It is one of the many memorable moments that make me smile so many years later!

I got really excited about the company conference, JBT had asked me for ideas on seminars and speakers. I wanted to run things like "How good is your hearse driver?" and "Embalming under pressure and run the David Bowie song" and a funeral word-search with a prize of a free funeral to the winner, but JBT, conservative to the end, changed them all and they were all incredibly boring. At one of the seminars I counted fourteen people fast asleep, even then I knew better.

On one remarkable occasion we were making a TV commercial for the product 'Dignity In Destiny'. Script writers could have huddled together in a room for many long years and failed to come up with a crappier title than that. It was discovered that one of the coffin bearers who should have been part of the filming had actually gone home early. Chris, who was partially in charge of producing the video (I forget his second name, so that saves him serious embarrassment), stood in as a bearer and immediately looked out of place. It was one of those wonderful moments when we all knew he was not the real bearer, but an impostor!

Chapter 11

Big Deals

Howard always managed to attract colourful personalities to his team and Simon Preston, a direct descendant of Lord Nelson, was no exception. I never met him in all the time I was there, but he was a key cog in the wheel of Hodgson success. I only ever met Pip Rosen his young, female sidekick, and the sight of her in tight black jodhpurs would cause JBT's arm to extend even wider and created a general sense of male hormone havoc in Head Office. Pip amused me greatly as she was so very casual about everything and she was fairly close to my age. Simon was treated rather cavalierly by Howard and whilst in many cases he was right and got a very good deal for the business, there were times when it all got a bit much. Howard referred to Simon rather derogatorily, he had a habit of doing this and it always made me wonder what he called me when my back was turned. Howard didn't really need a public relations team, by now he had perfected the art of talking about himself and Hodgson Holdings, and to his credit he did it extremely well. Those frantic months showed me a side of journalism that I was not impressed with. Many journalist ran the same game, they arrived at Head Office and always ended up writing the same sort of story, they could have just cut and pasted the previous article. It all got a bit of a bore really and showed me how lazy so many of them were.

In 1993 Pentos, who owned the retail book chain Dillons got into severe financial difficulties. A stockbroker wrote a damning report on them explaining how their outdated financial methods were covering up the fact that they really weren't going anywhere. He titled the article 'Pentosauras' claiming that their financial treatments were old fashioned and not in keeping with what should be being declared in the city. Before this though, we had our own Pentosauras moment. One of the city guys, who had been wined and dined by Russell Hodgson (Howard's brother), wrote an article indicating stockholders should hold and not buy Hodgson stock. He titled it "Running faster to stay still" and Howard was not amused.

Yet he had got it right at a stroke, we had to carry on buying as the firms we bought lost funerals almost immediately. It was a vicious circle. And yet it seemed that no-one, apart from this one sharp hack, had understood what was gong on. Acquisition accounting is complicated as each period could not be compared with the last because new acquisitions affected the figures. In fact the figures were confused whatever happened, most of the time we didn't know if we were coming or going or having a perm, as my granny used to say!

In many ways it was a sense of Emperor's New Clothes, Howard had to move fast, the first mover was important and if he grabbed a market share now, he could reflect and re-adjust later. But it would be interesting to see what has happened to the funeral numbers over the last twenty-five years since the acquisitions of those heady days. Dennis Amiss once brought the house down at a dinner speech by declaring that Howard didn't buy small firms, he just bought large ones and waited. Whilst it was a little bit of an exaggeration, there was a huge amount of truth in it.

It seems obvious now that much of the middle management felt they were "big deals", they had been good if not great funeral directors but they were not equipped for the middle management role they now held. They had a title of Director and a beautiful car, but not the minerals to go with it and this was inevitably terminal for them and the company, at some stage it would all come home to roost.

Dottridge Brothers was one of the last remaining large firms in London that was worth buying. They were very old, well established and conducted five thousand, seven hundred funerals through their scattered branches in London. In terms of rationalisation it was an important scalp for both Hodgsons and our main rival Kenyons. It came as no surprise that we were entering into a ferocious bidding war, which was to become rather nasty.

Simon Strudwick and Vic Taylor of Dottridge Brothers came to see us at Plantsbrook House. They were of course given the full treatment (barring JBT as he had been banished for the day) and seemingly agreed a price. Dennis Amiss was cock-a-hoop, it meant that on signing he would be getting around £12,000 in commission and everything was set for another good city announcement. The share price it seemed would be climbing again on this latest piece of news.

175

And then came the bombshell – a fax arrived claiming several things for the directors that had never been discussed in the original deal; £50,000 salaries for them both and a BMW each. It was a bolt out of the blue and a "try on" by their solicitors. Howard tried to tweak the deal, but even he could see the demands they were making were ridiculous in the extreme. I suppose you have to take your hat off to them for trying! So, we reluctantly pulled away from the deal, we had offered £9.5 million and in the end were told that we were way out of the bidding. Ron Middleton breathed a sigh of relief, it was going to be sold to someone else.

Things went very quiet, we tried to get on with other stuff but there was a hint of despair in the office amongst the people that would have got involved in the deal. Dottridge Bros was in the heart of Kenyon territory and they were determined not to lose out this time. In the end, Kenyon's paid £11.5 million and whilst Howard was furious he had lost a key part of his London expansion, he realised once the figures had been analysed that Kenyon's price earnings ratio had been diluted. In actuality this was a great thing to have happened, as in one year's time Dottridge would be his. In a very simple and clever way, the two guys at Dottridge knew they had a rare jewel to sell and maximised the price for it by getting the three main quoted funeral directors to bid against each other.

Most of the larger funeral directors regarded Howard as an amusement, they didn't look into what he was doing and how he was transforming the industry. One such guy who was a real player was Colin Field.

Colin was Managing Director of the Great Southern Group. He was younger than Howard by about three years, but always came across as being slightly older and much more pompous. Colin was a typical funeral director, but had also gone down the acquisition and expansion route himself incredibly successfully in the South East and now controlled far more funerals than Hodgsons. I knew nothing about Colin Field until the

Money Programme on BBC 2 ran a programme about acquisition and rationalisation in the funeral industry and fairly predictably interviewed Howard, Colin Field and Michael Kenyon. Of course the other two were as reticent as Howard was forward, they rather embarrassingly didn't look at the camera and had very different approaches. Michael, ever the gentleman, when asked to comment on Howard buying Ingalls for so much money commented that it was a matter for him and him alone. Colin Field smirked and said that in his opinion, the directors of House of Fraser had got a very good price for the business and when asked to comment if it was too much, repeated that statement, thereby obviously insinuating that Howard had paid too much for it.

It wasn't what Colin Field said but how he said it that people remembered. "Who was the little jealous guy on your programme last night?" was the comment frequently made to Howard in the days following such exposure. But it was clear to all TV people throughout the land, if you want a story, comment, interesting angle and someone who is going to make good telly, then don't bother with Michael or Colin, just call Howard. To his credit it was totally justified, he was funny, interesting, looked good and he was so much younger and snazzier than the others. The thought of Howard being installed with the President's Chain of Office at the National Association of Funeral Directors was just too ridiculous to imagine. The other two would suit that role perfectly.

The major turning point in the Hodgson story and to some extent a defining point in that of the Great Southern Group arrived when Ingall Industries was put up for sale by House of Fraser.

Ingall Industries was originally a coffin manufacturer which had expanded by purchasing funeral directors, many of them in the West Midlands, Liverpool and the North West. They were a ragbag collection of firms, some excellent funeral homes conducting thousands of funerals a year, and other small satellite offices that had just about run their course. It remained a great mystery to most of the people in the funeral business what a company whose main asset was a world famous quality department store in Knightsbridge would have to do with 156 funeral homes scattered around the UK. Indeed one day, House of Fraser made the decision that it did not form part of their long term plans and decided to sell to the highest bidder. There was of course huge interest. Howard more than most realised that opportunities like these did not knock every day and pursued it with a vigour bordering on the obsessive.

I was massively involved of course, a person prepared to work all the hours necessary (and even a few that were not), an obsession about detail, planning and making the Hodgson system work. I recall spending many a happy weekend working out how the rationalisation would work after the purchase, such was our optimism. Goodness knows why Ruth put up with all this kerfuffle on the weekend! But I was determined to make a great song and dance about all this and hammer a stake into the ground, I knew it was a seminal moment and that the business opportunity was there to be seized. I wanted to be as much a part of it as I could. So I worked long hard hours producing graphs, papers and suggestions about what we should be doing post acquisition in order to enjoy the economies of scale. They were great, fun, drama filled, heady days and they came to signify what working with Howard was all about.

At that time, Hodgson Holdings was a small publicly quoted company on the Unlisted Securities Market with a market capitalisation of £8 million. No matter how much Howard had impressed the city with his first real trading figures (and boy, they were very impressive), the city just would not allow him to purchase the entire House of Fraser group. At 23,000 funerals, it was more than double what Hodgson was currently conducting. So, Howard constructed a wheeze, that's all it was really, he got together with Bruce McDougall of the Co-op, reasoning that if one purchaser tried to buy the whole group, then the likelihood was that the deal would get referred to the Monopolies and Mergers Commission. But if two purchasers put forward a joint deal and carved up the cake then things could move forward.

The move got off to the falsest start imaginable as just before they put in a bid of approximately £30 million, they were told the business had been sold already subject to contract! Howard got hold of Tim Seymour from the Australia and New Zealand Bank to phone Alan Bond and told him "You're not a gentleman Alan!" The Australian hated that, so they were invited to put together one final bid. They bid £31 million, which was accepted and the other deal was dead.

That was one of Howard's skills, he was very good at getting the undoable done.

I guess that part of this had been learnt whilst he rebuilt the Hodgsons business from scratch, getting on with it and never blaming other people or bemoaning his luck.

There were of course legal issues and practical ones surrounding such a huge purchase. Even now, the deal was on and off with the frequency of a conjurer's hat. It almost stalled at the twelfth hour when even the dynamic brains of Simon Ramshaw from Edge & Ellison couldn't see a way around buying just the one section called Ingall Industries as the total value was too much for Hodgson Holdings capitalisation. Everyone tried to find a way around it and in the end, only Howard managed to discover a way forward, as he said much later "not because I was more intelligent, but because I wanted the deal more." I never, ever, ever forgot this comment which I was to repeat so many times for years to come. It is so true. Basically, he purchased Ingall Industries for £17.5 million, left the Creditors in the deal and therefore managed to keep the purchase price below £15.5 million, the value which would have forced him to go the to the shareholders first. In doing so, he managed to grace the Financial Times front cover with the memorable headline "Hodgson buys Ingall Industries for £15 million".

I know, because I went out and bought the paper with such a headline. I showed Howard and the board of directors that bright and breezy June morning. Even I was impressed, there was a certain cache about the pinkness of the Financial Times that made it all seem very real and exciting.

It was the single most major move that Howard had made. The quantum leap in his business career, now he had a platform of 23,000 funerals on which to pursue his rationalisation programme and prove to the city that he could deliver the numbers as well.

Although clear to me at the time, many people hadn't quite caught on to how the rationalisation following acquisition worked. This single move meant that Howard could now demonstrate what could be achieved with bigger numbers. From a flotation in June 1986, when we conducted just 5,600 funerals, one year later we were to conduct approximately 24,000 funerals per year.

To show how rationalisation worked and how profitable it was to the company's bottom line, it is good to look at the business of Coyne Brothers, conducting approximately 850 funerals from one main office and four branches. Now in the first instance, they would almost certainly have had too many vehicles, staff and wouldn't have been tightly co-ordinated in running their funerals. Immediately we would have put just one funeral arranger into each of the offices and taken all the equipment to the main centre. This then became the hub with the branch offices as spokes of the wheel. A full time coffin fitter would then work from the head office and prepare all the coffins for all the branches. All the funerals would be booked through one day book diary, remember no computers here in those hazy 1980 days. I realise this sounds like total common sense but it just wasn't generally happening in the industry. So, immediately upon acquisition Coyne Bros became more profitable and probably contributed about £100 per funeral in profit to the company's bottom line (now about £85,000).

Taking this a stage further, when Ingall Industries were acquired, Thompson Bros in Liverpool had fifteen offices conducting about 1,400 funerals. These would immediately all become branch offices and the total turnover of £1.4 million translate into about £300 per funeral nett profit (about £430,000) All the coffin fitting would still go an at Coyne's Hub and all the Thompson Offices would need only a funeral arranger. It was classic and was a very quick way of delivering immediate profit following acquisition.

This sort of doubling up in areas of operation happened many times following the Ingalls acquisition and Howard had been totally justified in paying what seemed to be such a high price. In retrospect it wasn't. His purchases afterwards were far, far too expensive, but Ingalls was a snip at £15 million as Thompsons alone would have paid back £420,000 of the interest in its first year of operation.

These funeral numbers were very large and this was really a whole new ball game now. Great Southern Group had taken fifteen years to reach its total of 23,000 funerals, whereas Hodgson Holdings had gone from 450 to 23,000 in just eight years, an extraordinary leap. Money was cheap and acquisitions were very much the name of the game. It was early 1988 and things were about to happen big time. Many businesses would have now slowed down, looking for a period of stabilisation and consolidation. Not

181

Howard, he flounced forward, share price having gone off the Richter scale, using paper now to fuel his ever increasing purchases. The high of acquisition had got to him and like a heroin user, once hooked, forever hooked, the down times were at this stage to be a long, long way away.

One of the potentially largest single purchases slipped through Howard's hands. This was the renowned James Summers in Cardiff. Paul, the owner, had decided he had enough of funerals and chose a good time to cash in. Summers was THE funeral director in Cardiff, with its own funeral chapel, they conducted around 2,000 per annum. It would have been a big prize. I recall Paul Summers came up to see Howard, we did the usual, lunch at Le Bon Viveur, the tour of Plantsbrook House and the waffle from Hodgson, Penrose and Amiss, then around 6pm Howard told me to drop Paul back to Cardiff – in his car of course, so I looked forward to the journey.

We chatted very easily until we got on the motorway and then I had this brainwave. Paul wanted to sell, why couldn't I say, "Don't sell it, let me run it and I can go back to Cardiff". My mind was racing at a hundred miles an hour. I was getting myself all ready for the conversation, but decided around Worcester way that I didn't really have the balls for it, after all if he knew Howard really well then he could tell him and that wouldn't look good. I often wonder what would have happened if I had made this proposal to him, and what would have happened if he had said yes. Again, another fork in the road...

His driver met him us at Monmouth and on the return journey I was cross with myself for missing the opportunity. And then three weeks later he sold the business to the Co-op. We hadn't expected that, but this chapter was now closed and I buried myself in work again.

It's worth pausing at this stage to mention Howard's solicitors. When I got to Head Office, Howard was in the final stages of negotiations with the solicitor Philip Dunn. Phillip had been Howard's father's solicitors and Howard had stayed with them. That was until it was discovered that Phillip had syphoned off some of his client's money to fund some wacky deal in the States. So, Howard changed lawyers and got in touch with the firm Edge & Ellison. They would mainly be handling acquisitions, which involved transfer of goodwill, commercial property and productions of leases. Simon Ramshaw, head honcho at Edges was a genuinely lovely guy who always seemed secure in his own skin. He was never overawed by Howard and appeared to be one of those rare breed of solicitors who got things done to a timetable and got it done properly. Simon together with Neil Pearson, Chris Rawstron and a couple of other commercial specialists were kept very busy for the next three years on Hodgson Holdings work.

I always liked seeing them, they were cheerful, young and very positive about everything. Neil did a substantial amount of work for me when I opened my first business much later. I saw Chris Rawstron and Simon Ramshaw a number of times. They didn't ever quite seem like solicitors really, it was rather strange!

I was in a very privileged position. I was the first port of call for any press contact at such a time. I spoke to the journalists on the phone, made the appointments to see Howard and entertained them with coffee, charm and chat. I met most of the leading financial journalists of the time, formed opinions about many of them and fell in love, albeit only for a few hours, with the dark haired, sultry and very beautiful Marina Cantacuzino who was freelancing for The Observer. I don't mind admitting I might have made myself a little bit silly over her! She was very sweet indeed.

As well as opening Howard's post and greeting and meeting the various personalities who came through the door at Plantsbrook House, I was responsible for a number of personal projects, a couple of which were doomed to failure. Howard owned a yacht "Fat Girl" and moored it at Port Grimaud in St Tropez, France. Howard's holidays were fairly infrequent as things used to grind to a halt when he did. One famous JBT tale is of a toilet being repainted at The Oaklands, but because Howard was on holiday, no one knew which colour to paint it, so they didn't decide until he came back! He would take the yacht off and sailed out to anther point on the coast. Often he didn't want to sail back the same way, so I was instructed to find a skipper who would bring the yacht back for Howard at a fair price.

I managed to get hold of a skipper, then he seemed to have innumerable problems with the boat, firstly unable to get the engine started until spare parts had been ordered from America (Howard predictably poked his nose in and the whole thing was delayed for another two weeks). Then the skipper managed to lose a member of crew overboard when he slipped on a rope, and then the skipper had a problem with the entire electrical system which culminated in him receiving an electric shock whilst astride the toilet. Of course I was the messenger for all these disasters and I felt somewhat at a loss to know what to do, as trying to control a project so far away from home had rather stretched my capabilities. Regular updates were imperative for Howard and this meant much amusement was brought on a frequent basis to quite serious meetings with financiers and merchant bankers.

Then there was trying to get the Director's cars washed at one of the funeral homes. This, the most simple of things to achieve you would have thought, quickly turned into a nightmare with tales of lost keys, scratched door panels, hearses stuck behind Jaguar XJS's and being delayed for their funerals, the wrong car brought back, the young coffin fitter who moved the car and bashed it into the limousine... It seemed that nothing could be achieved without the maximum amount of faff and foodle, and I was left carrying the can. I worked very hard to control these things, even taking the car to the funeral home, waiting whilst it was washed and returning it myself.

All this should have prepared me for running more than one restaurant in the early 1990's. If you weren't there on the spot, things didn't go according to plan, people made different decisions to the ones you would have made and that in turn affected your plans. It was the oldest rule in the book, but I was still learning, would I ever remember when it got to my turn?

I was also responsible for booking lunches at Le Bon Viveur, the restaurant just up the road in Sutton Coldfield. Most days Howard seemed to have someone for lunch and I frequently joined him when there was two people to entertain. This was always fun for Howard as he would explain my reluctance to drink alcohol (at the time I was a teetotaller) due to the fact that I was a recovering alcoholic. I always enjoyed the lunches, yes, I had a bit of a non job really, but I could converse with people a lot more experienced than me on matters I knew rather a lot about and it gave me chance to flash off my double cuff shirts and pink braces and generally look the part. I did rather enjoy the whole appearance thing but equally enjoyed the fact that I was right next to the action. Some weeks we must have doubled his turnover at the restaurant, there was always someone to meet. Lesser mortals like David Tonks from Thorley Smith weren't allowed to meet Howard, but instead got JBT and me for lunch. Having lunch with JBT was a bit if a nightmare as he wasn't the best socially and he didn't eat very much so it was all a bit of a non-event.

David Tonks came down one day to discuss the price of gowns. I was on a self avowed mission to get them down to £3.75, we were currently being charged £4.20 by Bill Fry, who was a long standing friend of Howard's. For the uninitiated, the classic coffin gown is a little like a vaudevillian costume, it is just a wrap around (or over) and doesn't possess a back. Made from taffeta or silk (we were mainly taffeta because of the price), they were stapled to the top of the coffin inside and then went around the arms and tucked in around the neck. On rare occasions clients provided suits to dress their deceased relatives in, it always looked far more dignified for men, there was something a little strange about dressing a six foot man in a lady's nightie. Anyway, David came down and we didn't particularly get on. He quoted a slightly better price, but I didn't drive him hard enough and I allowed him to get away. A couple of years later, we did change suppliers and saved a load (after all 75,000 funerals a year saving only 50p makes a huge difference).

I still felt desperately sorry for John Mould, only a year older than me, he was still fated to conduct funerals from The Oaklands, which meant there was a good chance either Howard, Marianne or a friend of a friend would make some comment about the speed of the cortège or the dress of one of the bearers. It really did seem very unfair, by comparison I had rather fallen on my feet. And I understood by now how difficult it was to lose a label once one had been acquired. This certainly did give me an early warning so I was careful to make sure that if anything like this started to happen to me I stopped and checked!

Chapter 12

At the crease with Dennis Amiss

In 1066 William strode the English lands conquering villages, towns and ultimately the throne at Hastings. Only a mere 930 years later, a direct descendant of his burst on to the Hodgson scene, his sights set not on thrones or kingdoms, but that most traditional of motivators, cash! David Kynaston Mainwaring of Kynastons was as barking mad as they come. David was large, rotund and his hair was greased and slicked back. He always gave the impression of being extremely successful and at image he certainly was. He had the most enormous plum in his mouth, wore loud pin striped suits and squeaky shoes which always gave him away when he was approaching the reception at Plantsbrook House. He was the stature of Hercule Poirot, no mystery about him though, David was in it for the money. He strode the country meeting funeral directors, having lunches with them, swilling a lot of port (mainly on his side of the table) and persuading small town funeral directors that there really was a deal to be made by selling their business to this upstart Hodgson. He was delightfully charming to me as he was always trying to speak to Howard, but I ran a tight ship and guarded him pretty well. He had come across Howard at the Royal Automobile Club and was now actively engaged in making approaches to as many funeral homes as possible in order to act as an agent for Hodgsons. If Hodgsons ended up buying them David would earn a commission. David had a sidekick who was chalk to his cheese, a Scot who was never as slick or professional as him and in fact became rather a laughing stock at head office.

You see Ron McAllister had been entrusted to deal with the admin of David's approaches. This required a cool head and an organised brain, McAllister had neither of these. He continually forgot who David had contacted. One time he was in negotiations to buy a business in Surrey and kept increasing the price as the funeral director had been speaking to someone else. It took a couple of weeks and the rapid increase of many offers before Ronald Middleton one day discovered that David Mainwaring and Ron McAllister had been bidding against themselves. It was so funny. Ronald didn't really have much of a sense of humour (to be fair if you had been Finance Director during these silly times then you probably wouldn't have had one either) and was seething with rage. We all just found it very funny and managed to milk it for as much as possible. There were only a number of occasions when things like this happened but we all fought for a ringside seat when Howard discovered it as we were always hugely entertained by his response.

In addition to having difficulty with general organisation, Ron McAllister had great difficulty adding up, this didn't exactly endear himself to

Howard. There was a small section in the acquisition form where the items to be sold could be added up, and he invariably got this wrong. Because he worked out of a northern office somewhere, not in Head Office, we quite enjoyed making fun of him. He and David seemed to be very much the odd couple, they were highly entertaining and it meant that the days whizzed past.

"Get Mainwaring on the phone" was a frequent shout from Howard's office, it was all an act really. Yet Howard was clever in getting huge support at grass roots level from the funeral directors and drivers (in the main) right through to the movers and shakers he got in to help as he built such a monumental funeral chain.

But one day it all came to an end; David Mainwaring had somehow had his day, after too many cock ups and too few good leads Howard decided to terminate their agreement. He had him on speakerphone in the office and David was desperately trying to claim as many of the potential acquisitions as his, should they ever complete. It really was most amusing; Howard had agreed a list of companies that David could have commissions on, but like a drowning man clutching at straws, David was desperately trying to add others. One firm he mentioned caused Howard to pause and smile at me.
"No David, you can't have that one."
"Why not Howard? We have an appointment to see them next week!"
"David" Howard paused for dramatic effect, "we bought Ann Bonham & Sons four years ago."

That really summed up David and Ron, they were a class double act. I did miss him coming to see us at Head Office, there just didn't seem to be the characters there any more. With JBT having left, and now Mad Ron and David Mainwaring, what were we mere mortals going to do for entertainment next?

Every day at Hodgson Holdings could bring excitement, but for me there was nothing as exciting as seeing one of my heroes walk through the door. Another visitor on the seemingly endless list of people to be shown around Plantsbrook House. Dennis L Amiss had captivated me when as a schoolboy he had bravely stood up to the bombardment of the Australian cricketers Lillee & Thompson and the quartet of the West Indies, staying put as an opener (my preferred cricketing position) and scoring a memorable 276 against them at the Oval. I used to keep score with pencil and paper in front of the TV and compare my notes to the official scorecards at the end of the day. Oh yes, heady times in Cardiff all right!

Dennis was now forty-two, just recently retired, he had been awarded an MBE and had a superb Test Average of 42.26 (cricketers in this category are regarded as truly great). Howard was a great cricket fan and he had a job in mind for Dennis, to join his team in heading up the Acquisitions Department. Before this, Howard had coped with David Mainwaring and Ron McAllister and their scattergun approach. Now Dennis, or DLA as he soon became known, would target the largest funeral directors in the country and meet them over lunch to offer a free valuation. Well everyone loves a free lunch don't they? Thus began the most aggressive and, it has to be said, brilliant of Howard's moves. Dennis and I worked in tandem, me controlling the initial contact and him meeting, greeting, wining, dining and eventually signing.

Well I was happy, it was a promotion. I think the title Acquisitions Executive sat rather neatly on my pompous head for a while and Dennis was easy to work with. He realised he needed me to get his feet under the table and was very helpful to me. Kindly, he gave me his old boots, shirt and trousers to wear as I was just starting to take an interest in cricket again. He was also very free with advice, such as time when I had been out for five runs after only two overs.

"Talk to yourself" Dennis said. "Hit everything back in the V between mid off and mid on for the first twenty minutes, build your innings slowly. Keep talking to yourself."

Very wise advice and many years later when opening up for my local village in Devon and I scored an unbeaten 76. I mailed him and got a very sweet reply.

We bought firms all over the country, and very nearly one large Norwegian firm from a completely insane Norwegian. I still can't remember how we got hold of the contact, but Mr Tittee (yes, we made as much mileage from the name as we could with much furtive giggling) came to see us at Plantsbrook House. We spent weeks poring over numbers and detailed accounts, never fully understanding what he did, how many funerals he conducted and whether or not we could extract the canning business from the limited company before we bought it. It was more than a little bit of a wild goose chase. It was about this time I realised we were quite often faffing about with stuff we should have had no interest in. To get the business to flotation and beyond, Howard had been extremely single minded, which had been essential to get to this point. We frequently fell out with suppliers (many times due to lack of communication) and often forgot the niceties of doing business with people. One such firm was Folium Press run by John Steed, a charming gentleman who reminded me of his namesake from The New Avengers. He was all politeness and courtesy and when we managed to foul up a proof reading rather magnificently (to my dying day I will say it was JBT's responsibility, but he will say differently!) all Howard would say on the matter was "We're not paying the bill". It was clear that we were to blame, but not which one

191

of us it was. So the relationship with these fine people deteriorated and it was such a desperate shame as I felt it didn't have to be like that.

Dennis was good at what he had been brought in to do, he was entering the job just at the right time. Funeral directors were beginning to understand the amount of money that could be realised from their businesses, even if they were currently running at a loss. Howard didn't care about that. He knew (and this was his simple genius) that by applying his strict formulae and banging up the prices he could turn the business around and make it profitable immediately. It was a shrewd move, Dennis and I moved swiftly to exceed even the ambitious targets that Howard had set.

Working for Dennis was very rewarding. I still had an inflated sense of my own importance, but the skills I had were useful for getting inside a funeral directors' mind and Dennis had the charm to deal with anyone. I took the trouble to explain to Dennis in great detail how funeral directors operated, what equipment they would need and whether or not certain funeral homes would be good acquisitions. I located the targets on a map, explained the theory and the practical issues of rationalisation. A potential buy in a cluster where we already had a presence was of greater interest to us than a new area. Dennis was neatly targeted to concentrate firstly on the largest firms and then the ones which fitted neatly into our existing structure with very little hassle.

Continuing to hone it all down, we had constructed a neat system of lists; List 1 were those businesses we had agreed to buy and were drawing up contracts. At our peak we probably had about forty on this list.
List 2 were those businesses we were in negotiations with, even if that was only a visit from Dennis when he was in the area. Of course he was never really in the area, we just planned trips for him to see as many as possible.

List 3 were those businesses not currently available for sale, but would be happy to be contacted in two months time.

List 4 was a main database of businesses we had not yet contacted.

List 5 were businesses we had blacklisted, never to be spoken of again.

Simple, but very effective. The Amstrad PCW 9512 was kept busy each Friday with an update for Howard as to what was going on in this most important of departments.

Dennis was always keen on new technology and although he wasn't there when the first fax machine was delivered to Plantsbrook House, he was always keen to look to move forward in such clever ways. Thus happened the most classic of all Hodgson cock-ups and one that brings a wry smile even now, many years later.

Christine, Dennis' secretary, was typing out letters. To save time where she could, she was using the very latest tech available at the time, the Mail Merge facility on the old Amstrad PCW 9512. This would print different addresses atop the same letter. Dennis was familiar with this, but then worked out that he could take it a stage further. If he found out a funeral director's wife's name, he could drop this in too, making it all seem more personal. So, the letter would read;

> *Dear Leo, We would be delighted if you and your wife Gabrielle could join us at the company conference for a slap up meal etc etc...*

Class suggestion really! It was only a bit unfortunate and perhaps highly predictable that of the fifty-six leading funeral directors in the UK, only one of them (Leo McKenna) had a wife named Gabrielle, yet an almighty cock up on printing meant that all letters were printed in this way. Of course they were not checked before going out to the addressees and so once again - great idea, poor execution.

This was the 1987 conference, memorable for, amongst many high-lights, the performance of Kit & The Widow as hired cabaret for the evening. I was sitting at a table with a number of large funeral directors, including Robert Pargetter, a boring old fart if ever there was one. We had spoken briefly over the phone, I hired all the vehicles from his firm for the Nutkins Funeral, as the family had demanded Rolls Royces. Then there was the colourful and unpredictable Simon Truelove whose gorgeous wife displayed her ample charms. It came as no surprise when I discovered she had been one of Hugh Hefner's Playboy Bunnies. Simon was Managing Director of WA Truelove, his large family firm in Surrey. Howard had decided, through Dennis, he would wine and dine them, to show them just what a great bunch of guys Hodgsons were. However, Simon already ran a budget of several million pounds, to be wined by a spotty twenty-three year old (that's me by the way) and to see the clowns we had acting as managers wouldn't have impressed or overawed him. Howard would have been far better keeping all his expert links in the closet for another day.

It followed a familiar pattern. I would make the appointment, Dennis would turn up, charm the pants off them (he was extremely good at this), tell a few cricketing stories and have some lunch. Then, as the lunch progressed to further drinks, would ask if he could please give them a valuation as if he didn't Howard would be very cross with him. This always managed to elicit the information and Dennis would, in a seemingly disinterested fashion, jot the information down on a napkin. Thirty minutes later from his high-tech car phone he would convey the details to me where I put it all onto a bespoke acquisition form and ran into Howard's office to price up. The formulae was pretty much the same, unless the business was exceptional (and to start with all we bought was the disparate and near bankrupt firms). Howard would value the stock (normally about £5,000), give good value to the second hand vehicle (normally about £25,000), put a value of about £30,000 on the fixtures and fittings, value the property at a fair market value and then look at the goodwill in the business. With this calculation, the only really important figure was how many funerals the business was carrying out per year and how much they charged for the basic funeral. At that time, the average price was a round £600 per funeral. Howard would multiply the funerals by the average income (times one and half) and arrive at a goodwill figure. Together the average funeral home would be worth about £350,000, a figure most people would never be likely to see in their whole lives. Bear in mind that at the time, most of these funeral directors would be scraping by on £25,000 profit per year. Here we were prepared to pay £350,000 for the entire business and in many cases keep the owner on as a consultant at a rate of £15,000 per annum for a period of three years. They couldn't have had a better offer. Howard had the cash, Dennis had the charm and I had the pushy nature on the phone with the wit to keep one step ahead and get many deals signed.

I needed an extensive knowledge of funeral homes in the areas we were looking at, were they Co-op areas or were they all independent operators who would benefit from our rationalisation programme? We had a couple of priorities, firstly buying up the larger businesses in the UK, as it was as much hassle to buy a small business as a large one. Secondly, buying those within Hodgson territory as they would immediately increase our bottom line.

My first port of call was the handbook of The National Association of Funeral Directors. This listed some, but not all, of the firms in the UK, and some of the firms that were part of a larger organisation like the Co-op. These could be crossed off straight away. Then moving into London and the South East it got a bit easier as we knew which firms belonged to the Great Southern Group, they also got disregarded. This left the independents, until we discovered otherwise by telephone. I loved the challenge and developed one of those wonderful maps which I kept in the board room showing where we had presence and then a further map in Dennis' office which showed where we were in discussions with people. It all looked rather impressive, until the day the overnight cleaner knocked the skirting board and all the pins dropped out. She tried to put them back in the correct places, unsuccessfully! At this time we were buying businesses every week we never managed to get on top of the map again, it is probably lying dormant in a funeral home in the Midlands now with people occasionally taking it out and wondering what it was all about. At the time I could have given Peter Rogers and Gerald Thomas a script for "Carry On Head Office". It was bizarre and hilarious in equal measures, but never boring, oh no!

I had a serious crack at redressing the whole map affair when I purchased larger pins to mark larger funeral homes and smaller pins to mark the satellite branches. Over one weekend I carefully reconstructed the whole thing with a separate pin board to the side explaining who was who, the name of the main head office, names and subsidiaries of satellite branches as well as the number of funerals they were expected to conduct. Though I say so myself it was a great work of art and I was immensely proud of it. I remember looking back at it from very many angles to see how it would look from different views and was looking forward to showing Dennis on Monday morning. The pins were hammered into place, no worries there I thought, alas that weekend the cleaner knocked the whole pin board over again. I had to marry up as to who was where, so we were back to square one again. This all seemed a long way away from marking graves with certainty and giving quality service to grieving families. But thus we entered a twilight world where nothing was real, the money certainly wasn't real and we were buying for the sake of buying. It was to leave us with raw wounds for many years.

Later I was to read that David Meakin, one of Howard's mates who ran the Dignity In Destiny bit of the company was on record saying "Howard always got to the mountain top first, he never went the classic or the easiest way there. He often went down dead ends, but he got there in the end." I recognise that completely and would never have dreamt of trading my years at Hodgsons with The Co-op or Great Southern Groups despite the fact that they were probably far more organised than us. Working for an entertaining maverick had its hourly rewards and we enjoyed them greatly.

There were so many classic moments. One business we had been pursuing was Mannerings Funeral Service in Bromley, thankfully nothing to do with David Mainwaring. The two guys running it were Mike Dennis and Kenyon Gilbert. They had started the business three years ago and decided now was the time to sell. They were still very young and anticipated a good deal and lots of cash. Dennis Amiss was detailed to ring them up with the offer, I will remember it to this day. £570,000 - and this for a business operating out of leasehold premises. They weren't interested said Ken Gilbert.

"What figure did you have in mind?" asked Dennis. Ken responded "£720,000" "That should be all right" Dennis answered. "But I will have to get it past Howard."

Years later I bumped into Ken Gilbert and he confessed it was the first figure that came into his head. Such were the days of our tight rather woolly acquisition policy.

Of course there were the class abject failures as well. I think more particularly of Lodge Bros in London. We knew they conducted about 3,000 funerals, on speaking to the manager of their smallest branch office in Wandsworth the result was a flat "Get out of here now!" Then there

197

was E Sarjeant & Son in Slough, where as I recall, the phone call hardly got past the "Hello, it's Tim Penrose from Hodgson Holdings here…" before the dialling tone indicated the receiver had been replaced. It was all a bit crazy really, I mean there was no greater accolade than someone wanting to buy your firm and if you played your cards right, like Henwood and Son in Newquay, you managed to achieve a ridiculous price for the business, far above what it would be worth to anyone else, then negotiate (and this was the clever part) a retainer to act as consultant to the newly acquired firm. If you were extra clever then you whinged about selling the property (family birthright, etc) until Howard kept the price the same and you rented Hodgsons the property for about £20,000 a year. Thus you ended up with about £250,000 in cash, a yearly guaranteed income of £35,000 for five years and £20,000 per annum thereafter. In most of the cases it was more money than they had ever seen in their lives, many funeral directors with their business (pardon the pun) at death's door were only to eager to take us up on what was an excellent financial package.

Then there were the memorable visits from potential acquisitions, memorable in other ways. The Lymm-Rose family had been conducting funerals in Nottingham for almost ten years, they were posh, very posh (did it come with the double barrelled name?). George and Sheila were the matriarch and patriarch of the family firm. I knew their son Nigel, who rather bizarrely came back as a memory years later, when one of the girls in my Am Dram society in Sutton Coldfield explained that Nigel was her brother-in-law. Nigel was smooth and well dressed, suits cut to the quick, he had money and knew it, his every pore emanated charm and style. His sister was the one I knew more about – having a claim to fame, wait for it… of being the only female embalmer in The British Institute Of Embalmers. Jacqueline Lymm-Rose had appealed to me at the Brighton Grand, where we had been sent for some crazy conference. Not yet married, I was taken with her high cheekbones (sorry Jacqui, it's all coming out now!) and the stunning dress she wore to the ball that night. I did fancy her and I couldn't help thinking of her when George and Sheila came to Plantsbrook House to look around one day. I guessed they had no intention of selling the business, but wanted a glimpse behind the curtain to see what crazy schemes we were all up to. They didn't have to wait long as they had arrived on one of Howard's better days, he had just finished doing a news article with the Sunday Times. Dressed in fedora and crombie overcoat, he flounced into reception. "Hello! Timothy please show Mr & Mrs Lymm-Rose around…" and so it went on. I gave them the by now famous tour of the building, which in hindsight must have been incredibly boring. They met a number of directors, made small talk for a few minutes and then were waltzed down to see the administration department. It was probably light years ahead of its time, but looking back on it now it does rather embarrass me. We basically had two lines of desks in one long hundred yard office block. On the left hand side was the sales ledger team, reconciling and filing invoices for the management accounts. On the other side the purchase ledger team were doing the same, attempting to sort out the weekly payments made by the ever growing list of funeral directors. It was running at the rate of several a week now and they would go bananas every time Dennis and I bought one as it just meant more work, you couldn't blame them I suppose!

When we invited potential acquisitions to visit, I always ran the tour. It helped that I had been a funeral director as I could relate to what they were doing on a day to day basis. Meeting JBT was always one of my highlights, normally I would knock on the door of the particular director and wait, but with JBT it was different. I had started to enjoy this, I would wait until I knew he was on the phone, he was always most worked up when he was. Then I would burst in saying "Oh Sorry Mr Taylor!" This always elicited a "Bugger off!" from him followed by a great big grovel when he saw the clients standing behind me! His large arm would then quickly extend across his forehead (it really was most amusing) he would make a hurried apology and think of something to say to the guests. It didn't help that JBT wasn't one for small talk, he just didn't do it! His was a world of numbers, figures, absolutes and yes or no, he didn't do flannel or faff and I always thought more highly of him for this!

Barry Albin was one guy who, during the time I was at Head Office, didn't ever make it to see Howard. I had contacted Barry direct and we had arranged a classic Dennis lunch and chat. Dennis came back rather overawed by what he had seen. Dennis liked tradition and old things, he came back all fired up about Barry Albin and his empire in Bermondscy. There was a coffin manufacturing arm, old Rolls Royces, it was a firm and a half. Howard and I eventually put a price of about £1.2 million on it, leaving Barry owning the property which was rather a good deal. Barry spent a lot of time faffing about and we had him on the famous List 2 (still in negotiations with) for a good year. In the end he decided not to sell, I think he couldn't see the business working any other way, and had sons who were showing an interest in the business. Like Derek Tyler at Mangotsfield, Barry had developed his own little world where he was king, and anything that was likely to change in that world was probably not good news for him. Barry was an out and out showman, like so many of the larger funeral directors I met. He wanted to be in charge, to be the main circus ring leader, and he wasn't going to take instructions from anyone. If he had sold, the Rolls Royce fleet would have gone, Barry would have been demoted to third coffin bearer or something similar, it would never have worked. Of course Barry kept his business, he died not too long ago and the management team which purchased it following his passing is indeed expanding it and is probably pleased with the decision not to go down the Hodgson sale route. In fact Howard would have been better off buying a failing firm, rather than one that was making money anyway.

Then there was the incident of not buying (although we had agreed to in principle) the firm of Rom Massey in Dublin. The price agreed was several million punts (this was before the euro had taken hold), but we had agreed to buy the limited company and as this was a separate legal entity, we would have been liable for any back taxes and monies owed to any other government departments. This situation is normally dealt with by the seller giving and providing warranties that no such monies are owing, but Rom Massey wasn't prepared to do any of that. So from a rapid promotion to List 1 (we had agreed terms with these businesses and were about to buy them), they vanished to the immortal List 5, funeral directors whose names were never to be mentioned again in the presence of the almighty Howard.

Chapter 13

Spending £34 million pounds

David Hendry was unlike any funeral director I had ever met and I was effervescent in my praise for him. I immediately spotted David had fizz and bubble, and was streets ahead of the regional directors we had appointed. He just had to run the whole of Scotland and the North.

There was just something about David, his suits sparkled, his ample frame exuded confidence and poise and he talked a good game. Always guaranteed to get you into Howard's good books. David had sold his business to us and carried on working in the area as a regional director, managing Pagan of Dumfries and all the little Scottish firms we had acquired including the rather odd business of Alexandra Armours in Ayr. I got on well with David from day one, we weren't that different in ages (bear in mind most of the funeral directors I had met to date had been in their late fifties or early sixties) and we got on extremely well. I hadn't caught up with David until writing early drafts of this book in late 2008. I was pleased to see he had become hugely successful and I dare say, all of it deserved. My Penrose antenna all those years ago was spot on.

Trying to organise the Scottish businesses we had acquired was a bit of a hoot. There was something rather cute and quaint about them as they made a huge fuss about funerals being different in that part of the country, often declaring they were a different country. But, blustering apart, it was the same as it had always been. Howard kow-towed to them and allowed them to create the rather wonderfully named Caledonian Funeral Service. It had its own limited company and board of directors, but I wasn't fooled or even amused. I had seen it all, through Cardiff, Bristol, Hereford, Northampton, London, St Albans, Dunstable, Berkhamsted... and just as Howard had forecast many years ago "Everyone you met will tell you their town or city is a little different and how it is special there. It's not. A funeral is a funeral is a funeral. There are a few quaint traditions, but its generally all the same." To his credit he had been spot on; John Smallbone had said it to me, Alan Bradley had said it to me and I heard the words echoing in my head when I had heard them for the umpteenth time. People wanted to feel that their area was special, but it wasn't.

We also courted Richard Steel's revered funeral business in Winchester. It was over a hundred years old. Richard was very young, perhaps mid-thirties and the business was conducting about 850 funerals per annum. Howard made an extraordinarily generous offer, from memory about four million pounds as it included some rather juicy property. But they came, saw and declined.

Jonathan Harvey in Glasgow was one Funeral Director I will never forget meeting. He flew down from Scotland to meet Howard on a potential acquisition. Dennis and I had done our spade work and Ron McAllister had been to see him. Harvey was a serious funeral director, I don't mean that he treated everything very seriously, just that he did in excess of 750 funerals which was well worth us getting out of bed for. He was intrigued with the Hodgson set up, keen to meet and chat further. Howard knew about it in plenty of time, but yet again the "Mr Howard's running late" had become rather a boring and tired strap line. Most people would just grin and bear it, mindful of the swelling of their coffers months down the line, but Harvey was not amused. I have to say you can't really blame him, here he was, a serious businessman who had taken the day off, and travelled down from Scotland to be greeted by a twenty-three year old with pink braces, red socks and a flashy yuppie suit. He had been shown around a Birmingham office block and been talked at for two hours by a guy who knew a lot about Hodgson operations, but little about the outside world. He left early, and didn't ever get to meet Howard. Of course Howard was cross with us about it, but I think Jonathan's decision had been made well before we had gone through the JBT routine, but it certainly hadn't helped.

One business we did buy in the South was the business of H A Harrold and Shearings of Salisbury and Fordingbridge. It was the only acquisition that had been concluded whilst Howard was on holiday. As was normal in the acquisitions, the key people, either the owners, or managers were always tied into the business post-acquisition through signing of personal restrictive covenants. One of the key pointers to this deal was that the owners no longer worked in the business, and one Ian Newman had held it together. Ian had always been anti-acquisition and certainly anti-Howard. He was declining to sign the agreement in the last few days leading to completion. Howard left explicit instructions that unless the agreement was signed, then the business would not be acquired. Upon returning he discovered Graham Hodson had signed the documents without Ian Newman's agreement and two weeks after the acquisition we had a rival funeral director with all the goodwill not half a mile down the road merrily taking the funerals away from those horrible people in Birmingham. It always made for an excellent sob story.

Many years later finding myself in Salisbury Cathedral I got talking to one of the vergers who had helped organise Sir Edward Heath's funeral, his ashes are interred in the Cathedral, he had lived just across the road. I asked who the funeral arrangements had been entrusted to (as you do) and he told me there had been an unholy war as Ian Newman had carried out the cremation and had been arguing right up to the last day about who would be carrying Sir Edward's ashes down the aisle. I couldn't help laughing, it was just typical of all of us funeral directors, we all wanted our moment of stardom and here was Ian Newman being denied by a lowly verger. Every time I hear Salisbury Cathedral or Sir Edward being mentioned I grin at the thought of a most unholy tussle taking place down the aisle. I didn't ever hear of a battle between the verger (just think Mr Yeatman from Dad's Army and it is even funnier) and Ian Newman at the rear of the hearse "He's mine" "No let go, give them here" – but my imagination allows me to do quite wonderful things and it makes me smile every time I think of it.

News never got out about how Howard had taken the insubordination shown by his Number 2. They had interconnecting offices, so I suspect some toing and froing went on in the first weeks following Howard's arrival back from holiday. But Graham didn't wear his heart on his sleeve and I suspect being so unlike Howard in that respect was one of the reasons they got on so well… until that day.

The Ian Newman fiasco was really the icing on the cake. By now with the Ingall acquisition, we were having weekly battles with managers or senior funeral directors who were deciding to leave and set up their own businesses. It has to be recorded that most of them were extremely successful. There were notable battles with Ian Hazel when he left the family firm of A Hazel and Sons in Erdington to set up as Ian Hazel Funerals in Mere Green, just down the road from my flat. Then there was Chris Waldron of Roberts & Brain who left to set up as Brain & Waldron. I rather liked that, it was a bit cheeky and clever!

Ian Hazel's departure from the huge firm of A Hazel caused the most fall out. Hazels were conducting approximately 1,200 funerals a year. Ian left within six weeks. I can't say I blame him, he had inherited the ruddy-faced panicker Brian Phillips as his Senior Manager and Ian was not amused. Within four weeks of Ian's new venture opening, Howard instructed JBT to see what properties were available in Mere Green; we were going to meet him head on.

The situation regarding the Mere Green property came up weekly at the Monday management meeting at Head Office. Howard was there with Graham Hodson and JBT. Velma always went along with Beryl Smith and by now Jeff Hickman had joined in the fray. Nick Denslow would be there for finance and I was there to report on Vehicles, Stock and other bits and bobs. The slightest mention of Mere Green by Howard brought JBT's flailing arms across his forehead with style. It had become a bit of a standing joke. But the saddest part was that the subsequent property acquisition, refurbishment, opening (and shutting a year later) could have all been avoided by a little more diplomacy from the Hodgson empire. It was conceivable that Ian was going to set up on his own anyway, but these set backs damaged the numbers and got the management team tied down in quite ridiculous battles over territory and funeral numbers. Having said that it always livened up the weekly meeting so from that point of view they were good news.

Dennis Amiss who had been hired by Howard to buy funeral businesses was now becoming highly successful, though not popular amongst the other directors. To Dennis' credit he had been given few, if any guidelines and it didn't matter to him whether we paid £30 or £30 million for the same business. If the business was conducting 250 funerals a year, then he would receive £2 per funeral, so £500. The fact that the prices we were paying were now ridiculous didn't overly concern him and his push for ever more firms to meet and do deals with meant we were burning through all the money we had been allotted, but nobody told us to stop!

I occasionally got out and about to see people, though they all felt rather short changed the minute they saw me get out of the car and not Dennis, it was a case of poor relations really. I went to the Lake District, Scotland and Cardiff where I saw the hilariously funny Pidgeon brothers who were just like Laurel and Hardy, in stature, looks and it has to be said, entertainment value. They had developed some sort of bizarre hatred for Howard. After an interesting thirty minute conversation during which James (the fat one) complained that Howard was a prat because he used Ford hearses and not Daimlers. I returned to my car seriously wondering whether or not they had let the tyres down.

There were a few successes, I saw funeral directors in Bromley, which we eventually bought and then had the most surreal weekend with John Weir (nicknamed John Weird by our local funeral directors) as we discussed the options of buying his business. I remember an evening dinner at Chilston Park where all the main house lights are turned off at night and the place is lit with candles. I recall being served Calamari which tasted like rubber bands and becoming quite close to John as we chatted about funerals, Howard and acquisitions. In the end John didn't sell his business but expanded and has probably forgotten all about the precocious twenty something that turned up on a mission to get a foothold in Kent!

I tried quite hard to get out and about and see the businesses that were in rather nicer areas, hence Scotland, the Lake District etc., but was often rumbled by Dennis. I then despatched Dennis to Hartlepool (where in my defence he bought a firm called Mason & Martin conducting 750 funerals a year) and Clacton-on-Sea where he met the terribly posh and delightfully mannered Jeff Titford and purchased Titford Funeral Service. A number of years later Jeff became a Conservative MP and I could see him doing that very well indeed, a very nice man!

For some unknown reason, Howard once again took leave of his senses and sent JBT to Guernsey to meet Pitcher and Le Quesne. Peter Pitcher was the funeral director on Guernsey and made rather a lot of it. JBT being JBT couldn't wait to get out of there with the details of the business taken down. He wouldn't have done it in a Dennis way, with a long drawn out dinner and all the flirting and fluttered eyelashes that Dennis employed. He would have said "Right, tell us how many funerals you are doing and I'll phone you next week with a price." Diplomatic and sensitive JBT wasn't.

JBT asked me once to drop him into Birmingham City centre. If I remember correctly he couldn't drive, Joan was away for the week and he needed to get to his hairdressers in deepest Digbeth. Now if you know Birmingham you will know that Digbeth is more than a little rough. Now it has the Irish quarter, and yes, the revitalised Custard Factory, but this was many years before they had even been thought of and Bird's were still churning out their eponymous product from the building and not music and fashion. I dropped him off, circled the block and literally within five minutes, he was out. JBT had what I called a "Bobby Charlton", that is generally bald, with a wisp of hair over the top. The hairdressers were J Page, many years later I was to meet the owner of this firm in much changed circumstances. Don, who I met whilst performing in Gilbert & Sullivan's "The Yeoman Of The Guard" remembered JBT fondly and how he was always on edge, panicking and looking terribly, terribly stressed. It was something that was to blight the appearance if not the life of JBT all the time I knew him!

Working with Dennis continued to be hugely entertaining. He had persuaded Howard that rather than forcing the potential acquisitions to watch the corporate video in the board room, Dennis could have a TV and show them the video in the luxury and comfort of his own office. Well it was a great wheeze from day one, Dennis still loved cricket and was always reluctant to miss a moment's play during the Test Matches. He developed a very good habit of watching the TV whilst I kept an eye open for Howard coming in the doorway.

One day I was finalising a visit to an important funeral director in Norwich, DG Barber, partially through a dare from Howard. I had contacted Graham Barber as he was the current President of the NAFD and was now thrilled to have got a positive response from my phone call…. Then Dennis shouted "Tim! Tim!" I dashed into his office expecting there to be something urgent.

"Look" said Dennis, "Gower's out, he played straight across the line!"… there were many such moments and I loved it. Dennis was the first one to not take Howard terribly seriously. He played the game as far as it went, but was never afraid to have the finest wines when dining with potential acquisitions and Ron Middleton would often blow a gasket when examining his expense claims. I used to really enjoy playing piggy-in-the-middle and sympathising with both Dennis and Ron and then talking to Howard about it, well you've got to take your amusement where you can!

Dennis liked being out of the office, he was born to travel and charm people, he was very good at it. He wasn't fussed about being in the office, except when he had to sign letters and catch up with other mail. But our system worked very well, he was out and about, I was in and in control (well most of the time). Dennis' writing was rather rapid and scrawly, he was tut-tutted by Mr Graham (whoops sorry Graham Hodson) on more than one occasion when we were trying to decipher his spidery scrawl.

The reality of being paid an excellent salary and a good commission was beginning to wear on some of the other directors. Ron Middleton didn't want to buy these firms, Graham Hodson was irritated that Dennis was getting more than him, the regional directors were irritated because "he wasn't a funeral director" and it was his acquisitions that were causing more work for them. Honestly I should have delivered a gross of handbags to them all and let them slug it out! I could see everyone's point of view, but Howard was clear that we had to acquire and of course the situation has been the same since acquisitions began. Upon acquisition you will lose market share and therefore you had to acquire more to replace the ones that you have lost. If you were to include all the funeral firms we ever bought up to 1990, then we should have been conducing about 45,000 funerals on an annual basis, instead we were doing about 38,000. So we were 7,000 funerals down, which would have been worth about £12 million at those prices of the day. This was to become known as the famous Hodgson black hole.

As I had been moved to work with Dennis, the role of Howard's PA had been given to a wonderful character called David Flett. We didn't know much about David when he came which made him all the more mysterious. We did gather he was an old army friend of Arthur Abraham and this was enough said, there were going to be some gems here for sure. He fitted into the culture quite well initially, as it was based a bit on bullying and threatening people, but he was so hopelessly disorganised! He used to try and speak pidgin French on the phone to Pompes Funerbres Generales and this caused utter hysterics as it was an open plan office and we all got to hear him strangling the death out of the language. On more than one occasion, desperately using an old phrase book, he referred to

Howard's housekeeper not as a nurse, but as a nudist, and when trying to tie up a major coffin deal informed the wholesale arm of PFG that he had high regard for their "large logs". Hearses were called "Coffin Trains" and he, like Ron McAllister, was not terribly organised with his phone list and was continually getting peoples names and office locations mixed up and ran a very confused desk. It was just like having Officer Crabtree in the building and so we used to greet him with a cheerful "Good Moaning!" He had not one ounce of a sense of humour and all the time he was there I don't think he had a clue we were taking the mick. He was in his mid-forties, clearly had a sense of order from the army (I didn't ever find out what regiment he had been in, but we safely assumed it was not the SAS) but no social graces, nor any ability to be close enough to people to win friends. I passed on all the information I had which didn't take too long and he was left to well flounder really… but again it was so entertaining. You see David, a little like Arthur, had a rather inflated sense of his own importance, he referred to himself as "Mr Flett", one of my pet hates. It was just not done, I had been taught by my father at an early age to announce yourself with your name and let people give you the title. Arthur did the same, it grated on me and I know it also irritated people like Jeff Hickman who knew how these things were done.

Chapter 14

The Ever Moving Budget

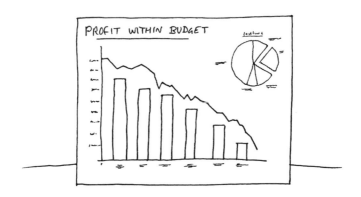

1984 was the first time I met Graham Hodson when he arrived at SA Evans to supervise the takeover of the firm. The plan was that I would work there for two weeks with him and then be left to get on with it on my own (they were very trusting people you see).

I completely failed to fathom Graham Hodson in all the years I knew him. As Churchill said about Russia "a riddle, wrapped in a mystery, inside an enigma". He was certainly that and more. Shy and a particularly good foil for Howard, but I couldn't ever work out what it was he actually did. Years later when I was working with him at Head Office, he used to keep a tightly organised (he was certainly organised) filing cabinet and in it was all the details on funeral directors we had agreed to buy. But it always seemed so slow, and Graham was most reluctant to advance you, give you some slack, trust you or get you working with him. Some of the managers and directors called him Mr Graham and this was nervously upgraded to

Graham in a rather high and squeaky voice when they became directors. But in early 1986, I decided I would call him Mr Hodson and leave it at that. Saying "Mr Graham" was a bit poncy really and didn't flow off my tongue. He gave the impression of being cool and suave, but it was clear he was in awe of Howard. One day he had to cancel a day out shooting just because Howard had said so, he was unhappy about it and I was taken with the fact that he didn't query it. It was ridiculous in my view, but he just let it go.

He was very kind to me though, and I remember having the hots for one of his daughters. Amber I think it was, or was it Abbie? She did have the most beautifully warm brown eyes. Hi Amber, you are probably fifty now!! Anyway, Graham worked fairly closely with me at Bradley & Sons in Manchester. One night asked me to go and collect my new car from his place in Stafford. I had finally graduated from a run down Ford Escort to a new Ford Fiesta – very snazzy! Although it wasn't exactly a car which would pull in the women, it was very nice to have a new one! A reward for my hard work? Probably. It was also nice staying overnight in his Home & Gardens house in Stafford and then driving back up the motorway in this new beast. His wife Wendy was particularly kind in a motherly way!

By now, Howard was having severe difficulty in getting any sense out of the numbers presented to him daily by Ron Middleton. All the time he complained that the figures didn't seem right or were down on his annualised expectations. To each query, we got the reply from Ron "Well, we are on budget" and that seemed to ease Howard's concern. It took a good six months before the Finance Department admitted that each month they would revise the budget downwards! So we had in fact an ever moving budget which moved in line with whatever the latest fall in numbers were. Most funeral firms we owned were losing numbers and the pattern was repeated throughout the country. I'm only sorry I was in Scotland the day Howard found out what had happened. But did anyone's head roll? No. That is the sadness of it, perhaps if they had then we wouldn't have ended up in the mess were to end up in almost twelve months later. Sandy Fraser (to come) and I still chortle at length about the "ever moving budget".

There were still comical moments that I had begun to milk for all they were worth. One Friday, Howard told me that a Mr William Fanagan from Dublin needed collecting from Birmingham International Airport with his brother, on Monday. This was a significant potential acquisition of perhaps 2,000 funerals. I made a note and thought no more about it until I got to the airport on Monday and realised I didn't have the largest of cars. Of course, William Fanagan was built like Big Daddy and seeing him and his equally ample brother squeeze into the Ford Fiesta was a farce which must have been hugely enjoyable to the casual observer. I knew before we even started that we would not make this acquisition; first impressions count for so much. Even now I recall David Fanagan's head pressed tightly against the roof and the pained expression on his face as I trundled the car into first gear and started the fifteen mile journey back to Plantsbrook House... another day, another dollar!

And then there was of course the love affair with SCI. The Service Corporation International was the single largest provider of funeral services in the world, conducting some 250,000 funerals, five times what we were doing at this stage. Howard had persuaded SCI to come over to the UK, have some hospitality and talk about how they could work together. So, a few weeks later, Buddy Hunter (don't you just love that name?) and Kyle Guinn, Chairman and Chief Operating Officer respectively, were jammed in the back of Howard's XJS as I picked them up from Birmingham International Airport. I liked them tremendously. There was an aura about them, they were streets ahead of any crackpot director we had employed. I have always liked Americans and I think I managed to name drop Wilber Krieger into one of my wackier conversations with Kyle Guinn. They appeared to breeze along, secure in their own skin. Why, for a couple of days I envisaged myself stowing away with them and vanishing to America for a year or two to further my own career. They were staying at the Plough & Harrow, once a byword for style and elegance in Birmingham city centre, but now having seen better days. I joined them for breakfast one morning as they discussed the industry and the rationalisation going on in it.

They stayed for about a week, just long enough to deduce that we were an excellent target for their brash acquisitive policy. I fawned around them and was entrusted with the sacred job of delivering them back to catch their plane.

They came back into the game a few weeks later when they agreed to provide the funds to dig us out of a hole. We were to sell them 9% for a goodly sum, until the phone call came. Kyle Guinn had called Howard direct one afternoon to say that SCI's share price had collapsed for no significant reason (they were quoted on the NYSE) and that they now needed the funds to buy their own shares to support the share price.

Sandy Fraser had joined us from Philips & Drew, he had got his teeth into the cash flows and they showed, not surprisingly, that with the funds we had already committed to agreed acquisitions, we were going to run out funds in a few months. It really was dire straits! Then Dennis came to the fore. He convinced Howard to let him have a day off to play golf, under the pretence that he would be able to make some helpful contacts there. Howard made the most of this, mocking, laughing and making sure people knew exactly what he thought. Dennis left, I ran the office on my own for the day, and that was that.

So now, in Howard and Hodgson's hour of need, Dennis said, "What about speaking to John Gunn at British & Commonwealth Holdings?" B&C were a small bank, lending in high risk situations. Dennis had of course met John at the golf day, as was Dennis' charm he could make the contacts very quickly and then use them to great effect later.

So it transpired that only four weeks after Dennis' golf game, B&C came up with the readies to allow us to carry on trading. Not long after that B&C went into administration. Many years later I spoke to John Gunn as I tried to raise funds during a similarly dire situation, although the funds involved were not nearly as high!

Through all this, acquisitions of small funeral homes, and the loss of Dottridge Brothers, Howard continued to look long term. He was immensely focused, as only he could be, on his plan to take over Kenyons. It was always referred to as a 'merger' but in reality it was a hostile takeover. It had been plotted over twelve months and came to fruition the moment Michael Kenyon was on holiday. It was the product of greed, ambition and an awful lot of business sense.

Ever since 1986, Hodgsons ran at a nett profit margin of 17%. Great Southern's was 11% and Kenyon's a paltry 6%. What everyone wanted was Hodgson & Kenyon's numbers under Hodgsons management style and to deliver the same resulting percentage nett profit. The shareholders were the key as they would get a much higher return than they had done previously.

There was many a phone call with the wonderfully named Herve Racine of Societe Generale Bank. With Pompes Funerbres Generales (PFG) owning such a high concentration of Kenyon shares, Howard only had to get hold of their agreement and the merger would be binding. Of course this had all come about since the Dottridge acquisition. Kenyon's had funded it through selling shares to PFG who now owned 25% of their enlarged company. PFG seemed to have cash to spare and were happy to have fingers in English funeral pies.

PFG were 25% owned by the French water company Lyonnaise Des Eaux and were rapidly increasing their market share through expansion in France and now in Britain. It was PFG who had invested several million pounds into Kenyon's when they were looking for the money to buy Dottridge Bros, but having lost 25% of their company it proved to be a big mistake.

Howard always liked everything French. His wife, the cigarettes, the language, the holidays in the South of France and the directors from Societe Generale and PFG. Through Societe Generale and then Credit Lyonnaise, he opened up talks with PFG explaining his plan for a joint bid to merge Kenyon and Hodgson, with of course, Howard as Chief Executive.

It was extremely ambitious, but very sensible. The merger would offer huge head office savings and other cost centred savings. The main problem was that the management infrastructure wasn't there to cope with it, it was lazy, over ambitious and not sharp enough. We were playing with the big boys in terms of turnover and stock market listing, but we had managers and directors which quite frankly weren't up to running a small stationery company in Handsworth let alone the largest funeral directors in the United Kingdom.

When it was announced Howard sat on the left and Michael sat on the right of Claude Pierre Brosellette, the new chairman of Pompes Funerbres Hodgson Kenyon International. Howard had been asked by the French to be quieter at the press conference than he would have normally been, but of course Howard was Howard (and I confess to have loved him for this). The opening statements had been made and a Daily Mail journalist said "What worries me is the Hodgson valuation in all of this." Howard snapped back with "What worries ME, Michael is every time we make a statement you say What worries you, well if what worries you is the share valuation, then perhaps if you had not spent the last year mocking the Hodgson share price, then you wouldn't have to ask that question!" Then swinging the microphone over to himself, "Ah, yes, you in the blue tie – name and question please?"

He was a class act, but then he deserved it really. He had created a mega business through merger and acquisition. But what would happen now? Michael Kenyon looked bemused and the French embarrassed by the bad behaviour of the British press, Howard was on a roll.

We didn't ever see dear old Claude. He was clearly a figurehead who was designed to be the foil between Michael and Howard at the potentially prickly press conference. He was a respected French businessman who had been awarded the Legionne D'Honneur and what he knew about funerals could have been written on the side of one of the smallest coffin plates possible. So post press conference, he flew back to Paris and it was business as normal in the chaotic world of mergers and acquisitions.

None of us knew what the next few months would bring, but they were to be the most glorious months I had ever spent in the company of such funeral directors and people of Howard's empire. The months were to be fun filled, incredibly exciting, and hugely entertaining. They were to be memorable times, I would see situations I would never forget and be involved in the most ridiculous of projects. It was time to get the silliness to a new level.

Part of the problem was that although the merger had been initiated by Howard and the French, whilst a funeral was a funeral, there were many differences in culture, social graces and styles and it would be a long time before these were to be anywhere near reconciled.

In France between the hours of twelve and two the whole country stops for a lunch. And this is not an exaggeration. Workers down tools, shops firmly fasten their shutters and all retail outlets will say Ferme. They are obsessed with their food and the board directors who came to England were shocked. Firstly by the lack of decent coffee, and then by the lack of decent food. It was at times, almost like working with another species of human it was that bad!

I got talking to Ken Millard and Des Lee about the French in general, and explained that many French people ate horse, they thought that I was having them on. It was a completely strange situation. If we had a meeting or buffet lunch arranged one of us had to leg it down to the nearest cake shop for pastries and sandwiches. The French would examine the food critically and put it down again disdainfully. It would not be long before the differences in tradition and habit started to show in the way we practised running our funeral homes as well.

What I failed to comprehend until many years later was that the French had actually played Howard along and Howard had gone straight into their lair. They were no fools and were not going to have their enlarged investment business run by this nutcase. They had a strategic plan for people like Jean Neveau and also one for Howard and neither of them had a future in the enlarged empire.

You see, PFG had planned all along that once the merger was in place they would bring their own man in to run the empire. They were disorganised but had much more experience in running larger firms than Howard and his merry men. They clearly saw (through Neveau's daily ramblings) that the numbers would work together, that there were huge savings to be made, but that the management would have to be sorted out by them.

Chapter 15

The Board and the bored

My first view of Sandy Fraser was when I was showed him around Plantsbrook House one afternoon. I had the job of greeting people who were coming to have lunch with Howard. This was quite entertaining, although I must have had a huge sense of my own importance, with my dark glasses and city set get up. Quite frankly I must have looked a complete prat. But this was a huge education for me, no particular job description, but the ability to waffle and meet anyone. A skill indeed, which Howard rewarded pretty well; I was earning £18,000 a year and had a very nice company car and car phone (they were rather cutting edge in those days).

Sandy was working for Phillips and Drew in the city. Howard had encountered him while on a fund raising exercise and persuaded him to head up the corporate finance division of the company. Sandy was quite young and worked with Russell, Howard's brother, in the city. Sandy didn't move from London, but commuted from London by train. He was going to make quite a difference to my life, but I had little idea at the beginning.

Sandy was different, right from the start there was a quiet confidence about him. He spoke slowly and was deliberate about what he said, not a tall man, he flew under Howard's radar and got involved, I recall, as the only one with a modicum of common sense. For a while he and I worked on discounted cash flows, budgets split into different departments, and other mad-cap Howard instigated projects which Sandy would try to wriggle and worm his way out of, normally to no avail. He also had a great sense of humour, something that was always sadly lacking at Head Office. Everyone was terribly serious. Dennis liked a joke but was careful as he protected his position with a watchful eye, and there was no one else who would really let their hair down. Sandy was on my wavelength from day one and we got on very well. I knew he was good at his job; I hope he realised and saw that I was rather good at mine, but we ruthlessly mocked the people who were getting it terribly, terribly wrong (in our opinion of course)!

Sandy had been successful at Phillips and Drew the stockbrokers, despite being named as a third man in the Blue Arrow affair where his boss got beaten up with a big City stick due to insider trading. Many years later when I stayed with Sandy in Scotland with his delightful but mad family he pulled out a press cutting where one morning he had been photographed by the paparazzi from behind the hedge as the scandal broke. Never a dull moment was there? His son, who was probably only twelve then said "Why didn't you go to prison then Dad?"

Ronald Middleton had been appointed by Howard to the crucial position of Finance Director of Holdings a not insubstantial responsibility. He was a short man, on his first day I made him coffee and made small talk. There was something about the cut of his suit that didn't inspire me, a sort of short David Bonham. He didn't smoke granted, but there wasn't a confident dash (as there always was with Graham Hodson or Eric Butler) and I suspected this was going to be a very interesting appointment. Well, soon after Ron joined the board, Sandy Fraser was called up and at one monumental meeting, Ron said to Sandy "I just can't work out where all the cash is going!" Sandy asked about the company's cash flows. "Oh" said Ron, "that's a good idea!" It summed us all up really. We were belting along with money flowing freely, from director's Jags to huge acquisitions, and no one had given an iota of thought to the simple hard-nosed business fact that most businesses go bust simply because they run out of cash! A company can make losses or profits, but this is all totally irrelevant if they're out of cash at a given moment.

It appeared these cash flow scales had fallen off Middleton's eyes, so the juniors in the finance department were tasked to produce figures that made some sort of sense to the ever bewildered Middleton. To be fair to the old chap, he didn't have a hope really. On more than one occasion when asked for his opinion, Howard retorted with "Oh what do you know, you've never been a Funeral Director!" He was totally and utterly out of his depth and even to a finance novice like me it showed.

The sad thing is that Howard had done so well to a point, to save the family firm from liquidation, to take a company to the Unlisted Securities Market and raise millions of pounds, to return the best profit per funeral in the sector… he was right, most of the time. I'd had problems with vicars in the early days who didn't like that their Church Fee now came from Birmingham rather than cash in hand. Nor did they appreciate that in most of the acquisitions Howard had significantly improved the business and the capital equipment. There was still the feeling of mistrust and this was very unfair.

A minister had once said to Howard that, as a large business, Hodgsons couldn't possibly give the same level of service as the smaller independent ones. Howard asked why, and the vicar blathered on about impersonal organisations, local figureheads, the understanding of tradition and impossibility of control. Howard, totally unfazed, asked if the vicar gave a good service to his parishioners. "Of course!" replied the vicar. "But" said Howard, "you don't own your parish, or your building and you are part of the largest organisation in the United Kingdom, it is no different from you!"

One of the abiding memories of the time was the look of total bemusement on Ron Middleton's face as he discovered another black hole in the company finances or another dynamic wheeze that would leak cash. One of the more classic involved the cash being paid for acquisitions. There was one funeral director in Denbigh, Ivor Howatson, and we had somehow agreed (Dennis must have got Howard on a good day) to purchase the business for £525,000. The funeral home was conducting about 125 funerals at the time, the price was insane! As the day for exchanging contracts came nearer Middleton's face got redder and the whole affair was beginning to look like the famous Kennedy Khrushchev face down. In the end we didn't ever buy dear old Ivor's business, and for just a day Ron must have breathed a little easier. At least, until the next crackpot scheme was discovered.

One of them was not so much a scheme or scam, but a glorious misunderstanding that caused a cash leak for several years. Every firm we purchased had it's own fleet of vehicles. These would usually be surplus because of rationalisation or we would upgrade them. We programmed in new vehicles, and this was a substantial cost as at the time a new hearse or limousines were about £30,000.

Graham Hodson had done a deal with Bob Grey of Glenfrome Engineering. He agreed to take all our old vehicles en masse. This was good news as it meant we didn't have to faff about finding the best value for them, we had got better things to do like sort out the funeral home we had just acquired. It was only after six months of this policy that Howard asked to see where the income from the vehicles was being shown and Graham Hodson confessed that the money wasn't being passed over by Bob until he had actually sold the vehicles. Howard was not amused, there were many letters back and forth, at one stage there was about £100,000 outstanding to Hodgsons on vehicles that we had paid for, then sold to Bob Grey and not yet received the money. It was a bit of a shambles, but then things like this happened on a daily basis, it was all most amusing if you were outside of it.

I remember being intrigued that Ron seemed to be constantly surprised by everything. The finance director is a pretty important guy in a public company, yet he had working for him Nick Denslow, a man who was never the tallest, but would look smaller every day as the ever increasing things he took on his plate seemed to cover his huge desk. He had made a bit of a name for himself. Nick was a lovely man, but he couldn't run a bath let alone a department of finance where the figures had always been hard to ascertain. Nick had two guys working for him, leftovers from the Ingalls days, and Howard had relocated them to Sutton Coldfield. Ken Millard and Des Lee (who came every day from Derbyshire in a three hour round trip) slaved away at numbers trying to make sense of the merged figures. Both Ken and Des were nice guys and very sweet to me, but they didn't have the drive that a number of the Hodgson team did. They were both much older. Ken must have been late fifties and Des was about sixty-four, although he looked so much like Lurch from the Addams Family, he could easily have passed for eighty.

So here was dear Nick, attempting to make sense of the numbers that had suddenly increased from 5,600 funerals to 24,500 funerals and not having a huge amount of success. Nick had to deal with the wrapping up of the old limited companies we had bought, the collection of debts and payment of the creditors from the same. This also involved preparing accounts for each of the limited companies as they were entities in their own right, papers were arriving and leaving (although more arrived than left) on an hourly basis and Nick was the perfect example of someone who worked the longest hours possible, but didn't ever seem to achieve what he had set out to do that day. He was a hard worker, but could not seem to focus himself or his colleagues on delivering the results that were needed. I saw it and noted it, but thankfully I worked alone and only ever had myself to blame.

Nick was a dear chap, as kind as the day is long. I will always be grateful to him since he lent me his car one weekend as mine was in the garage when I needed to get back home to Cardiff. He still remained a friend even after I reported to him that the head gasket had seemingly blown on the way back to Birmingham. What a dear friend. But Nick was symptomatic of people at Head Office, all running around like the proverbial headless chickens with no organised plan as to what to do next. The ball kept moving, it was never still, but much of this was Howard's fault. He just couldn't leave people to get on with things, already notorious for interfering and fiddling about, he had created a culture that resulted in a mess and this was never going to help in ascertaining his financial position on such a fast moving company.

Sandy was truly the bright spark amongst a whole compost heap of Yes Men. He was never afraid to front up to Howard on some of the more bizarre schemes. The main protagonist in all this was a character who will live with me to my grave, he was quite extraordinary, one Jean Neveau.

When Pompes Funerbres Generales took a stake in Hodgsons they quite rightly demanded a seat on the board. Howard had comprised a junior board called Hodgson & Sons Ltd who were supposed to run the funeral operations, but they were staffed by a bunch of the most incompetent nitwits you could ever find. Even now, people's names are familiar to me, Arthur Abraham, Ken Purdy, Clive Summerscales, all of them dearly kind men and undoubtedly excellent funeral directors, but they had all been catapulted to levels of compete incompetence.

So, the plan was that Hodgson Holdings board would run the holdings company, making decisions on acquisitions, finance and general policy. Hodgson & Sons Ltd would run the funeral directing side. Of course it was flawed, most of the decisions that were made at that time were, and we were playing with a lot of money. In 1990, the year before I left, PHK turned over £100 million, a lot of money by any one's standard.

So, as these characters struggled to read balance sheets and generally had meetings for the sake of meetings, this was the period when Howard really started to lose it. He would have been far better off getting JBT to have all the reporting (at least you knew exactly where you were with him as he never minced words) and getting Johnny Mac to go and check that no bearers were drunk on the funerals and the Hearse Drivers were not past the age of eighty.

But this is of course all fine with hindsight. Howard felt it incumbent upon himself to explain how many of the managers and directors had come from humble beginnings and this all looked extremely good on paper. In practice it meant we had lost exceptionally good funeral directors and made them into completely incompetent managers. We would not be the first nor the last to do such a thing, it is a pretty classic management cock-up. People who had demonstrated they were rubbish in a position just stayed there as they weren't good enough to gain a promotion and so they stayed put! This wasn't ever going to change. Many years later when I spoke to Sinclair Beecham about Pret a Manger it was discovered that Pret had done a similar thing. All their great sandwich makers had been promoted to managers, predictably they had lost their best sandwich makers and inherited shitty managers. Who stayed there in that position which did not help anyone.

There was a department that did however manage to acquire many of the cast offs (funeral directors who had drink problems, managers who has been caught nicking) and that was the gloriously titled Capital & Revenue Department. Amongst all the monkeys working there I only ever had time for two. Jeff Hickman, who was an acquisition from Ingalls, clearly head and shoulders above most of the directors on the main board. The other was Pat Ramage (both I hasten to add not there for any of the afore mentioned misdemeanours) known locally as Pat Rampage for her brusque no nonsense style.

I liked Pat. She was straight to the point and extremely likeable. We got on very well and I continued to see her from time to time when she popped into Hudson's and had coffee. It was clear she was a grafter and had the intelligence to go with it; hers was not an easy task. She had the unenviable job of credit control. It was customary for all funeral directors to give credit, back when the company was a small affair with the culture

227

of Derek "Few Outstanding Accounts" Tyler flowing, we were well on top of cash flow. If anyone criticized Howard for late payments to suppliers he responded that whatever we owed them was vastly outweighed by the £100,000 owed to us. I was never sure if it was actually true or just Howard spin.

Now with the enlarged business, the credit situation was coming home to roost. In addition we were taking on credit in much poorer areas, and areas where people didn't think twice about ripping off the local funeral director. Whereas Hereford was rather an upright town, with most of our clients having plenty of money, some of the suburbs of Hackney, Clapham and Liverpool struggled to repay the debts as quickly as we would have liked. Pat was sweet really, and did an incredibly difficult job, she relished the nickname Rampage and indeed rampaged around Head Office trying to sort out these miscreant credit controllers called funeral directors. It would have been better to have specialists dealing with the account after fourteen days had lapsed. It was reasonable for the funeral director that had conducted the funeral to phone the family, after all this is the system I had employed to great success in Hereford. But at Ashton Ebbutt, the way they ran the business meant the Funeral Directors rarely saw the family until the funeral and so didn't build up any sort of relationship with them which made it much harder to collect the money.

Jeff Hickman had moved from his office at Ingall Industries to work with us at Sutton Coldfield and he had kept his company Jaguar. Clearly the product of a different generation, he was clever enough to play Howard, defer to him when need be and say the right things to the right people to get by. But Jeff was no mug and taught me more there in six months than I had learnt in twelve with Derek. He was extremely well organised, spoke correctly and worked very hard until late at night, he was not going to be accused by anyone of slacking.

Jeff made time for me. We played golf, chatted at length and he shared a number of his very private business thoughts with me. Jeff also taught me how to read a balance sheet, what a star! Jeff was very popular, he was known by everyone as a very lovely man. He would have been an ideal choice for a non-executive and would have probably stopped Howard going down silly routes on a number of occasions. It was disappointing to me that when Jeff retired, Howard did not see fit to hand him his old company Jaguar car. The banger must have only been worth £2,000 and Jeff had earned this mark of gratitude, yet Howard remained the hard man. A pity, as Jeff was one of the good guys and he deserved better treatment at the end of his time with us!

He died not long after he retired, old and full of years. I can still see his scrawling handwriting now explaining how balance sheets worked to my small, but nevertheless enquiring brain.

Vehicles were flying about the company now with gay abandon. Howard and Graham had a new Jaguar XJS every year. The vehicles were top of the range with leather seats and dark blue piping, car phones already installed (which were still a bit of a novelty) and the finest cassette player and radio, all very smart. I didn't complain as I got to pick them up from the Evans Halshaw garage in Birmingham city centre. Howard's vehicle one year was a soft top Cabriolet and I posed all the way back from Birmingham with the roof down. I was very cool and slick, until that is when the day was over and I had to return to my little light blue Ford Fiesta in the car park. All the directors had Jaguars, Dennis a XJ6, Ron Middleton an XJS (complete with the number plate RAM 102 from a previous funeral home acquisition) and the Hodgson & Sons Ltd Directors all had Jaguar saloons. It was all part of a brand building exercise, which perhaps in one sense had its value, but also its detractors.

The exercise was carried to its extreme when Howard appointed the Hodgson & Sons Ltd board of directors who were supposed to run the funeral directing side of things. This was known all over to be a huge giggle exercise. The only guy on the board that had the clout or the self confidence to shine was David Hendry, who moved over a couple of months later to the new one called Caledonian Funeral Services. The other people on the board were just very good funeral arrangers or funeral directors. Arthur Abraham would have gone through fire for Howard, he was always clear about that and Harvey Ewart was always heard to be saying that he owed Howard all he had. Howard had pulled many of these people up by their bootstraps. Whilst it worked very well with people who were terribly committed and prepared to work hard, you had to have some modicum of understanding about business and how to run such an expanding company. It just didn't sit together at all, they would come up for the whole day, faff about in the boardroom on fairly meaningless reports, have lunch (which I had to get from the local sandwich shop) and then have coffee and drive home in their Jaguars.

There are some things in life I will never understand, how to put up a shelf so it doesn't collapse, why some people enjoy explaining the intricacies of computers and Scottish men who wear kilts. However if you were into funeral directing, then there was a stage worse than this; Scottish men who wear kilts to Embalming Conferences. I mean, let's get a grip here, Funeral Directing conferences I can just about understand, but a conference for the British Institute of Embalmers? Subject matter rather limited I would have thought. Of course nowadays the word embalming is not referred to, all sorts of wonderful euphemisms are used including my all time favourite Hygienic Treatment. What embalming actually does in laymans terms is take out the foul liquids of a dead body and replace it with disinfectant. It's obviously a bit more complicated than that, involving instruments that could have graced any top surgeons Christmas wish list, but in a nutshell that is what is achieved. It has its unfortunate mythical links with the Egyptians, although what they did was vastly more complicated. They decided to really go to town and remove all the internal organs (including the brain) and replace them with sheets or sawdust. Nothing like that happens in a modern embalming.

Steve Gauld was indeed one of those men, Scottish through and through, who seized the opportunity to wear a kilt to these conferences and always did so with a sparkle in his eye. I thought this rather strange. He worked at Head Office and had an open home to whichever crackpot appeared in the office that week that needed to stay overnight. Steve and his wife Ann were legendary hosts, they appeared to have an unlimited supply of small talk for these occasions, although I wondered if it wasn't recycled somewhat. So, wacky Norwegian Funeral Director thinking of selling his funeral homes? Overnight at Steve Gauld's. New regional manager in the area who hadn't quite got accommodation sorted yet? Steve Gauld. SCI Executive to experience great British (well Scottish) hospitality? Steve Gauld. And so it went on. Steve Gauld seemed to have an insatiable appetite for entertaining, I rarely spoke to his wife so could never unfortunately get her angle on it!

Steve had been acquired when Howard had revisited the House Of Fraser/ CWS Monopolies & Mergers Commission and agreed to purchase Wylie & Lochead, a group of funeral homes in the North of Scotland. There was a line being touted around by Howard at the time, he realised he needed to keep what goodwill he had in the North and wouldn't be able to achieve it himself, so he told them "We are acquiring you, but you are getting Steve Gauld as well." By all accounts it kept them happy. So armed with this latest acquisition from the CWS's scraps table, Steve duly arrived at Sutton Coldfield and set up yet another directors office from where he could control his Scottish kingdom. He was always immaculately turned out, crisp double cuff shirts, smart suits, a well-creased moustache and a ready smile for anyone that dared cross the Scottish border. But I also couldn't help thinking that he wasn't the brightest button on the block, just a feeling that he lacked drive and …not ambition, most of the people we saw at Head Office were extremely ambitious. But not driven or hugely enthusiastic, unless it was for wearing a kilt at an embalming conference.

Chapter 16

"Ha Ha!"

So, anyway back to Jean Neveau. In my naivety I had assumed that when PFG took such a crucial stake in a large company they would send a cautious, upright and sensible man to be guardian of their stake. Not so. Jean Neveau was quite the most completely insane individual I had ever met, I revered him for three weeks, then was tickled by some of his more absurd suggestions for a further two weeks, the scales fell from my eyes on the next two weeks and thereafter I was desperately trying to get away from him as the mere sight of him reduced me to helpless giggles. He once brought a board meeting to a complete standstill when he suggested we should buy a boat, moor it at Poole and scatter ashes from it as "ze English zey are a maritime nation".

It probably didn't help that he looked like Heinrich Himmler and Howard had already christened him thus when he arrived. Short and with small excitable eyes framed by little round glasses, he was to be the biggest source of entertainment to me and my fertile mind in the last years of the empire.

Talking of giggles, Sandy Fraser was the worst. We had an appointment at Philips & Drew in Moorgate to discuss funding of crematoria. We had been looking at this project for a number of months, with a potential crematorium at Hinckley, Leicestershire as residents of that town currently had to use Nuneaton Crematorium, which was a good twenty-five miles away. Cremation Fees were rising and Howard saw a good opportunity that was already being exploited by PFG and now we were looking for a slice of the action.

We were told the night before that Jean Neveau had to come with us to make the presentation (probably because Howard was desperate to keep him away from another important meeting). We were mortified, Sandy and I knew that we would end up in a heap of giggles. Now bear in mind this was a presentation involving millions of pounds of company money, but we weren't worried about the points of the meeting. No, we were worried that a fellow director would cause us to embarrass ourselves!

It was always difficult working with Jean Neveau as he would get us giggling, but it was okay as long as you could furtively giggle whilst there were other things to deflect attention from you. Sandy and I knew two things, firstly that we would be on edge anyway, and secondly that our presentation to Philips & Drew needed to make bold statements about cash flow, income streams, asset based and revenue. These guys were from the city and did not want their long lunches sullied by talk of ashes, deaths and bodies, we knew that they knew that we knew that they knew we knew, but no one had told Jean Neveau. And now we knew it was all going to collapse around us like a deck of cards, in one way or another (and probably in all honesty in both ways), Jean would say the wrong thing, have us in fits of giggles and scupper the whole proposal. Why oh why was he coming?

Sandy and I met in the huge marble foyer of the building and walked up to the reception desk. "Uhhh Sandy Fraser and Tim Penrose here for the Crematoria presentation" Sandy declared.

"Are you expecting anyone else for the meeting?" the Receptionist asked. Sandy tried so hard to say the words Jean Neveau, but he failed, he collapsed in giggles as the words spluttered out. He apologised but I knew, we were doomed and we hadn't even set eyes on the man!

We recovered, still tense, and after ten minutes in we were hoping perhaps Jean Neveau wouldn't make it. We accelerated our presentation and then... a knock on the door. The little froggy glasses and excitable eyes arrived with an Adidas bag.

"Ha Ha" (He started all his sentences like this) "I 'ave something in my bag here for you" – it was getting worse – "'tis a little ashes casket. I have a little columbarium." It was curtains, we snorted and giggled our way through the presentation. I couldn't see Sandy's face, he was covering it with his papers, but I knew what was going on, the paper was shaking and shivering every second. And all the time Jean was oblivious, smoking his Galois ciggies and saying "Ha ha" every five minutes. It was like a bad Peter Sellers movie. It was without a doubt the most uncontrollable emotion of my life. I will never forget it.

And yet, perhaps it now all makes sense. If PFG had a completely insane director that caused all meetings to turn hitherto formal and upright executives into exploding giggling little boys out of control, then wouldn't you pack him off to the UK and get into someone else's hair? Perhaps they were not so stupid after all.

235

I found myself on a train with Jean Neveau (cue giggles), Michael Kenyon and Michael Roscoe from Waterloo to Charles De Gaulle in Paris and then on the TGV to Nantes, all to look at a crematorium that Pompes Funerbres Generales owned. To this day I do not see what was achieved by going out there, we all had rather a nice train ride and a jolly good French breakfast including one of the nicest espressos I have tasted in my life (lovely crema). Quite frankly one crematorium is much like another and despite the fact that the carpets were very clean and the brand new crematorium ovens shone, the reality of the situation was that it was very much like every other crematorium we had ever seen. We set off incredibly early, then had to double back as Jean had forgotten his passport which involved a huge faff back down the M42 in the middle of the rush hour. I was wondering whether we were going to make the train, but we got to Paris to take the TGV, and reached Nantes only seven hours after setting off. We wandered around the crematorium, made approving noises where we felt we should, stood in awe of the rather complicated booking system, stopped to see a cremation taking place in those bright new cremators and generally faffed about. It was yet another waste of a day. However the visit was memorable for one moment back at Plantsbrook House when Jean was explaining (once again to the wrong person in rather too much detail) how the crematorium at Nantes had this incredibly clever system which meant the family only had to choose numbers instead of titles for the hymns. For the life of me I cannot now understand how this was particularly ground breaking, but that was Jean for you.

His little froggie eyes lit up "Ha Ha, you zee, ze family zey have only to say ze numbers. We want number 12, number 4, number 5, and a number 7! Ha Ha!" The stockbroker remained completely unimpressed and just said "Ha Ha, and some prawn crackers." Of course this was totally lost on the French non-humour of Jean, but it was a joy to watch.

He was also famous in the company for forever talking about Columbariums. These were sections of the property like a walled chamber where ashes could be interred, rather than scattered in the garden of remembrance which brought no income. The families would receive the land in perpetuity and they would pay handsomely for it. It was just a combination of the accent, the way he called me "Timotei" which meant that whenever Jean mentioned the words "a little columbarium" he had us all falling about. This led to an internal competition to see who could get him on the subject as quickly as possible. It made the day go very quickly and he provided a huge amount of constant merriment.

One day, when Jean Neveau was ill, I was despatched at short notice to Inverness to tender for a crematorium. Of course I knew absolutely nothing about crematoria at the time. I was due to meet Gordon Webster whose firm we had just purchased in Aberdeen, I suspect he wondered what he had been lumbered with as I got off the plane. What was scheduled to be a meeting with three councillors turned into a full blown presentation with thirty-five councillors and some members of the public present. It was not one of my finest moments and I remember the plane ride home was as turbulent as the meeting.

Once, with Sandy and others egging me on, I spent part of the day telephoning the new Regional Managers pretending to be Jean with the mad froggy accent and dreaming up some completely crazy idea. It was always fascinating to see how they responded. Most of the time they were totally polite to even some of my wilder suggestions. I spoke to Peter Elms on his car phone and suggested we sold coffins with French flags on. Harvey Ewart to make the point that if we were careful we could use only two pall bearers on each coffin thus saving the company £2 million in costs and this would be fine as long as they were careful when lifting and putting down. Then there was the phone call to Michael Kenyon's son, Peter, telling him (posing as Jean Neveau) that he had spoken to "Timotei" and he thought I was a fool, and what did he think? It was all most amusing and fine but for the fact that I really should have been contributing towards running a large funeral company but I reckoned by now the writing was on the wall!

I also impersonated Howard's shirt maker, Jonathan Hart. I had met Howard's tailor on a few occasions, he had a little place down on Hagley Road in Edgbaston. He was charming and very funny, but very much the typical male tailor. Jonathan did make very beautiful shirts, they all had double cuffs of course and they were made of the finest Egyptian cotton. I can't remember why I decided to do it, just because I could I suppose, I had always enjoyed impersonating people (remember Don York?) I unfortunately got put through to Graham Hodson who rumbled me within a few minutes. He took it in good spirits though, I was quite surprised, most of the time he took everything very seriously. He was certainly shy and this amounted to people saying he was aloof, he wasn't really. I felt that Graham was very clever, he had an analytical mind and was the ideal foil to Howard, they had always got on very well but as the company got larger they, like many other characters in the group, just hadn't developed. And this malaise meant it had been passed on to other people in the company, there is no doubt in my mind that the culture from a large company comes down from the top. Just as a poor school will normally have a negative Headteacher, poor companies with a negative culture will have had it passed down through the ranks. It was clear this pattern would continue to repeat itself through the latter years of the Hodgson empire. Yet people like Graham had the opportunity to develop people who had a passion to get on, but they just seemed to want to keep them down in their little place, like little people, and it all seemed to me to be such a desperate shame.

However, since the merger, things had gone off the Richter scale of the bizarre and I had been introduced to Chris Henley. Chris was a little older than me by a few years, shared the same ridiculous sense of humour and was also post merger trying to carve out a niche for himself. Chris's father, Des Henley had embalmed Lord Mountbatten, Sir Winston Churchill, Judy Garland and George VI. Chris was now rapidly getting sidelined into a non-job since the advent of PHK (just like me) and so it was on such a non-job mission we found ourselves at GMEX in Manchester at a Funeral Exhibition.

Now explaining to non Funeral Directors what actually goes on at a Funeral Exhibition is a little difficult, people will look at you in an advanced state of incredulity. But people really do display the latest models of coffins, special snow chains for your hearse, the sleekest embalming equipment and super grip ties to tie the wreaths down in a force-10 gale. So there we were putting together an exhibition stand where we would be trying (yet again) to sow some corporate seeds of goodwill amongst the remaining independent funeral directors in the UK. Looking back on it now, I find it difficult to understand why I was so inured that these guys would be opposed to us. We had just bought out their competitors, raised the prices by 25%, dropped the standards of service by the same and got rid of the main protagonists the families knew and loved. They must have loved us coming to town!

So Chris and I, along with Dennis Amiss (who now basically had no job to do as cash was rather short to put it mildly) were entrusted with the job of putting on this exhibition. We worked hard all Wednesday and Thursday, so by Friday morning when the exhibition opened we did not feel it was essential to be there at the opening hour. Instead Chris and I were soothing our tired limbs in the hotel jacuzzi, telling ourselves that we had earned it. Unsurprisingly Dennis was not amused, he could sense that people would be looking for redundancies and was keen to impress. At least we could still conduct funerals for a living, the ability to cover drive extremely well would not cut any ice with the new Chief Executive of the enlarged group.

We had spent the best part of a week sorting out corporate colours and carpets, wallpaper with little oak trees on (I kid you not), Chesterfield sofas in just the right colour, bottles of wine with fancy glasses and making sure we had enough brochures, reports and accounts to entertain all the potential clients that would come to our stand.

We also had the rather tricky problem of trying to hide Jean Neveau on the stand. Someone had decreed he should be there to discuss potential acquisitions. Despite the fact that this wouldn't have helped anyone, Chris and I were helpless with laughter at the thought of it all. We knew if he got going then not only would we stand no chance with the potential acquisitions, but (and this was far more important) we would be collapsing with hysterics. The only saving grace was that Sandy Fraser wouldn't be there to fuel the laughter, as when Sandy, Chris and I got going on the subject of Jean Neveau, no sensible work could be carried out for several hours. We discussed things seriously, we even created a system to keep him away from everyone. Basically we would take it in turns to talk to him and hopefully introduce him to someone else in the funeral business from time to time, like a casket manufacturer, and make sure he stayed with them. The plan was coming to fruition when I started to feel giggly and said "Ha Ha! I have a little columbarium." Columbariums were one of Jean's favourite subjects, it was just the way he said it. We all started laughing, and I mean helplessly laughing, the situation had become ridiculous, here we were all fairly well paid executives trying to ensure that one of the main board directors did not meet anyone because if he did we would all be dissolving with giggles.

Most of the time it worked like a charm as we were sensible enough to understand what would happen if the plan went wrong – but then Chris came back late from lunch, I wasn't there and we heard the words "Ha" and we all dived behind the exhibition stand in giggles. We were all like silly schoolboys, it was all so daft and then try as we might, we couldn't come out as every time we tried to one of us would hear another "Ha Ha!" In the end Dennis discovered something was up and came and gave us a good talking to. As we sheepishly slunk out "Ha Ha!" and all three of us were back behind the stands in the giggles again.

Dennis was quite cross now, but slowly seeing the funny side to it all (he also thought Jean a little strange). He also got the giggles and then we were all at the back for a good ten minutes every thirty seconds dissolving into laughter every time we heard "Ha Ha!" By the end of the exhibition, it had got so bad we only had to hear Jean's voice for it to bring on another uncontrollable fit of the giggles, it was really very unprofessional, but I mean just what could we do? And did we achieve anything at this exhibition? Not really. But one thing remained, Jean had been elevated to cult status and that, amongst every other detail, is the strongest memory I have of working with funerals; not suicides, terrible deaths, mergers, acquisitions, just Jean and his "Ha Ha!"

Chapter 17

Getting away with Merger

"Is Harvey still on Line 1?"

One of the firms Howard had bought in Felixstowe was Gordon Rodwell and Sons, with the business came Gordon and his wife Ann. I quite liked them, I had been to Felixstowe in the first instance to get the details of the funeral business and they had sold for a good sum. Shortly afterwards, I was chatting to Stephen Heathcote at Head Office one day when I mentioned it seemed completely daft that all the limousines were stuck in the garages at night doing nothing. We had now accumulated a total of about 350 limousines in prime sites around the country and I proffered the thought that perhaps we could try and hire them out in the evening to executives for private hire. The next thing I knew it was on the agenda for a board meeting and for some unfathomable reason Ann and Gordon were asked to head up this division. Thus Ann Rodwell's travelling limousine became a bit of a party piece at these funeral director's exhibitions. We had a hamper at the back, packed full of good grub and a brochure mocked up with "PHK International Limousine Hire" on it, it was really rather posh. I wasn't there long enough to find out if we ever hired a limousine out, let alone made any money from it, but I do remember being a bit miffed that I didn't get the recognition that was deserved, I mean all I wanted was a thank you!

Chris Henley and I just gelled from day one, we were both seemingly the only people to see that the Emperor wasn't actually wearing any clothes and it amused us both greatly that there was a whole rack of senior management crawling to higher management in fear of their place in the company. From nowhere had come this guy who I was to spend only six months working with, but who was to leave with me the fondest memories of Hodgson Holdings or PHK. And perhaps this was a good thing because all the ups and downs meant that finally right towards the end I had a period in my life at Hodgsons that was truly memorable. Chris was great fun to be with and we just absolutely hit it off in everything we did and I miss him greatly, I must look him up and present him with a copy of this book.

Now following this huge merger, we were discovering areas in funeral directing that were completely new to me. One of the guys I met at the Brighton exhibition was John Nicholls. John was a legend in repatriation and emergency services. On call 24 hours a day and seven days a week, he took his emergency pager with him everywhere, and I mean everywhere, he never knew when he would be needed. He had been leading Kenyon's team for the last twenty years. Present at the Moorgate disaster, the Tenerife Plan Crash (over five hundred dead), the Isles of Scilly Helicopter Crash, Piper Alpha and the Herald of Free Enterprise Ferry. John had seen it all and was mentally built for the job, as it didn't seem to bother him a jot. Part of his portfolio was the photographs taken at the time of such disasters, I remember being slightly unnerved for the first time in my career at the photographs. First of Piper Alpha victims, remember John was only interested in the dead, so no survivors here, just corpses in their orange survival suits. More so, the Isles of Scilly Helicopter Crash where John merrily showed his photos of the dead people still in their seats with their seat belts on.

But these people were very interesting, they had stories to tell, they had information to pass on to the next generation, they needed young enquiring minds, in a way minds like mine. I wish now I had enough grace to have got closer to people like John Nicholls and Michael Kenyon, sadly the circumstances would not allow it as the Hodgson boys were deemed rather common and the Kenyon boys were deemed a bit posh and not really allowed to muck in with the rough lads.

Of course this was yet another situation where Howard felt it important to fiddle. The Kenyon's expertise were highly revered in many countries and the goodwill attached to their name was huge, far higher that anything we had had at Hodgson & Sons. Their Chief Executive Christopher Kenyon possessed a gold card which allowed him to hire a plane at a moments notice to go out to world disasters. It had a credit limit at the time of £60,000. Today such a value would probably be about £400,000.

They were in their way very successful people working for a very unsuccessful company. The merger of the funeral homes would, in time, bring huge savings even if the funeral numbers dropped by 15%, but many facets of the much higher torqued operation were running very well and needed little interference. It had been mentioned, with a glint in the eye, that all the executives would be losing their company cars in the merger, well it did happen in many situations. But, in actuality we just replaced one poor hierarchy with another, and they were all granted new director's cars anyway. Our own failed sense of worth had allowed sheer numpties to work their way into a director's position, in many cases it really was quite a scandal.

Amidst all this tomfoolery sat Michael Kenyon, completely ill at ease with the thought of a merger. He wasn't fond of Howard and was nobody's fool. But he had had his day. Playing on the fact that they were the royal undertakers and that they were Kenyon's, they classically relaxed, Hodgsons had managed to sneak up beside them and beat them to the tape. There was only ever going to be one Chief Executive of the enlarged PHK group and that was going to be Howard. He still had the drive and the publicity value, which meant that he alone, after a few well-chosen interviews, could get the company's share price to rise. Michael Kenyon was more miffed at the fact that the French had sold him down the river to Howard than he was to Howard himself. Whenever I saw the two together there was a sort of uneasy truce. They were just totally different characters, all the Kenyon men thought all the Hodgson people were completely insane (well in many cases they weren't far off the truth), there was huge animosity as we looked to work together to bring this merger even closer to being successful.

I met Michael a number of times after the merger and he just looked totally bemused by the high farce conducted from Plantsbrook House. I suspect he had been fairly badly advised by the merchant bankers on how to raise the money to buy Dottridge. By surrendering so much of the public company's shares, Michael had lost any sort of control. His personality was not one that could be relied upon to hold the shares when Howard was talking about a merger to create a higher share price, therefore higher profits for people who had bought at the bottom of the market. Howard had become known as the first funeral director on the stock market, but of course it wasn't like that at all. Michael had been there many years previously and had much to teach the young upstart

245

about diplomacy, tact and the nurturing of relationships. These were areas where Howard was always way behind other companies. His drive could never be doubted, his determination and fizz to get jobs done was outstanding, he just didn't listen. I felt sorry for Michael, he was quoted in the press as being "very much the stereotype of the undertaker", but having dealt with royalty (Kenyon's dealt with Mountbatten's funeral in 1979) he had the diplomacy and tact to grace an ambassador's office.

Once Howard had got Kenyon's on board he sniffed out the fact they had conducted enough business with the Royal Family to apply for a Royal Warrant. Howard thought this was fascinating and had thoughts of the wonderful crest adorning the PHK stationery. However a little research showed that a Royal Warrant had to be granted and it would not have been deemed seemly, so all plans were horridly dropped.

We had a bit of a faff as well over the launch of the Dignity In Destiny Plan – a pre-paid funeral plan Howard had got is teeth into and was drafting a brochure on. In a light hearted comment on the phone to Colin Field (he was never one to take a joke) Howard mentioned he had used Great Southern's Golden Charter plan, copied it and renamed it Dignity In Destiny. Solicitors letters flew back and forth suggesting breach of copyright, oh they were very much on their high horse and I guess they had a point! In the end it was all settled amicably as we destroyed the copies we had made and started again.

The happy-go-lucky Howard that had a clear vision of the future had continued as the company had grown to surround himself with freaks, yes men, funeral directors and people that had no experience in business. Most of the hugely successful companies have got there because at one point, the Chief Executive had taken the decision that in order for the company to grow with a sound base, it was essential to hire people that were better than him. Howard didn't take this route. He created layer after layer of management, so we had this convoluted system which seemed to control costs and quality but in its own magnificent way managed to achieve the opposite effect and stifle creativity at birth.

The way it worked was like this. John Smallbone at Hereford would telephone Derek Tyler in Bristol each evening at about 4.30pm and report the figures each day. He also went down a list that included about thirty-five items as a daily check list. I will never forget the first three items on the list as long as I live: Removals, Papers and Flowers.

John then would confirm with Derek that all was in order and that the Chapels were checked (this was the last item on the list), this would take about fifteen minutes. Derek would then phone JBT and give him the two reports, although I knew JBT and Derek were more switched on and could short circuit the system to "Everything okay?", then JBT would pass this report on to Howard. Now this was fine for ten, twenty or thirty funeral homes, but as more acquisitions were assimilated into the Hodgson format, it got insanely complicated. When the BBC came for the best part of two weeks to film for the programme "Howard's Way", I spent an hour setting up all the telephone extensions in Howard's office so they could see a nightly report-taking place. We then had the farce of "Hello, Harvey on Line 1" – "David can you hear me?". It all started to be a little like a sitcom, people started tripping over telephone wires and JBT on more than one occasion knocked phones out of sockets, so that after an hour of reports Howard would discover that David Bonham had never been on Line 3 after all.

But then, could Howard be blamed? He was learning like the rest of us, he was allowed to make mistakes (people often think the boss isn't allowed to), but he didn't ever seem to take advice from people and get things changed. The system didn't work, even I could see that. It had become non-productive, part of the urban myth surrounding Howard and the way in which he would control things. Control was there, but not to the extent that Hodgsons thought. Many years later I read that Howard had agreed having more layers of management than a carefully constructed wedding cake just made the whole system complicated, it wasn't something he would do again. Unfortunately too late to undo all the farcical shenanigans, but then it was always fun seeing JBT's gangly legs fall over the telephone wires.

By now, we were starting to lose really good people. We had always lost some people on acquisition, but normally we lost the dross first, many of which we were delighted to see the back of. But now, we lost pretty young things who just weren't prepared to be managed by a ruddy-faced lunatic like Brian Philips. I remember Darren Faragher, he set up on his own and took about 450 funerals from us. Ashley Saville-Boss, he took a good 200, and dear old John Mould who must have built up his business in Greet to about 400. All of them damaging the Hodgson bottom line but perhaps more importantly taking valuable knowledge and good skilful funeral directors out of the company. Remember this was only in one small area, but sadly the pattern was being repeated around the country. What had been built on a shed load of bonhomie and hype was now starting to fall apart and the business got itself caught in that terrible position of having to purchase new businesses as the ones that they bought were losing funerals, so the cycle continued. Even today it hasn't got any better, no one seems to be able to stop the terrible cycle on its dreaded and predictable path.

It was difficult working with Howard at times. He rarely let you get anything done and micro-managed to the extent that people were afraid to make any decisions for fear of being humiliated and shouted down. It needed people more important than me to stand up to him and to just be honest, but the larger the company got, the less likely it was to happen. It was a real shame. Occasionally I summoned up the courage to speak my mind about something but it wasn't just a question of not being listened to, you were made to feel that your opinion wasn't important and he did this to most people. Yet in a way, through all the acquisitions, all the different people we had acquired, there must haven been some wise brain cells in there, it was just a question of facilitating them. But it was too late now, it was a culture thing that ran through the company like veins through Blue Stilton cheese.

Howard always spoke in a rather strange way. For one, he rarely looked at you when he spoke, which I always used to find disconcerting. He sprinkled his sentences with the wonderful phrase "the situation is". I remember him saying to a journalist one day "Well if that is the situation, then we will be in a situation where we would have to see what the situation is!" Class, sheer class, but nonsense of course! He rarely complimented you on work done well. In a way it was the malaise of the 80's and not just of him. There were so many moments when regional managers were phoning in their nightly reported and they ended with Howard saying "give them a bollocking!" It wasn't a great way to manage, it had got us so far, but a little more thought with the senior management selection would have meant far greater rewards being reaped. With the acquisition programme Howard had acquired a whole host of different personalities who had different skill sets. Arthur Abraham was a grafter, Derek Tyler a charmer, Derek Capel brilliant with funerals, Don York fantastic for his history and legend, June Hemming her administration skills, all of them dear people, but all so very different. No one it seemed, had the intelligence to look at them all and decide where their strengths or skill sets lay. So they were all treated the same and very different results were received, many of them not palatable.

Steve Fox was one of those people who just turned up at Head Office one day, having got involved with Howard on the Dignity In Destiny arm. This was a pre-arranged funeral programme and we were now starting to write these across the country. Steve was odd, it was just as simple as that. He too had this horrendous habit of not looking at you when talking to you, I have since despised this and believe it to be a character flaw! He was known by the girls in the office to be surly, rude and off hand. Inevitably the product got tarred with the same brush, so Dignity In Destiny was not a popular word at Head Office for some time after that. Yet, Howard was again light years ahead of his time, he could see how much this guaranteed funeral numbers for many years to come and was a beacon of great light, particularly with our falling numbers.

By this time, Howard had parted company with John Kerr from the company SUMIT. SUMIT had taken a small stake in Hodgsons just before they floated on the Unlisted Securities Market in June of 1986. I guess John had made a good investment as the share price rose and rose on excellent results, as I recall the first twelve months after flotation, nett profits of £850,000.

John had moaned publicly about a board meeting he attended and Howard had been running three hours late. This was a regular state of affairs in those days. I liked John, he had shown a genuine interest in a young Penrose and chatted very politely. He was far more important than me, so I will always appreciate the fact that he took time to chat, most people at Head Office had little time for that. So, without John who had been the voice of reason Howard had a free run to have his own way. He still had on the board Eric Butler who I naively thought was a well respected and sensible business man, but after a few highly discursive meetings, I discovered that he too was a yes man who demurred to Howard's will. The whole point of course of having Non Executive Directors was to provide an outside view and some stabilisation for such quickly expanding businesses. If John had stayed and Eric had been made of sterner stuff, then perhaps we wouldn't have entered the silly season; with talk of ships to scatter ashes, £85,000 being spent on a small funeral home that arranged just seventeen in its first year and, best of all, the substantial offer on a supposed genuine funeral business in the North which turned out to be a guy who put business cards at a bus shelter.

From an outsiders point of view if it wasn't so hilariously funny it would be sad, or if it wasn't so sad it would be hilariously funny. Either way works really, but we had lost focus and all of us appeared to be in the same situation. There was nobody apart from Sandy Fraser that said whoa let's just stop and find out where we are, let's look at the individual profit and loss accounts for the funeral homes and find out which ones are making money and which ones aren't, also why don't we have a period of consolidation? Yes this was the sensible approach but Howard was first to get to such a huge number of outlets and that meant that he then had the power to conduct the merger with Kenyans an end up of course amalgamating Great Southern Group into it all. He was undoubtedly 'The Man' and I have never to this day met somebody so charismatic and extraordinary. Of course, people will tell you about his faults, but we all have faults. He had skills way ahead of his time and I do salute him.

Chapter 18

Destined for McGreatness™

I was totally bored. My thoughts were not at all logical and I moaned all the time to my wife. I enjoyed funeral directing, but here I was twenty-five, stuck working for a company which had grown so large it had little idea of what was going on on a day to day basis and had completely lost its way.

Things had changed massively in Sutton Coldfield. Howard had moved his part of the operations to London and so he, Graham Hodson and Dennis (who drove down and back every day) moved down to a small industrial estate in Shepherds Bush and left me (it was like a marriage break up) holding the acquisitions fort back at home. The job was specific, I was told there would be no acquisitions for the foreseeable future but I had to keep people warm. So, I found myself with Chris Tidmarsh in the office at Plantsbrook looking at lists day in out, with no real enthusiasm for the job anymore.

It was a massive change and the whole culture and flavour of my job had changed overnight and very dramatically. It was not fun. I could not quite believe that day after day I watched the clock, willing the time way. This was crazy, in Hereford my feet hadn't touched the ground, I was dashing from one thing to the next, the days just flew by. It had been a riot, a circus every day, but never boring. But bored was what I was, no doubt about it.

I had felt that all the decisions made in the last few years were terminal and of course all these changes were just momentary, things would change even more and I would have been a great beneficiary of these changes if I had the sense to "hang in there". But then some things are just meant to be, and be they were.

Since the acquisitions had got completely out of control, Dennis had been swiftly sidelined into a job title of "Corporate Development & Public Relations". It was one of those classic job titles where nobody knew what he was supposed to be doing, which honestly suited him fine. Dennis was a good man, but he smelled people blood-hunting and was determined to be busy. I should have understood this, worked my socks off and kept my head down, but I didn't. I was called into Graham Hodson's office one day by Ron Middleton and told the position I held was to be redundant in six weeks. I was asked very coldly by Graham (sorry, Mr Graham) if I could think of any other job I would be able to do. I suppose funeral directing was the obvious one, but after two years at the forefront of corporate operations, funeral directing was not on my mind. A shame really as it would have been a good solution for everyone, I would have vanished from Head Office. I had been a good funeral director, I would at least keep some income coming into the house. It was however, not to be.

Dennis had already moved to the London office although he drove every day as he loved Birmingham too much (and I reckon was a bit afraid of telling Jill his wife that he would have to move). So I saw nothing of Dennis, had the office to myself with Christine and we just sort of bumbled along. I cannot remember anything of value that we did in the six months we had on our own. I was just disinterested.

I didn't feel anything at the time, I remember being a little surprised, but my card had probably been marked for some time. I had in turn irritated Graham Hodson, Ron Middleton and Howard, mainly by losing my sense of focus and not having anyone to motivate me. I felt I had jewels in my life but they were still to be unearthed, oh it was a bit pompous – but I always responded well to encouragement and for over twelve months I'd had none.

I had also got a little closer to Mick Harris. Mick was in charge of IT at the company. This was a new position and I liked Mick. Amongst one of the things I had gathered at a meeting about security and IT was that Mick could sign in using his name and the password SECOFF (Security Officer) and so on more than one occasion I decided to do that, just because I could.

Seeing the screens at such a level meant absolutely nothing to me, I wasn't that bright! But I played around, had a look at what I could and had a nose. Ho hum, ah well. I must have done this three or four times and then one day got a call from Ron Middleton to ask me why I had been logging on as SECOFF. I was so green even then I hadn't realised it would show up on my log! I mumbled something about just having a look and was then asked to clear my desk.

It was more than a bit of a shock really. I had brought this on myself, I still hadn't yet grasped the fact that my wife and I had only been together eighteen months and were rather reliant on my £18,00 salary for the payment of the household outgoings. Houston, we had a problem!

The end of the beginning.

For some time I had been looking at the possibility of opening a sandwich bar. Whenever I went to London, mainly to meet up with Sandy on some madcap project I looked up the original Costa Coffee Bar at Baker Street tube station. Very simple, but a prawn sandwich and good cappuccino made my day, this was the late 1980's and this sort of fare was infrequently available. I used to enjoy having a coffee and snack, and reading a newspaper. This was the beginning of my imagination starting to run riot; I could do this I thought, this would be fabulous! It was the classic way to start a business and the classic way to have a business go bust, starting with no knowledge of the industry, zero capital, loads of confidence (well alright arrogance) and the knowledge that nothing could possibly go wrong.

The sandwich bar idea had progressed to the stage of me mocking up profit and loss forecasts (I had great experience of these by now) and of cash flows, of course these were all done from a logical and necessary point of view and on a trusty Amstrad PCW9512. I quickly got used to the word processor, but didn't ever manage to master the spreadsheets, so they would all have to be calculated by hand, altered and checked every time we made an adjustment. Like thousands of small business start-ups before and after me, I would never look at these again. I had discussed things with Ruth and we were moving towards the idea of me resigning, I frequently ran through the resignation conversation in my head and it was all looking pretty good. And then the axe fell and the decision had been made for me. The first thing I decided I would do was to get down to McDonald's and work for six weeks to find out how systems worked in this strange place called retail.

I arrived at the opposite end of the Gracechurch Centre with my Grenson shoes, Pinstripe suit, tie pin and pink braces, and saw Ramsey the manager.

I want a job, I said, I can start straight away. He recalled a few weeks later that he was looking around for the Candid Camera as I was not his normal candidate. Even now I don't quite know why I went to McDonalds. For fun? To amuse people? I really don't know. What I do know though is that within days I was enthralled by it all. The systems, the speed, the efficiency, the ability to work quickly under pressure.

So much of what I had been thrust into was hard, slogging work. I was scheduled to work on a number of close shifts. These were after the restaurant closed at 11pm and after the security had left. We had to take all the cooking utensils apart and clean them. It was known as "the Dive" by the staff who had been there much longer than me. The amounts of grease we had to clean off were indescribable! The utensils never seemed to end, would we be spending the night there? And then, when the manager finally agreed the place was clean enough for us to all go home, I had to get astride my lady's bicycle which had been loaned to me by a friend from church and struggle all the way home, all uphill I seem to recall, getting in at about two in the morning. We lived in a second floor flat at the time and I will never forget heaving my puffing body up the stairs and collapsing in a heap on the bedroom floor. Quite what Ruth thought at the time I didn't ever enquire. I suppose I was always positive, recognizing that this was a turning point in my life. I was at McDonalds to learn and learn I did. Actually it was all fantastic, it was preparing my body, both physically and mentally for the torturous work that I was about to start for myself. It was heart-breaking, slogging work, just the sort of work you should be doing to prepare you for your own business.

Was I thinking about my own business all this time? Yes I was, I was planning at home, marking on a map all the eating establishments in Birmingham City Centre and was feverishly looking to see where I could open up and start something on my own. I had been working on a business plan for more than a year and I suppose the potential to open a new business gave me an escape from the nightmare that was McDonalds.

The staff there mercilessly mocked me. I discovered one week after I had left that at least three of them thought I had been a plant from their Head Office, so I was not party to the normal banter with workmates that came so readily to most people. I suppose part of me was protective about my past, I wasn't proud of what I now had to do in order to put food on the table, but I was proud of myself. I struggled initially with most of the jobs, but once I had been shown things at least three times they stuck and I was heading towards that most coveted of symbols, a McDonalds Star. I was especially fast and dynamic on the tills which was where I tended to spend most of my time. It was far less knackering and I had the interaction with customers which made the day go quickly.

A few weeks later I served Ron Middleton and greeted him "Hi Ron!" I was amused to see he had not recognized me, which was rather fun!

So that, dear reader is the reason I was at McDonalds at the age of twenty-five on my hands and knees, I mean, you couldn't make it up! I guess the fact I had done so much by twenty-five, a little like Alice in Wonderland who had done "six impossible things before breakfast", I was ready for the next stage in my career to begin.

The End.

"It's not time to make a change
Just relax, take it easy
You're still young, that's your fault
There's so much you have to know
Cat Stevens

Epilogue

- Derek Tyler retired from Roy Preddy and moved to Paignton

- Grant Baynham is Managing Director of LT Baynham & Son in Hereford

- Don York died in 2009 at the grand age of 82. I wept.

- Graham Hodson left to form "Laurel Group". He has since sold it and retired.

- Sandy Fraser is Managing Director of n1 Singer in London and we frequently meet up and take turns to imitate Jean Neveau – "Ha Ha!"

- Chris Henley ran his own repatriation business in London and then became a parish priest – I still miss our time together

- Dennis Amiss has now retired from business I suspect he is still just as interested in cricket – thank you Dennis for helping me with my batting average

- JBT retired and I have not been able to trace him – I suspect he has died and is without doubt at the pearly gates organising heaven's entries with one of his lists

- David Mainwaring is still alive and no doubt enjoying a large port from time to time

- I strongly suspect Jean Neveau is somewhere, wherever causing chaos – I will never, ever forget him

- I met Nigel Lymm-Rose at Burleigh Horse Trials a number of years ago, I have fond memories of all his family, although Sheila and George have since passed away

- Michael Kenyon retired and I was saddened to hear he passed away in 2020. He was such a gentleman and always very kind to me

- After the PHK merger, the enlarge company acquired Great Southern Group, renamed itself Dignity and is now listed on the UK stock market and part of the FTSE 100.

- And Howard is still Howard, running Memoria he is back in the death business and no doubt the famous Hodgson diary system is still being run. – I wonder what the situation is?

Postscript:

I finally met Howard again - in 2017 - twenty-seven years after we had last seen each other and we had an enjoyable dinner in London with his young son George. It was a bit bizarre, as the scenario and setting had changed so much, but he was an enormous part of my life and it is to him I owe a huge amount. Howard, thank you.

*Most of the other characters in the book have
either passed away or not been contactable.*

Excerpt from the next instalment in a new book...

Provisionally entitled:

"How to build The Best Coffee House in the world from scratch"

I couldn't quite believe it, I was sat with one of my heroes in my Northampton "Hudson's Coffee House" one of four in my group chatting over lunch with Sir John Harvey Jones, the former ICI Chairman and now TV star through his *Troubleshooter* programme on television about how to keep staff motivated in a large group. I was cock-a-hoop because we had recently been awarded "The Best Tea House in the United Kingdom" by none other than the legendary Egon Ronay. It was quite a moment.

A couple of months earlier I had spotted that Sir John was going to be signing copies of his book in Birmingham where our first coffee house was situated. Ever the maverick I turned up, handed him a letter including a rather fabulous tie, for which he was famous. In the letter I requested that we might have lunch together some day (as you do) and he wrote a delightful hand-written reply saying he would be delighted to meet up and was full of thanks for my gift of a tie!

I had started the Coffee House in 1990, well, actually it started off as a Speciality Sandwich Take Out Shop, and less than three years later after as many false starts and cock ups as you can possibly imagine (and a few you couldn't) the renowned food critic saw fit to say that my original Birmingham branch had just been declared the best Tea House in the country. I was proud but totally knackered, it had taken a lot out of me, but it had been worth it.

It's not finished yet, but it will be a corker and I commend it to you.
February 2022